Y0-BEA-041

STEPHEN L. KLEIN
Attorney at Law
11 Center Street
Rutland, Vermont 05701

How to Prove Damages in Wrongful Personal Injury and Death Cases

HOW TO PROVE DAMAGES
IN WRONGFUL
PERSONAL INJURY
AND DEATH CASES

I. DUKE AVNET

PRENTICE-HALL, INC.   Englewood Cliffs, N.J.

Prentice-Hall International, Inc., *London*
Prentice-Hall of Australia, Pty. Ltd., *Sydney*
Prentice-Hall of Canada, Ltd., *Toronto*
Prentice-Hall of India Private Ltd., *New Delhi*
Prentice-Hall of Japan, Inc., *Tokyo*

© 1973 by
Prentice-Hall, Inc.
Englewood Cliffs, N.J.

*All rights reserved. No part of this book
may be reproduced in any form or by any
means, without permission in writing from
the publisher.*

Library of Congress Cataloging in Publication Data

Avnet, I   Duke, (date)
   How to prove damages in wrongful personal injury
and death cases.

   Bibliography: p.
   1. Personal injuries--United States. 2. Death by
wrongful act--United States. 3. Trial practice--
United States. I. Title.
KF8925.P4A96   346'.73'032   72-13212
ISBN 0-13-429407-6

Printed in the United States of America

HOW THIS BOOK CAN
HELP THE LAWYER

This book is intended to furnish the negligence trial lawyer with a handy tool, as well as with a reference source, in the preparation and trial of negligence cases—both in wrongful personal injury and death cases.

While its emphasis is on damages, it covers the entire anatomy of a negligence case from the very first contact with the client through the court's instructions to the jury and the closing argument at the trial.

The author has sought to orient much of his approach to the treatment of cases of modest value (i.e. musculo-ligamentous sprain of the neck or back). This should be helpful to negligence lawyers handling average cases. However, this is not done to the exclusion of the "big case," especially serious disability and death cases, which are treated in considerable detail.

The field of damages law has become much more complex in recent years because of the tendency of the courts to keep pace with the economic and social growth of our country. For example, the courts, in assessing damages, must consider the improved economic condition of wage and salary workers, and the likelihood of future increases in their earnings and fringe benefits. Fatal accidents, including plane crashes, frequently involve professional persons, business executives and other wealthy persons; this has added sophistication to the damage prayer through consideration of future increases in income and accumulations in investments.

Some of the salient features of this book are the following:

1. How to prepare your case for settlement and/or trial.
2. How to research and prepare for the medical phases of the case.
3. What to say in the opening statement.

5

4. Demonstrative techniques in the presentation of the medical and economic features of a case.
5. Scientific proof of pecuniary losses.
6. Sample requests for instructions to the jury, both for plaintiff and defendant.
7. What to say in the closing argument.
8. A thorough consideration and discussion of "No Fault" insurance acts and plans and how they will affect the law of damages and the negligence lawyer's practice.

It has numerous other bonus features, such as forms for investigating a case properly, where to try your case, how to pick the jury, how to understand medical symbols and terminology, and how to use the hospital records effectively; forms of hypothetical questions to be put to experts, such as doctors and economists, and mortality, work career and discount tables helpful in serious injury and death cases.

The book has value to both plaintiff's and defendant's lawyers. While most chapters deal with the proof of a case by the plaintiff, they also contain frequent comments and references to enlighten and to assist the lawyer for the defendant. It contains a separate and documented chapter entitled "How Defendant Should Word Requests for Instructions on Damages." Also, in the chapter "How to Pick the Jury," there is a checklist on *voir dire* examination for the defendant's attorney.

I. Duke Avnet

ACKNOWLEDGMENTS

Many persons have given me considerable help in the preparation of this book. Among these are: Samuel A. Culotta, Albert Avnet, August J. Brozik and Herman Shapiro, fellow attorneys in my office suite in Baltimore; David J. Farber, economic expert, of Silver Spring, Maryland; Professor William Schwartz, Esq., Boston, Mass.; and not the least my secretary, Leah Pasenker, who typed my ragged hand-script, and my wife, Beatrice, who lent valuable assistance in checking the manuscript for accuracy.

Gratitude is expressed to the following, who were generous enough to grant permission to quote material and/or references from the works noted:

West Publishing Company, St. Paul, Minnesota, for *Key Number Digest System* and *Corpus Juris Secundum*, and for the following books published by it: *Virginia Practice*, Volume 1, by Doubles, Emrich & Merhige; *California Jury Instructions–Civil B.A.J.I.*, 3rd and 5th editions; and *Federal Jury Practice and Instructions–Civil and Criminal*–by Mathes & Devitt. Also to The Committee on Standard Jury Instructions, Civil, of the Superior Court of Los Angeles County, California, through its consultant, the Hon. Philip H. Richards, for use of the aforementioned books on California Jury Instructions. Also to Burdette Smith Company, Chicago, Illinois, and to West Publishing Company for their permission to use *Illinois Jury Instructions–Civil–I.P.I.*, and to Mr. Louis G. Davidson, Chairman of the Illinois Supreme Court Committee on Instructions, of Chicago, Illinois, for use of the aforementioned book. Also to Judicial Conference of the State of New York for its permission to use its books on *New York Pattern Jury Instructions–Civil*. Also to Atlantic Law Book Company of Hartford, Connecticut, and to Judge Douglass B. Wright for their permission to use their book *Connecticut Jury Instructions*. Callaghan & Company, publishers, Chicago, Illinois, for their book entitled *Medical Trial Technique Quarterly* by Goldstein; and for use of *Trial Lawyers Guide* and an article therein by attorney Philip H. Corboy of Chicago, Illinois. Lea & Fabiger, publishers, Philadelphia, Pennsylvania, for book entitled *Comroe's Arthritis and Allied Conditions*. The Institute of Continuing Legal Education, University of Michigan Law School and Wayne State University Law School and State Bar of Michigan, for the book *Persuasion: The Key To Damages;* and to attorneys Samuel Langerman of Phoenix, Arizona, and Craig Spangenberg of Cleveland, Ohio for materials therein. Metropolitan Life Insurance Company for its chart on joint life tables. Sun Life Insurance Company for its Discount Tables. American Trial Lawyers Association and attorney Dean Robb of Detroit, Michigan for their book *Damages and Settlement Course Handbook*. U.S. Department of Health, Education and Welfare, Social Security Administration, Washington, D.C., and the Nation Center for Health Statistics, Washington, D.C., for their material on "Life Tables"; and to the U.S. Department of Labor, Bureau of Labor Statistics, Washington, D.C. for its material on working life tables. The C.V. Mosby Company, publishers, St. Louis,

Missouri, and Dr. H. Early Conwell, Birmingham, Alabama, and Dr. Fred C. Reynolds, St. Louis, Missouri, for permission for use of the book *Fractures, Dislocations and Sprains,* 6th and 7th editions, by Key and Conwell.

CONTENTS

CHAPTER 12. How Plaintiff Should Word Requests for Instructions on Damage (Continued)

CHAPTER 14. What You Should Know about No Fault Insurance (Continued)

How to Prove Damages in Wrongful Personal Injury and Death Cases

Chapter 1

HOW TO PROVE DAMAGES

IN THE MODERN WAY

Sec. 1.1   The Old Approach

It is still not unusual to see serious disability and death cases tried in the old manner, namely, with the emphasis on proof of liability and with damages given secondary consideration. As to damage proof in a back disability case, for example, plaintiff's counsel will call on the treating doctor and perhaps an orthopedic expert to show percentage of permanency in loss of use of the back; then the medical and hospital bills and the past wage loss will be proven. Defendant's counsel will offer his orthopedic expert to minimize the percentage of permanency and the plaintiff's counsel will ask a few guarded questions of him on cross-examination to show bias or partisanship, and then beat a hasty retreat to avoid clashing with him on medical knowledge. Plaintiff's counsel then will argue to the jury about his client's bleak future because of his back condition, often utilizing an emotional appeal in hopes of scoring well as to damages.

Sec. 1.2   The New Approach

The modern treatment is to give damages at least equal importance in preparation to that of liability. The reason? It brings in higher verdicts.

The basic items of change are the following:

(a) Research and preparation of the medical phases of the case, both for direct and cross-examination of the medical experts;

(b) Demonstrative techniques in the presentation of the medical and economic aspects;

(c) Scientific proof of pecuniary losses.

Sec. 1.3 How to Prepare the Medical Part of Your Case

The medical phase of the case has an important bearing on damages. It is one thing for your doctor to testify about 25 percent disability of the back due to musculo-ligamentous sprain and quite another to communicate its significance to the jury.

For example, recently the writer tried a back injury case before a federal court jury involving a 54-year-old railroad conductor who fell from a defective ladder during the course of his work.[1] His condition was aggravation of a pre-existing low back condition by the trauma, complicated by osteoporosis (softening of the bones).

An orthopedic expert was used and emphasis was placed on the mechanics of a back sprain and how it affected this particular man. The doctor related that damage was done to the soft tissue surrounding the skeletal structure of the low back and that this not only weakened his back but that it would be a perpetual source of discomfort and pain to him, especially when engaging in activity that required use and motion of his back, such as climbing on and off railroad cars. Medical charts were used showing the skeleton and the musculature and soft tissues over the skeleton, and the doctor referred to them to graphically illustrate what he was describing. In point of fact, he took on the image of a teacher with the jury as his class of students, and the jury and the judge were duly impressed.

While the railroad company's doctor sought to minimize the disability and the percentage of permanency, plaintiff's counsel had available for use, if necessary, various medical source-book authorities with which to cross-examine him on the role of the sprain and its relationship to the disability. These would establish the following: that a sprain is a tearing of the normal soft tissue (i.e. muscles, ligaments, tendons, blood vessels and nerves) which surround and support the bone structures and their movement; and that on healing, scar tissue forms to substitute for the normal tissue but that it is less elastic and therefore pulls on being stretched and causes discomfort, pain and the disability.

The medical data is readily available to the lawyer. There are numerous medico-legal books which explain in layman's language the medical condi-

---

1. *Ryan v. B & O.*, Civil No. 18805 (D.C. Md. 1969). The verdict was $70,000. The medical expenses were $1,142.42. The past lost earnings were $7,961.78. The plaintiff was still employed by the railroad in the same capacity and was earning about $8,500 annually at the time of trial.

tion involved, supply source material, and even present the line of questioning to be put to your medical expert.[2] These can be obtained at most
law libraries.

The source material is important for two reasons. First, it helps you to
understand the medical question better and to examine your own doctor
more effectively. Second, it supplies you with an arsenal with which to
cross-examine the opposing doctor. It is usually best to have well-known
textbooks to use for this purpose because, generally speaking, the adverse
doctor must first acknowledge that he knows the book before you can use it
for purpose of cross-examination.[3]

Sometimes it is necessary to do more basic medical research. For example,
recently the writer's office was confronted with a case involving the
development of multiple myeloma (a malignant tumor condition affecting
the bones) shortly after a bad fall. Because this is a fairly rare phenomenon,
the writer contacted one of our local medical libraries and asked the librarian
to assist him in finding material on the subject.

The task of medical research is not as formidable to a lawyer as it seems.
It is wise to ask for a medical dictionary and to use it as you read. When the
medical dictionary does not explain the term clearly enough, inquire of the
librarian. When complex medical questions arise, it is advisable to consult a
friend who is a doctor. It is recommended to use at all times, especially for a
preliminary review of the medical subject, the convenient small-sized book

2. *American Jurisprudence– Proof of Facts–Annotated* (1965), published by Bancroft Whitney Co.,
San Francisco, and The Lawyers Cooperative Publishing Company, Rochester, New York.

Goldstein's *Medical Trial Technique,* published by Callaghan, Chicago (1942). Good medical
explanation of different types of injuries; includes medical text-book references; also contains direct
and cross-examination of medical experts.

Lawyer's Medical Cyclopedia, published by The Allen Smith Company, Indianapolis, Indiana
(1962). Good medical explanation of different types of injuries; includes medical textbook
references; also contains direct and cross-examination of medical experts.

American Trial Lawyer's Journal (NACCA Law Journal), published by W. H. Anderson Co.,
Cincinnati.

Handling Accident Cases-by Albert Averbach (1958), published by Lawyers Cooperative Publishing
Company, Rochester, New York.

Belli–*Modern Trials,* published by Bobbs-Merrill, Indianapolis. Special recognition should be given
to Melvin Belli of the San Francisco and Los Angeles bars because of his pioneering in the field of
modernizing proof of damages, which he called "The Adequate Award."

Trial & Tort Trends, edited by Melvin Belli.

Cross-Examination of the Medical Expert, PLI (1968), by John W. Reese. Bound in personal injury
law and technique course handbooks, series 1968, Vol. 1.

Lawyers Guide to Medical Proof, by Marshall Houts (1966), published by M. Bender, Albany, New
York.

Trial of Medical Malpractice Cases, by David W. Louisell and Harold Williams, published by
Matthew Bender, Albany, New York.

Traumatic Medicine and Surgery for the Attorney, edited by Dr. Paul D. Cantor, published by
Central Book Co. (1959), New York City.

3. *Fidelity & Casualty Company of New York v. Davis* (Tex. Civ. App. 1962), 354 S.W. 2nd 228.
However, if the text is not specifically referred to, questions may be asked based on the medical text.
See discussion in Averbach's "Handling Accident Cases", Vol. 7, p. 707.

"The Merck Manual," which is published by Merck, Sharp & Dohme Research Laboratories, Rahway, New Jersey and West Point, Pennsylvania, and which is obtainable at practically any medical book store.

In the myeloma case mentioned, with the permission of the orthopedic expert whom we intended to use and who was a member of the library, we borrowed, in his name, the books we found helpful. These books supported the theory that trauma could aggravate a pre-existing myeloma and accelerate death.[4] We were content to build our damage case on aggravation and acceleration because it would be more tenable and therefore convincing at the hearing, there being much controversy, medically, whether single trauma can produce cancer of this type. We cited our authorities to our own orthopedic expert in advance of approaching him for his opinion. He agreed. We felt that our textbook authority references aided in obtaining the favorable opinion.

Another observation made is that busy doctors have little time for extensive medical reading, let alone research on a particular subject in their field; therefore, the lawyer who has done his medical research on his case has the advantage of surprise over the opposing doctor in cross-examination.

In a serious case, it is advisable to obtain an appointment in advance of trial with your medical expert and to go over the case with him in advance. If his deposition is to be taken by the other side, it is essential that you prepare the doctor in advance and he will invite your aid. You should compensate the doctor for the time consumed, else you will have an unwilling witness. If the disability in your case is not too serious and the medical expert has had previous court experience, then a thorough telephone conversation may suffice.

The examination of the doctor in the *Ryan* case, supra, inquiring about the mechanics and the effects of soft tissue injury, appears in Section 4.12, infra.

A sample of the cross-examination of a hostile doctor in a similar type of case, with the use of medical text-books and articles for refutation, appears in Section 4.9, infra.

An important item of damages in a wrongful death case is the pain and suffering which preceded death. Frequently this is shown through lay witnesses who were at the scene or by the ambulance assistants who saw him at the scene and on the way to the hospital. Any proof which might show consciousness and evidence of pain should be utilized. Some of these items

---

4. "Pathology of Tumors," 3rd, 1960, by Willis, p. 195; "Neoplastic Diseases" by Ewing, 3rd ed., p. 108; "Disease & Injury" by Brady, pp. 333-335; "Trauma & Disease" by Moritz & Helberg, pp. 173, 174.

are the following:[5] conduct of the subject which would suggest consciousness or pain, as, for example, by speech, groans, crying, gesture, movement, responsiveness to directions, reaction to touch, etc.

However, the most convincing proof would be that of a treating doctor. Frequently, a fatal injury produces shock and the layman juror tends to confuse shock with unconsciousness. This is not necessarily so. A detailed discussion on this point appears in Sec. 4.10 infra.

Sec. 1.4   How to Use Demonstrative Evidence

The ancient axiom that a picture is worth a thousand words is as applicable today as when it was written. Modern science and inventions have placed valuable devices in the hands of the lawyer to illustrate to a court and jury the human anatomy and its functioning. For example, there are X-rays, both the negative and the prints made from the negative, medical charts and plates, anatomical slides and pictures from medical books blown up in size if necessary, moving pictures, and skeletal models and aids.

The demonstrative technique serves two purposes: to dramatize and to instruct. A civil trial is fraught with much boredom for the average juror, and the darkening of the court room and the exhibition of color slides of an injured liver, for example, will rivet the attention of the jury a thousand times more than the prosaic description of the injured liver by a doctor. Also, the doctor takes on the image of an impartial teacher rather than of a partisan witness. His description will be more vividly remembered by the jurors in the jury room when they are pondering their verdict than if presented in the usual way.

Nevertheless, demonstrative evidence should not always be utilized. For example, if its use would create the impression of overstatement or redundancy, then certainly it should not be resorted to. For example, if a man has suffered a fractured leg and the fractured bones were secured by the use of a medullary nail, all of which the X-ray pictures reveal and which can be graphically illustrated by the medical expert, it would be prodigal and unwise to introduce a blown-up picture in color of the same thing.

In the average musculo-ligamentous neck sprain from a rear-end automobile collision, it would seem wiser to rely on medical charts to demonstrate the skeletal parts concerned and the soft tissues surrounding them rather than to introduce a skeleton or a part thereof.

In a serious disability case, as, for example, brain injuries, there should be no compunction about the use of a replica of a human brain to demonstrate

---

5. See Speiser "Recovery for Wrongful Death," Section 14:6, p. 759.

where the injury occurred and about the use of a skeleton model to demonstrate how the brain injury will affect the specific members, if such is the case.

The medical expert should be forewarned about your use of these aids. In point of fact, you should arrange a meeting at the doctor's office for this purpose and pay him for this conference. You should bring with you the aids you are going to use and display them for the doctor's perusal while going over the case with him. Bearing in mind how the demonstration will be executed in court, bring colored pencils to mark charts (but the marking is to be done in court), as the doctor refers to the various parts of the charts.

Sec. 1.5   How to Introduce Demonstrative Aids

In order to introduce these aids, it is recommended that a pre-trial conference be arranged with the judge and the other side present, and that you disclose what you intend to offer as demonstrative aids. This tends to avoid objections from your opponent and to allow you to argue their admissibility, if there are objections—all before trial.

Demonstrative proofs are fairly well accepted today and are usually allowed in evidence, although it is discretionary with the court.[6]

The preparatory examination of the medical expert in order to introduce demonstrative aids appears in Sec. 4.11 infra.

Sec. 1.6   Where to Obtain Demonstrative Aids

There are numerous kinds of demonstrative aids and several sources where they may be obtained.[7] Some law offices acquire a collection of them and

---

6. *Slow Development Co. v. Coulter* (1960 Ariz.), 88 Ariz. 122, 353 P. 2nd 890; *First Federal Savings and Loan Association v. Wylie* (1950 Fla.), 46 So. 2nd 396. See also discussion and authorities in Averbach's "Handling Accident Cases," 6:7 et seq.

7. Anatomical drawings and charts may be obtained from:

Clay-Adams, Inc., 141 E. 25th Street, New York City, New York 10010. (Frohse, Schick lithograph, Bachin and Dr. Michel charts).

Denoyer-Geppert Co., 5235 N. Ravenswood Street, Chicago, Illinois 60640.

Dr. G.H. Michel, Inc., 3808 Prospect Avenue, Cleveland, Ohio 44115.

Ciba Pharmaceutical Products, Inc., Summit, New Jersey (Ciba Collection of Medical Illustrations; Dr. Frank H. Nettler's drawings, "The Clinical Symposia").

American Jurisprudence, Proof of Facts, Vol. 2, published by Bancroft Whitney Co., San Francisco, California, and The Lawyers Cooperative Publishing Company, Rochester, New York (Photographic Appendix of anatomical subjects).

Lederle Laboratories, Division of the American Cyanamid Company, Pearl River, New York (Paul Beck's anatomical illustrations entitled "Atlas of the Human Anatomy").

Fred C. Rosselot Co., 216 E. Ninth Street, Cincinnati, Ohio (color prints entitled "Atlas of the Human Body").

The Bobbs Merrill Co., Indianapolis, Indiana (charts illustrating testimony of a medical expert in reference to the anatomy of whiplash injuries).

thus have them ready when needed. This can be rather expensive, however, so many lawyers order them as needed. There are catalogs with graphic pictures of these objects published by the dealers. It is advisable to have them so that you can pick and order. However, it is best to phone the dealer in any case to notify him what you want and to ask for his help. It will prove informative and less expensive in the long run. A fecund source for a specific type of medical or anatomical drawing to suit your specific case appears in *American Jurisprudence-Proof of Facts,* Photographic Appendix.[8]

Sec. 1.7   Demonstrative Aids on Economics

There are numerous exhibitory tools to prove mathematically what the pecuniary losses will be to the survivors. The general subject of proof of losses through an economist-statistician or actuary follows in Sec. 1.8. These exhibits are useful in his hands to make more graphic and saleable to the jury the figures which he projects. These take the form of blown-up charts and tables, and their nature is discussed immediately hereafter. However, the same technique can be used by you without the use of such an expert to illustrate graphically to the jury what the specific wage losses are of an injured litigant. This is also discussed immediately hereafter.

Sec. 1.8   How to Prove Pecuniary Losses Scientifically

The most accurate and effective method to prove the net losses to the survivors in case of death or to the victim in the case of serious injuries is by the use of an economist-statistician or an economist-actuary. This is a person who is expert in the field of analyzing the earnings of the subject, in projecting his expected future earnings, and in computing the estimated losses. He must be familiar with union contracts, pension and welfare plans, government census and other statistics, and life expectancy, work career and discount tables. Then he must know how to tie them all together and to

---

Plates generally can be obtained in color, as well as in black and white. It is advised that the plates be photographed by Eastman Kodak, Rochester, New York, or by yourself with a technical close-up outfit made up of a Kodak 828 camera with Kodachrome 828 film so they may be enlarged and mounted on a cardboard and used as a court-room exhibit. A projector and screen will have to be used in court. Prints can be made from the transparencies and offered in evidence without the use of projecting devices.

Moving pictures can be obtained from:

Ideal Pictures Corp., 58 E. South Water Street, Chicago, Illinois or 233-239 W. 42nd Street, New York, New York 10036. (Kinescope of television program showing open heart surgery on eight-year-old boy, and other similar movies).

8. Compiled in Averbach's "Handling of Accident Cases" 6:17.

produce a chart showing the exact losses. This is discussed hereafter in chapter 9, infra.

In the case where such an expert is not used, a scientific approach can be made to prove damages. This involves a carefully planned and executed system of record-keeping between the plaintiff's lawyer and his client at the very outset of the case.

As an example, in the *Ryan* case, supra,[9] the plaintiff, a middle-aged man, was a railroad freight conductor who had injured his back from a fall from a defective ladder while on his job, and he commenced to lose time from work. While he was earning about $8,500 per year at the time of trial, he could have been earning about $10,000 if he had not been injured. To show this, the plaintiff kept a daily record showing what jobs he was on and how much he earned. His record showed also what days he had to miss on account of his pain and treatment, and who took his place and what the substitute was paid. The plaintiff laid a foundation for the introduction of these records by stating that he could not remember the details of the wage losses and that he had to rely on his records, which were prepared contemporaneously with the events recorded, and that he remembered making these entries and that they were accurate and reliable. A summary sheet was made available so the jury could see and remember the final figures. The management-union contracts covering the periods involved were produced to prove the wage rates. The company's records were subpoenaed to verify the plaintiff's figures and his work attendance. Government-issued statistics were available to show what the increases in this industry were over the past few years, thus to lay the basis for arguing mounting losses due to plaintiff's inability to take full advantage of the probable future wage rate increases. The plaintiff's fellow employees were produced to testify to his inability to perform regularly and to their protective measures surrounding him when he did work. The plaintiff's records were then offered in evidence as exhibits so the jury could deliberate with them.

As to the applicable evidentiary rules of evidence, the plaintiff's wage records fit into the niche of "past recollection recorded." As such, these records could be used by the plaintiff from which to testify; this is an exception to the hearsay rule, very much as would be business records and dying declarations.[10]

---

9. See footnote 1, supra.

10. *98 C.J.S.*, Section 358, 358 (c); *Jones on Evidence,* 5th ed., Vol. 4, Sections 964-966, 974; *McCormick on Evidence,* Sections 9, 276, 277 and 278.

If the plaintiff could have testified from memory after consulting records, then he would not have been able to use the records from which to read as he testified and could not have offered the records in evidence because, theoretically, the records had revived his present recollection and were not necessary to a recollection of the events therein recorded. *McCormick on Evidence,* Section 9; *Jones on Evidence,* 5th ed., Vol. 4, Section 974.

In order to make such testimony acceptable as evidence, a foundation should be laid. The plaintiff should show that he cannot remember all of the details and therefore needs to use these records. He should establish the safeguards required by the law to filter out spurious and unreliable documents. To do this, he should show that the records were made by the plaintiff or by someone under his supervision or direction, and that the entries were made contemporaneously with his lost time or nearly so, in order to demonstrate that the information entered was fresh in his mind when he entered it and that the records are accurate and reliable.[11]

The fact that he had to rely on oral reports from fellow conductors on the time they worked while replacing him does not vitiate his records. Cooperative records and reports are acceptable as long as the plaintiff could testify that he made the entries contemporaneously with the events recorded and that they were accurate.[12]

It is particularly apt for the court to admit testimony based on such records and a summary of such records because of the voluminous details involved, which no one could be expected to retain in his memory; in fact, it would probably be error to refuse same.[13]

The records themselves were admissible in evidence after the plaintiff had finished testifying from them on the theory that they had become incorporated as a part of his testimony.[14]

Careful and contemporaneous bookkeeping by the client in relation to his wage losses resulting from personal injury can reap substantial dividends in a jury verdict. Therefore, the client should be advised to do this and the lawyer should check his records periodically. Where the client is not educationally equipped to do it he should be assisted, perhaps by an auditor, but this must be done as currently as possible with the loss of work time and wages by the client, in order to meet the requirements of the evidentiary law. Counsel should not wait until discovery pleadings are due or until trial time to prepare wage loss damage, because he will be jeopardizing the admissibility of records prepared that late in time.

Of course, not all cases merit such documentation, but those which do will richly reward the client and his attorney by this approach to proof of wage loss.

---

11. *98 C.J.S.*, Section 358 (c); *Jones on Evidence,* 5th ed., Vol. 4, Sections 966, 968, 970; *McCormick on Evidence,* Sections 9, 276 and 277.

Such records would be allowed as the basis for a witness' testimony even if he had no independent recollection of the facts mentioned therin, so long as he testifies that he remembers that at the time he saw the records, he knew the contents to be correct. This would apply, too, where the witness has no recollection of the facts mentioned therein or of the writing itself, but where he knows the writing to be genuine. *Jones on Evidence,* 5th ed., Vol. 4, Sections 966, 968, 970; *98 C.J.S.,* Section 358 (c); *McCormick on Evidence,* Section 277.

12. *McCormick on Evidence,* Sections 279 and 280; *Jones on Evidence,* 5th ed., Vol. 4, Section 968.

13. *Hyman v. Josephowitz* (N.Y.), 187 N.Y.S. 317; *98 C.J.S.,* Section 358.

14. *98 C.J.S.,* Section 363; *McCormick on Evidence,* Section 278.

Chapter 2

WHAT TO DO

BEFORE TRIAL

Sec. 2.1 Should You Take the Case?

This is the first problem the trial lawyer is presented with in any case. It is a very important one, whether applied to the experienced practitioner with an active practice or to the beginner. While the beginner cannot be so discriminating, neither wants to reject a case which has some promise of favorable results. The average lawyer is motivated not only by the desire for financial gain but with the wish to make a satisfied client and to create a source of future legal business. Then there are those of our profession who bear in mind the duty of the lawyer to serve the deserving and the needy in the interest of justice.

In any case, the cost of taking a case and preparing it for trial is no longer small and the lawyer must be careful to screen out the worthless ones. It has been estimated that if the time spent by the lawyer and his office, from intake through trial (three days) in an automobile accident case involving moderate injuries were properly recorded, the time would be about 100 hours.[1] Depending on what the lawyer charges per hour ($25-$50 per hour is an approximation of the current rate), the lawyer has $2,500 to $5,000 involved of his time, exclusive of expenses, in an average case. However, there is a countervailing consideration, namely, the possibility of settlement, which could shorten the time and reduce the exposure to expenses incurred

---

1. Sindell—*Let's Talk Settlement,* p.275, published by Matthew Bender & Company Inc., San Francisco, California (1963).

26

by the lawyer. It is estimated that for every case tried, thirty are settled.[2] Also, there is the challenge presented to the aggressive trial lawyer of the well-financed insurance company having the field all to itself in combat with the humble victim of an accident.

Generally speaking, it is wise counsel to take the sure cases and to concentrate your time and energy on them, and to carefully sift out the others. As to the latter, it is no disgrace to accept them and most active practitioners do. If you have a borderline decision to make in such a case, at the intake stage you may take it conditionally or refer it to another lawyer if you do not wish to lose contact with it completely. If you take it conditionally, you should so notify the client and that if you decide to withdraw from it, you will do so within sufficient time to allow him to get other counsel before the limitations period expires. To protect yourself, you should put the conditional retainer in writing and have the client sign it so there can be no incrimination later from the client.

Sec. 2.2   What Makes a Case?

The basic factors in any negligence case are liability, injuries and damage, and collectibility of the award. If any one of these is missing, the lawyer is wasting his time if he handles such a case. The usual case will have conflicts of fact in respect to liability and injuries. However, if there is a prima facie case made out, this should be persuasive in accepting it. But if the defendant is uninsured and without assets, you can satisfy no one by accepting the case.

However, even in the latter situation, the case still may be salvable. If the case involves injuries or damage incurred in an automobile accident, inquire if your state has an uninsured fund to cover such cases. In the case of a child wrongfully injuring another child, there may be coverage through a family liability policy carried by the parent. The victim in an auto accident may have an auto coverage policy which provides for some award in case of injury from an uninsured motorist or for medical payments for his injuries.[3]

The following are samples of borderline cases which may be accepted, but with emphasis on settlement consideration: restaurant patron who finds broken glass while chewing on a sandwich, requiring medical attention; the drinking seaman who is struck in an intersection cross-walk by a careless motorist; the good samaritan who is injured when he rushes into a burning

---

2. Belli–*Modern Trials,* Introduction by Prof. Fowler Harper, Vol. 4, p. vi.

3. In such a policy, the customary limit for uninsured motorist coverage is $5,000; for medical payment the coverage varies between $250 and $5,000. Also, the client may be advised to seek social security benefits if there is permanent total disability. Sindell "Let's Talk Settlement," pps. 141, 142.

house to rescue a person when the fire was caused by the landlord's negligence.

The following are examples of cases which should be refused: motorist proceeding in fast lane who was injured when he collided with a motorist going in the same direction in the curb lane as he tried to move over into the curb lane; the tavern patron who is struck on the head by a falling electric fan when the tavern owner, whose equipment is heavily mortgaged, is without insurance coverage; the brawling neighbor who is arrested by his neighbor because of a fight with him but who is acquitted; the auto guest injured due to the ordinary negligence of his auto host in a state which requires proof of "gross negligence."

As to malpractice cases, it is advisable to accept only those which involve serious injuries and where you can obtain an out-of-state doctor to support your theory of negligence. Customarily, physicians will not testify against each other in the same community. Medical experts can be obtained in such cases, but obvious expense is involved. As to the sources for procuring out-of-state medical experts in such cases, see Sec. 4.2.

Sec. 2.3   What Documents to Prepare When Accepting a Case

Assuming that you have decided to accept the case, the first document to have the new client execute is the retainer. It should be broad and inclusive in the powers granted to the attorney; it should specify the fee; and it should make the client responsible for the expenses.

Paradoxically, a lawyer is a very vulnerable target. The legal calling is the most closely policed profession of them all. Unfortunately, when a disaffected client makes an accusation against his lawyer, a presumption of guilt seems to attach and it behooves the lawyer to have proof, especially records, to defend himself, else his career could be jeopardized. Hence, there should be no question about the retainer agreement and its terms.

A suggested form for retainer follows:

POWER OF ATTORNEY

I, or we, the undersigned, do hereby authorize and employ _____
_____ as my counsel and on my (our) behalf to take such measures as said counsel deems wise and expedient and to institute and carry on such claim, suit or action as said counsel deems necessary against:

_____

_____

on account of_____
_____
_____

For and in consideration of professional services rendered and to be rendered in the premises, I, or we, the undersigned, agree to pay said counsel the following:

_____ percent of any recovery realized from the aforegoing, whether by way of compromise and settlement, judgment or award

or

a reasonable fee consistent with law where determination or approval of counsel fee by a commission, board, agency, Court or other tribunals is required by law, same to apply to any recovery realized from the aforegoing, whether by way of compromise and settlement, judgment or award.

No counsel fee shall be paid if there be no recovery. All costs of litigation and all expenses connected with the handling of the said matters are to be borne by me, or us, the undersigned.

As witness my hand and seal this ____ day of _____, 19____.

Witness: Name _____ (Seal)
              Address _____
              Phone _____
              Name _____ (Seal)
              Address _____
              Phone _____

The next documents to be executed by the client should be the medical and hospital authorization forms. The following is a suggested form:

Authorization to Furnish Hospital (or Doctor's) Reports

City _____ State _____

Mo. _____ Day ____ Year ___

TO:_____(Hospital

or

_____Doctor)

Kindly furnish my (or our) counsel, _____
or counsel's representative, with full hospital (or medical and surgical)

reports of examination and treatment provided for me (or us) by your hospital (or by you) from:

Mo. _____ Day _____ Year _____

to

Mo. _____ Day _____ Year _____

· Thank you.

Witness: Name _____
                            Address _____
                            Name _____
                            Address _____
                            Name _____
                            Address _____

It is suggested that a general authorization form be signed also, in case it is necessary to have it to obtain, for example, a governmental agency report pertaining to the case. Such a form follows:

City _____ State _____

Date: _____

TO WHOM IT MAY CONCERN:

This Will Authorize you to turn over to my attorneys, _____
_____, any and all records, data and papers requested by them, which you may have and which pertain to me (us). Further, I authorize my said attorneys to obtain copies, including photostatic copies, of such records, data and papers.

Witness: Name _____
_____   Address: _____

It is also suggested that a Power of Attorney form be signed, authorizing the attorney to sign the client's name, as for example if the client is a seaman who may authorize a settlement while he is at sea. It is cautioned to use it very sparingly and only if the client specifically authorizes such a settlement as by a separate letter signed by him specifying the minimum amount of settlement agreeable to him. Such a form follows.

POWER OF ATTORNEY
Know All Men By These Presents,

THAT _____

residing at _____

do(es) hereby nominate, constitute and appoint _____

to be _____ TRUE AND LAWFUL ATTORNEY for_____

and in _____ name, place and stead to _____

_____

_____

and giving unto_____ said attorney(s) full power to do and perform all other lawful acts and whatsoever requisite and convenient to be done in the premises, as fully as _____ might or could do were _____ personally present; hereby ratifying and confirming all that_____ Attorney shall in _____ name lawfully do, or cause to be done in and about the premises, by virtue hereof.

In Witness Whereof, _____ have hereunto set _____ hand and Seal, this _____ day of _____ in the year of our Lord one thousand nine hundred and _____.

Witness:

_____   _____(Seal)

State of _____, City (County) of _____, to wit:

On this _____ day of _____, in the year one thousand nine hundred and _____, before me personally appeared _____ _____, known to me to be the person described in, and who executed the foregoing Power of Attorney, and acknowledged the said Power of Attorney to be _____ act.

In Witness Whereof, I have hereunto set my hand and official seal.

_____

Notary Public

My Commission expires: _____

The author uses a form letter which he sends to each prospective witness promptly. It is surprising how often the witnesses will answer. While it is best to interview the important witnesses personally, this form letter can be sent to the others.

Dear Mr. _____:

I am informed that you were a witness to an accident referred to in the Explanatory Statement included herein. I would appreciate it if you would fill out the "Statement of Witness Concerning Automobile Accident" which is enclosed. For your convenience, there is enclosed a self-addressed and stamped envelope in which to return your Statement.

Thanking you for your prompt cooperation, I am

Sincerely yours,

_____

Attorney for_____

EXPLANATORY STATEMENT:

This concerns the occurrence of an automobile accident, which occurred on the _____ day of _____, 19_____ at _____(a.m., p.m.), at or near_____ _____Street and _____ _____Street, in_____ _____ City or County, State of _____ _____, in which _____

claims injuries were suffered and automobile was damaged.

STATEMENT OF WITNESS CONCERNING AUTOMOBILE ACCIDENT

1. Did you see the accident? _____

2. When and where did it happen? _____

_____

3. Where were you when the accident occurred? (If in the car, what part of the car? If on the street, how near the place of the accident) _____

_____

4. Locate as near as possible the place of accident with relation to intersecting street.

_____

_____

5. If you so desire, please indicate location of accident by marking diagram on reverse side.

6. How far, if at all, did the cars move after the accident and where did they come to rest?

_____

_____

7. If there was anyone injured or property damaged, please state extent of same. _____

_____

_____

8. Please give the names and addresses of witnesses to the accident that you know of.

_____

_____

_____

9. Did the police investigate the accident? _____

10. How were the injured persons removed (i. e. ambulance)? _____

_____

11. Are you acquainted with anyone involved in the accident? If so, who? _____

_____

12. Were persons involved in accident related to you? If so, who? _____

_____

13. How did you happen to be at the scene of the accident? _____

_____

14. What is your employment or occupation and supply the name and address of your employer or place of occupation. _____

_____

15. What is your age? _____

16. Were statements obtained from the persons involved or of the witnesses or others? If so, from whom? _____

_____

17. Please tell in your own way how accident happened. _____

_____

_____

_____

_____

_____

_____

_____

18. What was said after accident? By whom? _____

_____

_____

19. What in your opinion was the direct cause of the accident? _____

LABEL EACH STREET OR HIGHWAY BY ITS PROPER DESIGNATION.
SHOW VEHICLES THUS ▬▬ SHOW PEDESTRIAN THUS ●

Indicate points
of Compass
N E.S.W.

Date: _____   Signature _____

Place of work: _____   Home address: _____

_____   _____

Phone number at work· _____   Home phone: _____

Sec. 2.4   How to Arrange the File

At the outset of the case, it is advisable to arrange your file as though you are preparing it for trial. At the trial, your papers should be so organized that you can pick them out promptly as needed without fumbling unduly. The author uses a simple method: a file containing folders, each of which is tabbed with a subject. These subjects are: *General Data* (for the memorandum of facts, public agency reports, witnesses' statements, and photographs of the accident scene); *Medical Data* (for the medical and hospital reports); *Expenses and Settlement Discussions* (for all expenses and careful notes on each settlement conference, whether by telephone or otherwise); *Pleadings & Law;* and *Correspondence.*

These will suffice for the average case. In the big case, the over-filled folder can be further broken down, as for example, "General Data" can be further divided into "Investigation Reports," "Witnesses' Statements," "Photographs," etc.

When the file becomes bulky and another is required, mark same "I" and "II" respectively and put an index on the outside of each so you will know the general contents of each without opening it.

When you go to trial, you can line up the folders on the trial table and refer to each as needed with the knowledge of what is in each one.

Sec. 2.5   How to Investigate and to Prepare the Case

The first interview with the client should be thorough and the fullest memorandum of the facts should be then taken. His memory of the events and details is then fresh. It is advisable to have before you a questionnaire form containing the questions which should be answered. There are numerous such forms. The following one is very exhaustive:[4]

Dear Client:

Since you are probably unfamiliar with the usual process of a negligence matter such as yours, we would like to acquaint you with the general pattern of how these cases are handled. We feel it will be helpful to both our clients and to ourselves if they know in advance what to expect and the step-by-step procedure of their case.

After your file has been opened in our office, the facts are first investigated to determine the value of the case from the standpoint of the extent of damage and injury to you, and the extent of negligence and liability on the part of the defendant.

Generally, discussions are first had with the defendant's insurance company for the possibility of negotiating a settlement without starting a law suit. If the insurance company is not interested in settling the matter, or will not settle for an amount which is fair and reasonable, then suit will be started.

Starting a suit involves serving a summons on the defendant(s), filing a Declaration, and waiting for an answer from the defendant's attorney. This process usually takes about one month. In some cases there is the necessity of further pleadings which must be filed and which, of course, takes more time. After all initial pleadings are filed, the case is put on the court docket, and your attorney has nine months in which to prepare your case for trial.

During that nine months, further investigation is made and when necessary, periodical medical reports are requested to enable us to follow the progress of your physical health. Also during this period

---

4. Taken from *Damages & Settlement Course Handbook*, American Trial Lawyers Association, 6 Beacon Street, Boston, Massachusetts. Prepared by Goodman, Eden, Robb, Millender, Goodman & Bedrosian, Detroit, Michigan.

See also a questionnaire prepared by Charles N. Segal, Esquire, 111 Pearl Street, Hartford, Connecticut; taken from Belli–*Modern Trials*, Vol. 4, p. 45. A thorough checklist in a death case appears in Speiser's "Recovery in Wrongful Death," p. 1015 et seq. Another source is *Legal Check-lists* by Becker, Sprechter & Savin, published by Callahan & Company, Chicago, Illinois. A brief one-page questionnaire is "Settlement Brochure" prepared by John J. O'Conner, Baltimore, Maryland–Belli *Modern Trials*, Vol. 1, Section 106, Chapter 6, 1966 Supplement.

depositions may be taken. The attorney for the defendant will want your sworn testimony of the facts surrounding your case, and we will want to take the testimony of the defendant. Your attorney will explain this to you in more detail when they are scheduled, and will review your case with you at that time. He will, of course, be with you when your deposition is taken.

One of the most difficult requests we make of our clients is patience. The completion of a law suit takes about two years. In other words, if a case is put on the docket in June of 1961, it may not come to trial until June of 1963. This applies mainly to cases in Wayne County, and if your suit is in the court of a less populated county, it will probably take considerably less time. We realize that it is sometimes difficult for our clients to understand that much of the time required in the handling of his case is due only to "waiting", but the dockets in Wayne County are extremely crowded and each case must wait its turn. We hope that some day this situation can be remedied, but this is the condition at the present time.

We do want to point out that although suit may be started, the possibility of settlement is always there, and if we feel that a settlement can be made which is in your best interest rather than waiting to try your case, we will make such a recommendation to you.

Please read the preface of this booklet before beginning to answer the questions. We are providing you with two copies; this one for you to fill out and retain, and the second is for our office and should not be completed until you have carefully checked your own copy and made corrections. If it becomes necessary to file suit in your behalf, the defendant will probably send us a list of questions called Interrogatories for you to answer. Your own copy of this questionnaire will help you answer those questions.

We would also like to draw your attention to paragraph I, J, and K. Please be sure to send all of your bills and expenses relative to your case which we do not have or are not included on the list of damages in this booklet. Also, please keep your attorney advised of any changes in your address, telephone number, changes of employment, physical health, and any other new information which may be helpful to us in preparing your case.

Your cooperation with your attorney is essential in bringing your case to the best possible conclusion. We welcome your help and suggestions.

> Sincerely,
> Goodman, Crockett, Eden, Robb & Philo
> By: _____

PREFACE

The answers you give here will be held strictly CONFIDENTIAL. If you wish, this booklet will be returned to you when your claim has been concluded.

Answer every question FULLY AND ACCURATELY. Success in this case depends upon mutual confidence and complete cooperation between client and attorney. It is imperative that your attorney know as much or more about you, your history and your activities, then the Defendant WILL KNOW by the time your case goes to trial. You MUST ASSUME that the Defendant will then know as much about you as you know, yourself.

ONE SURPRISE at the trial, produced on your attorney by the Defendant, because of an incorrect answer here, CAN RUIN YOUR CASE. That cannot happen, IF your attorney knows in advance every possible move that the Defendant can make, and has an opportunity to PREPARE YOU AND HIMSELF. Do not fail to answer a question fully, even though it may be embarrassing, or you do not think it is important, or you cannot understand why it has anything to do with your case.

This booklet is divided into major headings. Although it may appear long and complicated, each question has some importance to your case. In each instance we have provided space for you to fill in the answer. The success of your case will be governed by your cooperation.

* * * *

I—General Information

1. What is your full name?
   Present address:
   Telephone No.   If you have no phone, where can
        you possibly be reached by phone?—
   Social Security No.

2. List here addresses where you have resided during the past ten years, and give the period of time at each residence, including dates.

3. Have you ever used, or been known by any other name than that shown above?

If so, list each such other name, and state when and why you used such other name.

4. Where were you born?
   a. Date of birth
   b. Have you ever used any birthdate or birthplace other than shown above?
   c. If so, list here each such other birthdate or birthplace, and state when and why you used each.

5. Are you married at the present time?
   If so, what is full name of your wife or husband?

6. List the names, ages, and addresses of all those, including children, who are dependent upon you for support, and your relationship to each.

   Name   Address   Age   Relationship

7. Are you and your wife or husband living together at the present time?

8. Have you been divorced or legally separated at any time?
   If so, from whom, when and where?

II—Work Background

The amount of your recovery in this case will be affected by loss of earnings and earning capacity, so please outline carefully your work background.

1. Were you employed at the time of the accident?
   If so, state name and address of your employer.

Telephone No.

2. What was your job title, or the type of work you were doing?

3. What was your rate of pay?

4. How many hours per week were you working regularly immediately prior to the accident?

5. When were you first employed by the company for which you were working at the time of the accident?

6. Have you remained in the same job since that date?
   If not, state the reason for the termination of your employment, and name, address and telephone number of your present employer.

7. Have you missed any time from work as a result of your injury?
   If so, give dates you missed work because of injury:

8. Did you lose wages for the periods of time missed from work?
   If so, state the total lost to date:

9. Have you received any increases or decreases in your pay since the accident?
   If so, explain:

10. If you have changed jobs since the accident, give a summary of your present job, showing name and address of employer, rate of pay, your type of work, etc.

11. List your employment record as far back as you can remember. Your past employment record is important in determining your disability from an occupational viewpoint.

Name and address of employer	Employed From	To	Job	Reason for Leaving

12. What did you earn in the last year prior to your accident?

13. Have you filed income tax returns for the last three years?
   a. If so, where?
   b. Do you have copies of them?
   c. Will the figure shown in No. 12 be the same as shown in your return?

III—Background

We must know your background because your educational and physical history will have an important bearing upon your case.

A.   EDUCATION. What education have you had, including any special employment training?

B.   PHYSICAL EXAMINATIONS. List here EVERY physical examination you have ever had, for employment, promotion, insurance, selective service, armed forces, etc., stating the date, place, name of the doctor, and result as fully as you can recall.

Date   Place   Name of Doctor   Purpose   Result

C.   OTHER ACCIDENTS AND INJURIES. Failure to mention other accidents or injuries can undermine your lawsuit, no matter how trivial they may seem. List here every such incident, whether it resulted in a claim for damages or not, stating the date, place, nature of the accident and extent of your injuries. If none, so state.

Date   Place   Nature of Accident or Injury   Extent of Injury

D.   ILLNESSES. No matter how trivial an illness, either before or since your accident, we must know about it. This is particularly true if there is any connection with your present physical complaints. The defendant will have available at the trial, by medical and hospital records, veteran's records, insurance records, etc., a complete history of your past physical condition.

Date   Nature of Illness   Duration   Treated by   Hospitalized

E.   CLAIMS AND LAWSUITS. Any lawyer knows that there have been many cases damaged beyond repair by a history of other claims and lawsuits which he did not know about. It is NOT the fact that one has had other claims or lawsuits that is important, for he will not be penalized by a Court or jury if the claims are reasonable and genuine. It is the DENIAL of previous claims and suits which damages the case. List here EVERY claim you have ever made for personal injury or property damage, and fill in the details.

Date   Against Whom Nature of Claim   Suit Filled   Result

F.   POLICE RECORD. It is the law in this state, and elsewhere, that if a man has a criminal record, no matter how long ago, nor how mitigating the circumstances, that fact may be proven against him and commented on at the trial of his case. Most defense attorneys will NOT bring up a man's criminal record if they believe he will readily ADMIT the facts when asked, since to do so will hurt, rather than help, the defense. However, if they believe that a man will DENY conviction for a crime when the fact is otherwise, they WILL NOT HESITATE to use it against him. The defense will make a complete investigation of your background, and we must be PRE-PARED AGAINST development of unfavorable evidence. List here every arrest, and state the date, place, charge, and result.

Date   Place   Charges   Result   Confined

G.   ACTIVITIES SINCE THE ACCIDENT. If you suffered a serious injury in the accident, it is possible the opposing side already has or will in the future, take MOTION PICTURES of you. This is done with a telescopic lens, so that you never know it has been done, until the pictures are presented in Court to show that you ARE able to do something which you have either denied or neglected to mention that you are able to do. List here all your usual activities which you have NOT been able to perform since the accident, such as cutting grass, and recreational activities, such as golf, tennis, fishing, bowling, etc.

H.   WITNESS. Our law firm believes that besides presenting medical evidence that describes your injuries, it is very important to have as witnesses, various people who have noticed the effects of your injuries in your everyday life. Please list all of the people such as relatives, neighbors, co-workers, nurses, friends, etc., who might be able to compare your health before and after the accident.

Name   Address   Telephone   Relationship

I.   DAMAGES. Please list all of the damages and expenses to date that are a result of your accident. Where possible, please include dates, addresses, and enclose the bills.

                                                                                            Amount

J.   PHOTOGRAPHS. If you have them, we would like to have any or all of the following photographs:
        1. Pictures of you before the accident.
        2. Pictures of vehicle damages.
        3. Scene of accident.
        4. Pictures of your injuries—if someone else (such as insurance adjuster, friends, witnesses, or news photographer) let us know immediately so that we can try to secure copies.

K.   INSURANCE INFORMATION. Please send us:
        1. Your automobile policy.
        2. Homeowners liability policy.
        3. Your Blue Cross or other hospitalization insurance policy.
        4. Policies of any group insurance or special insurance such as newspaper insurance, accident insurance, etc.
        5. Give us a list of all other insurance policies issued to any other members of your family or household. This last item is very important.

L.   You should send to your attorney any subsequent bills for repairs to your car, doctors' bills, medications, braces, transportation to and from hospitals, doctors' offices, etc., household help required, baby sitters, etc.

M.   In our office, prior to trial, there may be several attorneys working on your case. One of us will be assigned the primary responsibility for preparing your case, but if you need help, any of the attorneys in our office can help you. IF YOU NEED TO CONSULT YOUR ATTORNEY PERSONALLY, regarding your case, be SURE to call him or his secretary for an appointment BEFORE COMING TO THE OFFICE. This will save your time and his. It is assumed, of course, that there will be taken information as to the "Accident,"the "Nature of the Injuries," and "Medical and Hospital Treatments."

ADDITIONAL DAMAGES AND OTHER INFORMATION

A very able and experienced trial lawyer once said that in every negligence case he feels much like David in his battle with Goliath. This biblical analogy is somewhat apt. The defendant is usually insured by a large insurance corporation which has unlimited means to investigate and to contest the case. David's slingshot may have been a modest weapon but it accomplished the defeat of the mammoth Goliath. The average lawyer has to be thrifty in his investigation but he must come up with the evidence to prove his case. In the usual auto accident case with modest injuries, the lawyer can investigate the case himself. It means getting the motor vehicle agency reports of the accident, the pictures and measurements of the accident scene (it is recommended that a Polaroid camera be used so you will know instanteously if the pictures taken are good ones), the statements of the witnesses, and the medical and hospital reports and bills.

It is important to visit the scene yourself because factors relating to proving negligence will be more obvious than from a picture. Time is of the essence. It is axiomatic that the one who gets to the witnesses first will get the better reception. A prompt investigation may beat the insurer's investigator, who usually has a case load to handle. If the case is of a higher magnitude, then a professional investigator may have to be brought in.

For example, suppose you are representing the widow of a motorist who was killed. Hypothesize further that while driving on an expressway, a truck driver going fast in the opposite direction lost control of the truck when a tire blew out and struck the vehicle which the deceased was driving. You should locate the defective tire (and get an order of court to sequester it at once for inspection, if necessary) and get an auto tire expert to inspect it to ascertain if the tire manufacturer was at fault and if the truck owner had made proper inspection of the tire, and if it was fit for use at all.

Another example, if you are representing a widow whose husband was a railroad conductor who was killed while assembling cars in making up a train, it would be wise to call in a railroad expert, preferably a retired railroad engineer, so you may be advised on what to look for to spell out a case of negligence against the railroad.

Still another example, if you are representing a patron who was seriously hurt at a beach resort when he dove into shallow water from a platform used by other swimmers, you should look for water safety experts to supply the indicia of negligence on the part of the resort owner.

If you are having difficulty locating needed experts, there are professional sources which can supply practically any kind needed.[5]

In the case involving wrongful serious injuries and death, the role of an expert to prove adequate damages has become almost essential. This type of expert is called an ecomionist-statisician. His function in the case and where he can be located are treated in chapter 9, infra.

The complete hospital and medical reports should be obtained. This is necessary in order to lay a proper evidentiary foundation for the medical expert you will use. For further details on this point, see Sec. 4.6, infra.

The matter of proving lost wages and income is vital to damages. This can be a big factor in the case where there has been lost time from work and where there is the likelihood of more lost time to follow, due to a permanent injury. Reference is made to the *Ryan* case in Sec. 1.8 to develop the wage loss data fully. In that case the author obtained a $70,000 verdict in a case of a sprained back occurring to a railroad frieght conductor. The large verdict was accounted for by the careful records kept by the client of his day-to-day wage losses.

Liberal use should be made of the discovery rules of court, whether state or federal, to obtain the data which you may need to flesh out your case. For example, in a case previously referred to in this chapter of the railroad freight conductor who was killed while assembling a train, the railroad was compelled to provide the plaintiff with an opportunity to take pictures and to make measurements of the accident scene and of the car types involved,

---

5. Technical Advisory Service for Attorneys (TASA) states that it provides expert witnesses for consultation, investigation, and court appearances in the following fields: safety, chemistry, aviation, construction, automotive, metallurgical, biological, electrical, textile, traffic, machine design, athletic, and engineering fields. It lists offices as follows:

- 253 Broadway, New York, New York, 10007 (phone: area code 212 732-2736)
- 1528 Walnut Street, Philadelphia, Pennsylvania, 19102 (main office) (phone: area code 215 545-8525)
- 3045 W. Liberty Avenue, Pittsburgh, Pennsylvania, 15216 (phone: area code 412 343-0888)
- 1000 Connecticut Avenue, N.W., Suite 9, Washington, D.C., 20036 (phone: area code 202 223-3555)
- 918 Fidelity Building, Baltimore, Maryland, 21201 (phone: area code 301 752-2424)
- 11420 Balboa Drive, Sun City, Arizona, 85351.

Another professional source is Expertise Institute, 130 N.W. 79th Street, Miami, Florida, 33138 (phone: area code 305 757-5594).

to produce the names and addresses of all witnesses, to produce them for the taking of their depositions, to produce their witnesses' statements (this was compelled because of court decisions in federal courts appertaining when the widow started her investigation late)[6] and to furnish the wage and employment records of the decedent.[7]

While the investigation and preparation of the case is underway, careful note should be made about the running of the Statute of Limitations in your case. No risk should be run of offending the limitations period because this would mean a premature end to your case.

Sec. 2.6   When Should Suit Be Filed?

There is much diversity among lawyers on this question. There are those who would wait until settlement discussion has been explored. There are others who believe suit should be filed promptly and settlement possibilities explored thereafter. The author is an exponent of the latter school of thought. The exception is where the case is a really dubious one, either on liability or damages or both, and it is desired to avoid time and expense spent on pleadings and discovery. When the suit is delayed, time drags and the client becomes impatient and often disenchanted with his case and his lawyer. Insurance companies set up a reserve for each case and wish to dispose of it fairly promptly in order to free that reserve. Nevertheless, many adjusters procrastinate to take the momentum out of the case and to dampen the enthusiasm of the client and his lawyer for a fat settlement. Adjusters have only very limited authority as to the amount they can offer. The defending insurance laywer usually has a better grasp of the exposure in the case and often has more influence in getting a higher settlement offer. In the lowest ranges, of say up to about $1,500 value, it is probably best to work with the adjuster for a settlement, rather than to spend the time and effort on filing suit and the follow-up work. In the cases valued above that, it is probably best to file suit promptly and to talk settlement afterward.

Sec. 2.7   How to Effectuate Settlement

After you have the evidence in your file to prove a prima facie case, you are in an effective position to talk settlement. Do not hesitate to call the

---

6. *The Guilford National Bank of Greensboro, etc. v. So. Ry. Co., et al.* (4 CA, 1962), 297 F.2d 921; *Reynolds v. U.S.* (3 CA, 1951), 192 F.2d 987, reversed on other grounds 345 U.S. 1, 73 S. Ct. 528.

7. The basic federal discovery rules are to be found in Federal Rules of Civil Procedure, Rules 26-37.

other side to discuss settlement. Nothing is lost by doing so. There is no concession either in pride or money to do so first. There are few cases which are 100 percent fool-proof. The average client wants to settle rather than to go through what is for him the ordeal of a trial.

The author recalls only one case in his trial career that appeared to be the perfect fool-proof case. This involved a back injury sustained by a merchant seaman during World War II in the engine department of the ship, of which he was a crew-member, when he was caused to slip and fall on oil negligently left on the engine room deck. However, the company had three witnesses who would testify that there was no oil on the deck at the time. He was treated for the back condition at the local U.S. Marine Hospital and the doctors on each side of the case allowed him some percentage permanent loss of use of his back. About one month before the scheduled trial date, the ship was torpeodoed by the enemy and went down with all of the company's witnesses. As the author eagerly approached the trial date, the client called and insisted on a settlement. The case was settled at a lesser figure than it would have brought at the trial. The client was satisfied; his lawyer was not. In retrospect, the author sees it differently now. Experience teaches the trial lawyer that the client usually has good reason when he insists on a settlement. It may be his jittery nerves which would make him a poor witness; it may be that he is concealing something, even from his lawyer, such, for example, as a previous injury affecting the same part of his body; or it may be some dark chapter in his past which he fears may be exposed. If the trial took an unexpected turn and the verdict were adverse, the client would probably look at his counsel (and his malpractice policy) with a jaundiced eye. The client's wishes in respect to settlement should come first.

On the other hand, if counsel feels that the case should be settled because, for example, liability is precarious, counsel should use all of his persuasive powers on his client to accept his recommendations. Counsel is better qualified to weigh the risks than his client is. If, despite this, the client refuses, it is advisable to obtain a letter from the client, signed by him, in which this state of things clearly appears. The letter may come in good stead to protect the lawyer if the client gets an unsatisfactory verdict. Recalcitrant clients have been known to turn against their own lawyer in such cases by complaining to the bar association grievance committee.

Before you talk settlement, you must fix a price value on the case. This ability comes with experience. Perhaps there is some intuition employed, too. There are some aids or yardsticks to help the lawyer, whether he is the veteran or the beginner.

In the average automobile accident case involving some musculo-ligamentous strain of the back, there are the special damages (i.e. medical, hospital and drug expenses, lost wages, and auto damage), the permanent injury, if any, and the pain and suffering. The first item presents no difficulty. It is important to remember that because the plaintiff received his full wages from a generous employer or received weekly disability insurance benefits under a policy he had, or received payment for medical and hospital debts because of his own insurance policy, the defendant is not excused from paying it again.[8] The value to be placed on the last two items can vary considerably. An important factor is the local standards in such matters. This is influenced greatly by what awards the juries and judges are returning in similar cases in that forum. Frequent contact with the courts and with negligence lawyers trying such cases will help to furnish this valuable information. There are sources which furnish a compilation of past verdicts in similar cases.[9] In Sindell's "Let's Talk Settlement," a slide-rule formula is used to arrive at the value of a case.[10]

A settlement proposal sheet which the author would use in discussing settlement in the back injury case just mentioned would look as follows:

Plaintiff's Settlement Figures

Special Damages:		
Sinai Hospital	$ 350.00	
Dr. A.B. (treatment)	$ 200.00	
Drugs	$ 20.00	
Lost Wages (1/6/70-2/6/70, 4 weeks @ $150.00)	$ 600.00	$ 1,170.00
Permanent Disability:		
10% loss of use of back		$10,000-$15,000
Pain and Suffering:		
First 2 weeks @ $50.00 per day	$ 700.00	
Last 2 weeks @ $25.00 per day	$ 350.00	
	$1,050.00	
Future pain and suffering	$1,500.00	$ 2,500.00
		$18,670.00

---

8. See "Collateral Benefits," Sec. 12.8 infra.

9. Jury Verdict Research, Inc., Cleveland, Ohio; McBride "Disability Evaluation," (1953), 5th ed., published by Lippincott Company, Philadelphia, Pennsylvania; Belli—*Modern Trials,* Vols. 4-6.

10. At p. 288. The formula assumes a maximum jury award in a similar case in the forum where the case would be tried. Then on a point system basis for various items (i.e. liability, injuries, age of plaintiff, type of plaintiff, type of defendant, and the special damages), it arrives at a percentage of the maximum. This is the recommended settlement figure. For information forms, see p. 297 of the Sindell book, published by Matthew Bender & Company, Inc., San Francisco, California (1963).

Determinative of the amount to settle for is the nature of the liability and how authentic is the permanent disability rating. If the liability is weak, the requested gross amount should be reduced proportionately. For example, if the case is 50-50 on liability, the gross should be reduced by 50 percent and the demand would be about $9,000. If the 10 percent permanency rating is doubtful, this should be reduced proportionately. For example, if your doctor has indicated that the symptoms are entirely subjective and that his evaluation is generous, and if the defendant's doctor states there is no permanency, then it may be in order to reduce the permanency figure to $7,500 or less and to omit future pain and suffering as an item.

If both liability and permanency are dubious, settlement is almost compulsory and the goal should be something above the special damages—perhaps in the range of $1,000—for an overall settlement of about $2,000-$2,500.

The impression the plaintiff would make as a witness should figure in the estimate of value. Similar consideration should be given to the defendant as a witness. The expected performance of each can be visualized if their depositions have been taken. However, these last two items are the least in importance in fixing the price-tag on the case, unless your client or the defendant makes a particularly bad impression; as for example, if the plaintiff makes a negative impression and has a long record of personal injury litigation, or if the defendant has an abrasive manner about him.

The technique of settlement presentation is more or less conditioned on the personalities of the opposing sides. Some plaintiffs' lawyers advocate the giving of as little information as possible in the settlement discussion. Some are exponents of the "race of disclosure" technique advanced by Melvin Belli, the noted torts lawyer.[11] This is a fairly complete disclosure of your case and in brochure form; it puts emphasis on frankness in the statement of the claim and discountenances "surprises." Some plaintiffs' lawyers, who are advocates of the latter school, use the brochure style and include in it copies of all of the bills to support the special damages, medical reports to support causal connection and disability, documents to support proof of lost earnings, and even pictures of the damaged vehicles and copies of statements from witnesses to establish liability. Some claims adjusters and defendants' lawyers are impressed with this approach; some simply exploit it where possible.

The author feels that in the final analysis, it depends on the nature of the case and the defendant's representatives whether to use one or the other of the techniques. If your case is a strong one and if you feel the defendant's representative is acting in good faith to achieve a fair settlement, then the

---

11. Belli—*Modern Trials*, Vol. 1, Sec. 106, p. 695 et seq.

complete disclosure tool may be used. Otherwise, it is wiser to play the settlement game "close to the vest" and to furnish the defendant with a minimum of information, and to put as little as possible into writing. The day is not yet here when both parties are nobly disposed toward each other. It is the rare insurance company which will not try to settle as cheaply as possible, rather than for what the case is actually worth; and any plaintiff is considered fair game in this match of strategy.

Should you use your rock-bottom demand figure at the first settlement session? Some plaintiffs' lawyers do; most do not. The reason that most do not is because they wish to allow some room for bargaining or for retreat on the price requested. The average defendant's representative will bargain and will hold back on the full authority given to him to settle; there are exceptions, however.

In the case involving wrongful serious injury or death, it is frequently advisable to call in an economist-statistician to adequately present the damages. This expert can prepare an estimate, especially for the settlement discussion. This entire subject is discussed in chapter 9, infra.

Should the lawyer keep his client posted as to the original estimate the lawyer places on the case and of the figures submitted by either side in the course of the negotiations? The author advises against it. The client is not a law specialist and is not familiar with the mystique of settlement discussions. The original estimate may build up his notion of the case's worth to a point where he will not readily yield. The ebb and flow of the figures exchanged during the negotiations may mislead him and make him suspicious of the whole thing. However, when counsel feels he has obtained the top offer for settlement from the defendant, he should promptly present it to the client with his recommendations and he should promptly notify the other side of his client's response.

Where settlement figures are submitted in writing, it is advised that the plaintiff's lawyer submit his figure as his own recommendation, rather than that which the client has agreed to take. This will avoid the awkward situation of having the client renege on his commitment. It is more acceptable and understandable to the defendant if a client refuses to accept his lawyer's recommendation; the possibility of an increased offer by the defendant is not entirely closed out then.

Sec. 2.8 How to Prepare for Trial

If settlement efforts have proved fruitless, the next step is final preparation for trial. The word "final" is used because it is assumed that much of the trial preparation was done before settlement was considered. From the time the case was accepted, the trial attorney should have been mentally focusing on the trial of the case, rather than on its settlement. If settlement had come, then it would have been felicitous; but even when settlement was being discussed, it should have been undertaken from a position of strength based on thorough investigation and preparation of the case by plaintiff's counsel.

A firm trial date should be obtained and every effort should be made to adhere to it. To avoid misunderstandings about it and to deflate glib excuses from the other side for postponements, send a letter to the defendant's attorney confirming the trial date. It can be frustrating to plaintiff's counsel, his client, and his witnesses to be put off by numerous postponements.

The witnesses should be alerted well in advance to be ready to appear on that date, especially the medical experts. A form letter used by the author's firm reads as follows:

Re:

Dear _____:

I represent the above-named in connection with injuries sustained in an automobile accident which occurred on _____ _____. This case is scheduled for trial for _____ _____ in the _____ _____. We would like you to be available to testify in this case and will issue the usual subpoena for you.

Because we are not certain whether the case will be reached as scheduled, you should phone us a few days before the trial date.

Thanking you for your cooperation, I am

Sincerely,

Each lawyer must find his own method of briefing for the trial. Some use rough notes, some an outline, and some detailed typewritten questions to be put to the witnesses, inclusive of examination and cross-examination of the medical experts. If the case is a big one, the lawyer may be working with another lawyer or lawyers in a team. In any event, the case and its steps from the conference with the judge and the opening statement to the closing argument and the request for instructions should be fully prepared sufficiently in advance of the trial to avoid unnecessary pressures. Each case has enough surprises before and during trial to take up counsel's spare time and attention without having to worry about preparation for trial in this crucial period.

The author is a firm believer in the preparation of a brief memorandum of authorities to support your position on anticipated evidence issues and on requests for instructions. This is particularly advisable where the case is somewhat off-beat, as for example a suit by the good samaritan on account of injuries suffered by him in a rescue or the suit involving the injured seaman or railroad worker. It is impossible for the judge to know all of the law. He will appreciate your help in directing him to the applicable authorities. You will feel more ready and confident by reason of this additional preparation, which simply capsulizes what you already have researched.

At a time close to trial, the client and his important witnesses should be called in and the case gone over with them. At this time, the client should be conditioned for the role he is to play and for the court's atmosphere. For a full discussion on this important subject, see chapter 3, infra.

Sec. 2.9   The Theory or Plan of Action

Counsel should have his theory and plan of the case well thought out in advance of trial. For example, the author recently represented a seaman who was knocked down by a U.S. mail truck in a cross-walk at an intersection. The seaman had been drinking. He suffered injury to his chest cage area. After he was released from the hospital, he had bouts of severe pain in his rib area and had to undergo a minor nerve block operation to stem the pain. The U.S. Marine Hospital doctors, including an orthopedic specialist, where he was treated, found no permanency and indicated the complaints of pain were largely illusory. The doctor who was treating the plaintiff was in Long Beach, California (the trial was to occur in Baltimore). The deposition of the doctor was taken at his office. Although he was a general surgeon, it was developed that he had had numerous experiences with this type of injury. Medical charts were used in conjunction with his deposition and they were carefully marked by the doctor in different and prominent colors to illustrate what he meant as he described the particular nerves which were injured by the trauma and how they reached the pain points in this man's chest. The deposition was carefully read by counsel at the trial and the medical charts were displayed, and a pointer was used by counsel to correlate the doctor's testimony with the charts. The plaintiff made a frank statement that he was a fairly heavy drinker when ashore but that he was sober enough to know that he was crossing on a green light when he was hit by the mail truck. Counsel had the seaman's wife come with him for the trial to confirm her husband's pain and to testify what a good husband and father he was, despite his drinking. The court, sitting without a jury as is required in a Federal Torts Claim Act suit, found for the plaintiff and awarded him $17,500.

The theory was to present plaintiff as a hard living, but a hard working and good family man, who was worthy of belief when he testified that he had the green light at the crossing and when he said he had pain. Further, the theory was to overcome the negative U.S. Marine Hospital medical testimony, made up of young resident doctors, by the clear and graphic testimony of an experienced surgeon who had actually found the pain on the plaintiff and who had relieved it by an operation. The judge accepted the plaintiff's position on all counts.

Another example. In a chain auto collision, John Stepac (fictitious name) suffered a whip-lash type of injury to his neck and back, and was hospitalized. He suffered a musculo-ligamentous sprain. Following his release from the hospital, he complained of severe pain and discomfort in the neck area and received considerable therapeutic treatment, but with little apparent relief. He lost much time from work, was often late in reporting for work, and became argumentative with his foreman. Eventually he lost his job. He obtained another job and lost it, too. Then be became idle but complaining and odd. He was a young bachelor and a refugee from the recent Hungarian revolution. The plaintiff's doctor prognosed about 15 percent permanent disability in the neck and defendant's doctor none. The offer for settlement was $2,000, which was rejected. Plaintiff's counsel theorized that John was more emotionally than physically affected by his accident and brought into the case a neurologist, who testified that John had suffered substantial permanent disability to his body as a whole on account of emotional difficulties flowing from the accident. John was a sensitive person whose emotions had already been strained by his previous war experience. Our theory was that the accident was the straw which broke the camel's back. The jury verdict was $25,000.

In short, once counsel is in full command of the facts, he is then in a position to study his case as an entirety and to see its true contours, its shallows and its depths, and then to project the course which his handling should take. This theory and plan should be followed from the opening statement through the closing argument. The judge and jury become the interested onlookers as you pursue this journey before them.

Chapter 3

HOW TO PREPARE THE PLAINTIFF
FOR THE WITNESS STAND

Sec. 3.1   Preliminaries

By the time the case is ready for trial, usually the plaintiff has answered defendant's interrogatories under oath and has given his deposition concerning the accident and his injuries. The defendant's answers to interrogatories are in and perhaps his deposition, too. The issues and trouble points are already fairly known. Counsel should have all of this at his fingertips when the client is called in shortly before trial to prepare him for the witness stand. In fact, the plaintiff's counsel should have the entire case ready for trial, so he can relate to his client what his theory and plans are and what witnesses he proposes to produce and when, besides what he will ask the plaintiff. Of particular importance is the pointing to the precise pages of the discovery records so the plaintiff is prepared for any seeming conflicts which will arise in the trial and so he is prepared to reconcile them. By this time, counsel has a rather accurate conception of what kind of a witness his client will make and what his strengths and weaknesses are as a witness.

Sec. 3.2   What General Instructions to Give

Some trial lawyers issue printed instructions to their clients on general guidelines to be observed at the trial.[1] While this may be helpful, the author prefers not to do this because there is a tendency for the witness to tighten up and to become a rule-book witness rather than a natural one.

---

1. See "Your Day In Court," published by Lawyers & Judges Publishing Company, 4156 E. Grant Road, Tucson, Arizona, 85716 (1970).

The plaintiff and his spouse, and other important witnesses, should be called in for the final trial preparations. The plaintiff should be instructed particularly that the jury does not know him or anything about his case and that they will do what they think is fair and just. Hence, it is important for the plaintiff to impress the jury first and foremost with his truthfulness and sincerity. He should avoid evasiveness wherever possible. This will have particular aptness when he describes what pain and suffering he has and is enduring, because usually this is on a subjective basis.

They should be instructed to act naturally and politely (even to the opposition), to be truthful, and to speak audibly. It is advisable to notify them to address the judge as "Your Honor." They should be cautioned against guessing and to act on recollection only when it is reliable. They should be instructed not to answer a question until the objection has been ruled on by the judge. They should not speak to the jurors during recesses. They must be cautioned to observe their conduct both outside as well as inside the courtroom.

To exemplify how important the last instruction can be, the author recalls an experience he had involving a ten-year-old boy who had suffered a skull injury in an automobile accident while a passenger. It was our position that the child had become emotionally unstable as a result of his head injury. His mother, who sat with him in the courtroom, was an hysterical type. As she sat behind us in the audience section and oblivious to us, she grimaced throughout the trial, made audible comments, and on a few occasions was restrained by her son as she arose to protest a statement made by an adverse witness or by opposing counsel. The jury brought in a low verdict. In speaking with the jurors after the verdict, they remarked that they were impressed by the boy's poise and control in pacifying his neruotic mother and therefore did not accept our neurologist's opinion that the boy had sustained emotional disability.

The plaintiff should be cautioned against certain trap questions, which are frequently put by opposing counsel. One of these is if he has spoken to his lawyer before the trial and if so, what he was told to say. The client should be instructed to answer that he has, and that he was told to tell the truth. Another trick question is if the plaintiff knows any of the important witnesses. If he does, he should not hesitate to answer in the affirmative, and if further questioned as to whether they discussed the case, to answer "yes" and that the witness was asked only to tell it as it occurred.

Sec. 3.3   What Your Client Should Wear

The plaintiff and his witnesses should try to make a favorable impression on the jury. To this end, they should be neatly and not poorly or garishly dressed or groomed.

If the plaintiff is a workingman, he should be told to wear his dress suit, with a tie and perhaps a white handkerchief in his lapel pocket. He should have his shoes shined. Juries are not impressed today with a plaintiff who appears in tatters in what may be considered a transparent effort to appeal to their sympathies. Besides, such a person is not inclined to qualify in their eyes for high damages, since his appearance denotes a low standard of living.

Be sure to inquire about the color of his apparel because counsel may be rudely surprised. If he does not have a dress suit, take him out and buy one for him and charge it as an expense item.

If the plaintiff is a white collar worker or even a business or professional man, do not hesitate to make similar discreet inquiries about his dress and grooming.

Where the plaintiff is a youth who is embellished with extraordinary long hair and/or a flowing beard, the author has no hesitancy in asking him to look like a "square" just for the period of the trial. While his lawyer may not object to his "hippy" appearance, it is certain that some jurors will. Why invite unnecessary risks?

Where the plaintiff is a woman, she should be asked what she plans to wear, even to the heels on the shoes. Her dress should be moderate in style and color. Extremism should be avoided—whether being overdressed or spinsterish in appearance. The hairdo should be moderate in style and color, also. It is important for her to avoid wearing especially high-heeled shoes, particularly if she is complaining of neck or back pains from an accident, since obviously these two items do not go convincingly together.

If the plaintiff is a child, he should be dressed up and should be carefully supervised in and about the courtroom. As he tires, he should be taken out of the courtroom. It will not do to have a child who has been allegedly permanently disabled upsetting the courtroom with his agility and antics.

Sec. 3.4   What Preparation the Plaintiff Should Make for His Testimony

The plaintiff should be aware of the answers which he gave in his answers to interrogatories and in his deposition, and should be cautioned that if confronted with a conflict between such statements and one which he makes on the witness stand at the trial, he should not deny the previous statements. To reconcile the conflict, he can say that his current recollection is the correct one. It is common knowledge that man's memory is not infallible.

As an example, the author had a case recently in which the plaintiff had injured himself when he fell over air ducts in a warehouse. The air ducts had just been removed for repair but were left on the floor in the path of the plaintiff as he opened the door to go from the office into the warehouse. But the plaintiff had testified in his deposition that as he opened the door, he was looking behind him for persons who might be following him so he could politely keep the door open for them, too. This obvious element of contributory negligence was explained away by his saying that he recalled that even though he did look back, he nevertheless took note of what was ahead by use of his peripheral (outward focal) vision.

As to details and dates which would be difficult to remember, as for example, medical and hospital treatment and bills for same, days lost from work and the sums lost thereby,[2] the client should write these down with the assistance of counsel and use these notes to refresh his recollection at the trial. It is important that the notes be in his own handwriting, else their use may be objectionable as hearsay. Counsel should photostat the client's notes to provide a spare, because it is not unknown for clients to lose or to forget them on the day of trial.

A blackboard or other exhibits should be used in counsel's office to illustrate the diagrams and exhibits which he will use. For example, in an automobile accident case, the client should be asked to point out how the accident occurred, using the diagrams. In this way, the client will not get confused by the diagrams and on geographical directions indicated therein.

At the conclusion of the interview, counsel should ask the client if he has any questions. Surprising inquiries sometimes are made, for example: whether he can ask the cross-examiner questions; if he can voluntarily give information directly to the jury in the form of a speech; or if he can bring out that he would have settled the case for the medical expenses alone if the defendant had the decency to inquire about his physical condition.

The witness should be cautioned against volunteering information beyond that requested by the question put to him. In this connection, it is important to appraise your client's characteristics. Is he loquacious or inarticulate? Is he excitable or dull? Be frank with him about his predispositions and caution him accordingly. His wife can remind him in these respects.

He should be cautioned not to try to memorize details, especially material he gave in the deposition. Memorization will make him sound rehearsed, and the effort will make him even more nervous.

As to pain and suffering, liberal use should be made of the hospital and medical records, and especially of the nurses' notes to remind the plaintiff of the discomfort and agony which he endured.[3] Nature mercifully enables

---

2. See the discussion in Sec. 1.8, supra.
3. See the discussion in Sec. 8.6, infra.

human beings to forget. Ordinarily, the most intensive suffering occurs during the first few weeks following an accident. A higher demand for damages should be made, therefore, for this period.[4] Try to have your client strike a happy medium between understating and overstating his pain and suffering. The jury may tend to ignore his pain and suffering if he adopts the understatement, and it may react against him if he overstates it.

Sec. 3.5 What Precautions to Take Against Your Own Client

It is advisable to remind the plaintiff that the defendant has means of checking on plaintiff's previous accidents and disabilities.[5] Hence, he should mention now any oversights, as for example a previous back injury in a back injury case. It is not unusual for a person to forget such a thing if it occurred many years before. Also, people who were involved in previous accidents tend to focus their recollection on the most serious aspect of it, as for example, injury to the right leg when there was injury recorded to the low back also. In such cases, it is advisable to procure the hospital or medical record of that previous accident to reassure yourself and to avoid surprise from the other side in the trial.

If there has been an offer of settlement made which the client rejects, the author strongly advises that counsel get his client to sign a letter in which he states that he rejects it and prefers trial. This is for counsel's future protection if an untoward verdict is returned and your client turns on his own lawyer. This is not farfetched.[6]

Sec. 3.6 What to Do About Surprises

Anticipating now unpleasant turns of events at the trial, suppose that in a back injury case, the defense surprises plaintiff's counsel with evidence of a previous back injury which the plaintiff has up to now denied. The author was confronted with this nightmarish experience in a seaman's injury case. The way it was handled was to get the plaintiff to retake the witness stand and to concede the mistake, but he explained that he did not mention it because he had forgotten it, since it had occurred many years before and since he did not consider it a serious disability. The jury thought better of him, I am sure, because of his manly confession, but it still decided the case against him; but this could have been accounted for on other grounds.

---

4. See the discussion in Sec. 2.7, supra.
5. There is a service available to insurers to check on previous claims made by a person.
6. See discussion on this point in Sec. 2.7, supra.

Another surprise ordeal? The author was representing a middle-aged fire-fighter who was compelled to retire because of a serious back injury sustained in a rear-end automobile collision. The defense produced a surprise witness—a female investigator—who called at the plaintiff's home while he was recuperating, on the pretext of conducting a census on men's hobbies, induced him to take her below to his workshop and to demonstrate how he operated lathes, saws, and other equipment in pursuing his hobby of woodwork. To add insult to injury, she subtly got him, a married man, to invite her out to dinner. On the way a tire was mysteriously flattened and he fixed it. I cross-examined her aggressively to show the jury that she purposefully used her female wiles on the plaintiff to get these calculated results and that she actually let the air out of the tire (which she vigorously denied). I was prepared to put him back on the stand to admit his human weakness in falling for her deceptions but to reaffirm that while he could engage in some physical activities, he did so with considerable discomfort and that he could not do it on an eight hour basis. Nevertheless, I settled this case before I put him back on the stand and then had to act as mediator between him and his enraged wife. I fully earned this fee.

What does counsel do when the defense produces footage of motion pictures of your client, who is claiming a permanently injured neck or back, showing him doing some active work like changing a tire? If the pictures are not inconsistent with your client's previous testimony, namely that he can do some physical labor but not on an eight hour basis, perhaps it is best to do nothing about it and to argue that the pictures in no way refute his position and previous testimony. If, however, he has denied ever changing a tire since the accident, it may be advisable to have him retake the stand and to admit it and to explain why he denied it, as for example, because he did not think it significant and that he suffered pain from it later. Whether to put the plaintiff back on the stand in these circumstances is a visceral judgment which plaintiff's counsel must make, depending on how good a witness the plaintiff makes and how plaintiff's counsel believes it will come off.

Sec. 3.7   Checklist of Items on Preparing Plaintiff for the Witness Stand

1. He or she should be instructed to dress and to be groomed moderately to impress the court and jury with being neat, tidy, clean, and to be accustomed to a decent standard of living.

2. Plaintiff should act naturally and politely, and speak audibly to impress the court and jury with his demeanor.

3. Plaintiff should be truthful and sincere, and avoid evasiveness where possible to impress the court and jury with his credibility.

4. Plaintiff should wait before answering once an objection has been made by either side, until the court has ruled on the objection.

5. Plaintiff should not volunteer any information, but answer the question and stop.

6. Plaintiff should not guess and should rely on recollection only when it is reliable.

7. Plaintiff should remember that his conduct is under observation by the jury while outside the courtroom during recesses as well as inside the courtroom.

8. Plaintiff and his witnesses should not speak to the jurors out of the jury box.

9. If asked, Plaintiff can mention that he has discussed the case with his counsel and his witnesses previous to trial, and that he and they were urged to tell the truth.

10. Plaintiff should be cautioned not to deny having made seemingly conflicting statements in the previous discovery proceedings (i.e. in the deposition of his testimony), and he should be prepared to reconcile them with his courtroom statements. In this connection, counsel should have the case at his fingertips so as to direct plaintiff's attention to these points immediately while preparing plaintiff for the witness stand.

11. Plaintiff should write out in his own handwriting dates and information which he cannot remember (i.e. admission and discharge dates from hospitals and doctors, bills for same; lost time and wages from work) and be encouraged to use them at the time of trial to refresh his recollection.

12. Counsel should use a blackboard and exhibits to familiarize the plaintiff with the diagrams and exhibits which will be used in the courtroom to describe the accident and other factors, and to acquaint himself with them and with the geographical directions appearing, particularly in the diagrams of the accident.

13. The hospital and medical records should be used to remind the plaintiff of his previous pain and suffering.

14. Plaintiff should be carefully questioned again about previous accidents and disabilities affecting the particular area of the body concerned in this accident.

15. Plaintiff should be warned about spying and surveillance techniques which the defendant may have used against him in the period before trial.

16. Plaintiff should be cautioned not to memorize the deposition or any of his statements, so his testimony will sound natural and not rehearsed or artificial.

17. If the client rejects the settlement offer, counsel, for his own protection, should obtain a signed letter from the client rejecting the settlement offer made by the defendant, stating that he prefers trial.

Chapter 4

HOW TO PREPARE

THE MEDICAL WITNESS

Sec. 4.1 What Medical Expert to Use

In Sec. 1.3, supra, there is a discussion on how to medically research your case. Much of that discourse is applicable here.

In many personal injury cases, the patient is treated by a general practitioner or by the hospital staff doctor and then referred to a specialist. If it is possible to use these doctors to testify in your case, even as to evaluation, then certainly this is to be desired. The reason is that the judge and jury should be impressed with the fact that they are impartial and objective because they came into the case quite by accident, literally.

However, it is frequently necessary to call in an expert for the purpose of assessing the degree of disability. Generally speaking, the treating doctors are not experienced in litigation and are fearful of the court room. They are not inclined, therefore, to be fully cooperative, and tend to be indefinite and to minimize the injuries and disability. What is worse, they make poor witnesses by being maneuvered on cross-examination into making damaging admissions and concessions, because they wish to appear impartial or because they do not wish to refute the opposing doctor. The defendant's attorney will have his own medical expert testify if he finds that the reports of the treating doctors give the patient substantial disability.

The necessity exists, therefore, especially in a serious disability case, to produce your own expert. There are two prerequisites for an effective medical expert. He must be well qualified in his specialty and he must be experienced in court trials. The omission of either condition could be very costly. Lacking the first requirement, his testimony can be eviscerated on cross-examination. Lacking the second precondition, it is more likely than not that he will make some unnecessary and damaging admission or concession on cross-examination. If you are going to use a newcomer as your medical expert, you should go over the case very carefully with him in advance of the trial.

In the less serious cases, if you cannot locate a specialist, a qualified surgeon or a specialist in internal medicine and diagnosis, who has had experience with your type of case, would be a good choice.

If your case is serious enough and if you cannot locate such a qualified witness in your own locality, then you should bring one in from outside, preferably from a large community near your own.[1] You must be prepared to pay him for examining the record and for preparing his opinion as well as for the expenses and time he spends in court. To reduce your costs, make arrangements in advance with the court and your adversary to have your case tried at a time certain, so you can put on your expert at a pre-arranged hour.

It is important to have him examine the plaintiff in advance of trial because the jury will not be impressed by the expert who is testifying about the disability of a person whom he has never even examined. Of course, in a death case, this is impossible.

Sec. 4.2   How to Locate a Medical Expert

The most convenient method is to consult fellow counsel who try similar cases. You may inquire of your local medical association and of the local university (medical center) about the specialists in the field with which you are concerned; however, you should inquire also of fellow lawyers about these doctors because, unfortunately, doctors, like other human beings, have predilections, tending either toward a conservative or a liberal viewpoint, medically speaking. If you are representing the plaintiff, naturally you will want a doctor who is at least sympathetic to the injured plaintiff and who will give him the benefit of any doubt in relation to causal relation and to the extent of disability. On the other hand, if you are representing the defendant, you will want the conservative-minded doctor. Some courts have a panel of doctors who are available to them as impartial expert witnesses in their field of medicine. Many Workmen's Compensation Boards in the various states have similar panels. Inquiry can be made of these sources.

---

1. In a malpractice case against a local physician and/or hospital, it is usually necessary to show that an outside medical witness is familiar with the usual and customary practices prevailing among physicians and surgeons in the same locality where the defendant committed the alleged malpractice. *Wells v. McGehee* (La.), 39 So. 2d 196, 202 (La. App. 1949). See discussion in Louisell & Williams *Medical Malpractice*, 8:04.

Again, the lawyer is cautioned to ask his fellow lawyers in the field about the expert's predispositions of thinking before finally choosing him.

If all of these efforts are unproductive, inquiry can be made of various other sources. There are numerous medical directories published in the many fields of medicine which name specialists and which usually mention something about their biographies. There is the American Medical Association (A.M.A.) which, through its Directory of Medical Specialties, names over 76,000 certified diplomats of the 19 specialty boards. There are others, the most prominent of which are detailed in *2 Am. Jur. Trials,* pages 361-369.[2]

Sec. 4.3   What Basic Questions to Put[3]

The fundamental questions which should be put center about the following points:

   (a) the doctor's qualifications as a specialist;
   (b) his familarity with the case (i.e. with the hospital records and with the plaintiff through his physical examination, covering the history of the accident, his symptoms, and his past medical history);
   (c) prognosis and disability;
   (d) causal connection with the accident.

These ingredients should be incorporated into a hypothetical question if the medical expert was not a treating physician in the case. A discussion of this subject will be made hereafter (Sec. 4.8).

---

2. For publications in the special fields of medicine which may be consulted for leads as to experts, see *2 Am. Jur. Trials* at pps. 371-407.

3. There are numerous books and publications on examination of medical witnesses. For a recent and succinct article on the subject, see "Direct Examination of Medical Experts in Personal Injury Actions" by Joseph B. Kelly (Professor of the Dickerson Law School), appearing in the *Daily Record,* Baltimore, Maryland, September 27, 1970, citing the following sources: Frost "Preparation of a Negligence Case" 28 (1946); Dooley "Technique of Increasing Plaintiff's Verdicts" in Successful Jury Trials, A Symposium 398 (Appleman ed. 1952); Appleman, Cross-Examination of Physicians, p. 381, supra.; 4 Busch Law & Tactics in Jury Trials (Encycl. ed. 1962); Fricke, Planning and Trying Cases (1952); Houts, Lawyers Guide to Medical Proof (1966); Goldstein, Trial Technique; McKelvy "The Proper Use of Cross-Examination in Successful Jury Trials", supra, p. 252; Gazan, Trial Tactics and Experiences (1954); Plant & Olender, Pain and Suffering in Damages in Personal Injury and Wrongful Death Cases (Schreiber ed. 1965); Groce, Preparation for Settlement or Trial by the Defendant, in Successful Jury Trials, supra, p. 51; Gair, The Trial of Negligence Action (1946); Neustade, When Your X-rays Go on Trial, Medical Economics 286 (Nov. 1957); Schweitzer, Trial Guide 1294 (1948); Belli, Modern Trials (384) (1963); Canter, Psychosomatic Injury, Traumatic Psychoneurosis and Law, 6 Clev. Mar. L. Rev. 380 (1957); Cox, Relation of Trauma, Disease and Law, a Symposium, 7 Clev. Mar. L. Rev. 22 (1958); Overbach, Causation; A Medico-Legal Battlefield, 6 Clev. Mar. L. Rev. 209 (1957).

Sec. 4.4   How to Present the Medical Expert's Fee

There are other incidental questions, such as the arrangements made to pay the doctor. Some defendant's attorneys inquire about this in order to generate a suggestion of bias. If you think that it might damage the expert's image if it is not mentioned by you, then you should go into it on direct examination. This is a judgment matter to be made often at the trial table. This inquiry may be presented as follows:[4]

Q. By the way, Doctor, you have been in . . . . . . since last Friday, have you not?

A. Yes, that is correct.

Q. And I have promised you that you are going to be paid for your time away from your work, and for your expenses in coming all the way from . . . . ?

A. Yes, you have.

Sec. 4.5   How to Present the Medical Expert's Qualifications

As to the doctor's qualifications, these should be gone into very thoroughly, even if opposing counsel agrees to concede your expert's qualifications as an expert in his field. It is much more impressive on the jury this longer way. It is advisable to have your doctor send you the list of his qualifications in advance, so you will know what to emphasize; as, for example, that he has written medical articles or that he teaches the subject in a medical school, or that he was in charge of a field hospital while in the service. For example, show that to belong to the American Board of Surgery, it was necessary to qualify by passing certain practical and written examinations in surgery.

Sample questions concerning the medical expert's qualifications appear hereafter (Sec. 4.8 and 4.12, infra).[5]

Sec. 4.6   How to Familiarize the Medical Expert with the Case

In the inquiry concerning the doctor's familiarity with the case, it is

---

4. See footnote 3, supra, Kelly-"Direct Examination of Medical Experts in Personal Injury Actions."

5. See also Averbach "Handling Accident Cases", 6:158.

desirable to bring out that he has read the hospital records (which you should have sent to him in advance of his physical examination of your client). Do not be satisfied with summaries of the hospital records, which the hospitals are prone to send, but insist on a photostat of the *complete* records. This will avoid any surprises and will defeat your opponent's objection to your doctor's testimony because of lack of an adequate foundation having been laid.

Go into some detail concerning the tests used by the doctor to illustrate that there is a sound basis for his conclusions. For example, if he used the straight leg raising test,[6] have him explain it.

Above all, make certain that the doctor translates all medical terms into layman's language. A good test to use as to clarity is whether what the doctor is saying is clear to you. An illustration of what not to do follows:

> Q. Doctor, in language as nearly popular as the subject will permit, will you please tell the jury just what the cause of this man's death was?
>
> A. Well, in plain language, he died of edema of the brain that followed a cerebral thrombosis, or possibly an embolism that followed, in turn, arteriosclerosis, combined with the effect of a gangrenous cholecystitis.
>
> A Juror: Well, I'll be g.d. . . . . . . !
>
> The Court: Ordinarily, I would fine a juror for saying anything like that in court, but I cannot impose a penalty upon you, because the court was thinking the same thing.

Before examining the doctor, you should be careful to inquire into your own medical knowledge on the subject by a discussion with your expert or with another doctor, so that you will know the substance as well as the rhetoric of the medical area to be covered at the trial. Do not wander beyond this subject, because your knowledge is limited. This has particular application on cross-examination of the opposing medical expert, who should be presented with rhetorical questions suggesting a "yes" or "no" answer rather than with "why" or "explain" questions, to shut off opportunity for making jury speeches.

A sample examination of how to present the expert's familiarity with the case appears hereafter.[7]

---

6. With the patient lying prone on his back, the leg with the knee straight is pushed up as far as it will go, thus to test for pain in the back and shoulders, and limitation of use of the leg.

7. Sec. 4.12 infra (*Ryan* case medical testimony).

Sec. 4.7   How to Present the Treatment Received
by the Patient

As to treatment, your medical expert should be encouraged to explain an operation so the jury can be made to realize its gory and grisly nature. For example, if it is a laminectomy and spine fusion operation, have him relate the size of the incision, the clipping away of the bone, and the bone graft.

Dialogue as to a laminectomy and spine fusion operation follows:[8]

Q. Doctor, does this man need further medical or surgical care?

A. He does.

Q. And what would be the nature of that?

A. The nature of that would be a removal of this space-occupying lesion that I showed on the X-ray there, and this to be followed by a fusion from the segment above that, which would be the third lumbar vertebra down to the sacrum.

Q. Now Doctor, could you take one of the X-rays and tell us what will have to be done surgically?

A. Well, surgically, this, the space-occupying lesion, would have to be removed and then he would have to have bone removed from a portion of his ilium. It is part of the pelvis, I guess you would say generalized region of the hip. And, transferred to his back, and this area from the third to the sacrum, third lumbar vertebra to the sacrum would have to be stiffened to form one bone. In other words, it would be fused so it would not move.

Q. Now Doctor, what is the surgical procedure to accomplish that?

A. The surgical procedure?

Q. Yes.

A. Laminectomy and fusion.

Q. Now, what do you do as his surgeon?

A. You make an incision from the middle of his low back down to the flat part of his pelvis, it is behind, and we carry and we strip the muscles off of the bony prominences that are there and we open up the space between the third and fourth lumbar vertebrae on the right by removal of a little bone, and we retrack the root and also the spinal cord and remove that space-occupying lesion which is the disc. Then after that is accomplished we take all the hard bone away from the outer

---

8. Goldstein's *Medical Trial Technique Quarterly*, 1965, pps. 420-422.

surface and we remove some bone from his ilium, which is the bony crest that you feel around your pelvis, and that is cut up into small, very small pieces and laid just like shingles, in shingle fashion, across from the third lumbar vertebra to the mid portion of the sacrum and then that in time goes through a bony change; at first blood comes into it and it is softened, and then by the parent cells newborn cells are · formed and it changes into one solid sheet of bone and will be stiff in those joints.

Q. Now Doctor, approximately how long is the incision that you make?

A. Oh, in this case it would be about eight inches.

Q. And then about what area of the spine, what distance of the spine is fused and made solid?

A. Oh, four inches.

Q. Now Doctor, will the surgical removal of the disc and the fusion be done in a single operation or does it mean two operations?

A. No, it means just a single operation.

Q. And, following the surgical procedure, about how long would the man be in the hospital?

A. About twenty-one days.

Q. Would he be fitted with any kind of a support or medical contrivance?

A. Yes, he will first be fitted in a cast from approximately the nipple line down to his hips and he will wear that cast for approximately four months, and after that he will be fitted in a brace which he will wear for approximately two months. He will be able to remove that, however.

Q. Will he require further medical treatment beyond that point, Doctor?

A. Well, just physical therapy to kind of limber up his back again and education of his muscles, sort of rehabilitation program to make him a useful and working citizen again.

Q. Now Doctor, will he have pain in the future?

A. Yes.

Q. And, will he have pain for as long as he lives?

A. To some extent.

Q. Doctor, will he have any impairment of the function of his back?

A. Well yes, the fusion operation is not the answer to everything, it is the lesser of two evils, and they have some disability after a fusion, their back is limited and ordinarily they have to go to lighter work.

Q. Doctor, in your opinion, do you have an opinion as to whether or not this will constitute an impairment to his ability to work as a pipe fitter?

A. Well, my opinion, I don't know all that a pipe fitter has to go through, I think they would probably have to do a great deal of bending and getting into odd positions, I think it probably would.

Sec. 4.8   How to Frame the Hypothetical Question

As to the inquiries about prognosis of the disability and causal connection with the accident, it is required usually that the answers be made with reasonable medical or surgical probability or certainty.[9]

If the medical expert was not the treating doctor, the hypothetical question is usually required if the defendant objects to an opinion expressed without it.[10] However, it is advisable to try questioning the medical expert about the history he got of the accident and thus to lay the foundation for his opinion later on the causal connection, without putting a hypothetical question. The reason is that some experienced trial counsel for defendants, knowing the opinion will come in hypothetically eventually anyway, will not object to its coming in naturally. In point of fact, the hypothetical question, when used by the plaintiff skillfully, can be more damaging to the defendant's side than the natural question because the plaintiff, in effect, is capsulizing the argument of his case in its medical aspects, even before the closing argument.

In any event, it is essential to have the hypothetical question in reserve, written out in advance of the trial, and to have it made available to the medical expert so he will know what to expect. To do it otherwise is to risk confusion and failure.

A sample hypothetical question, with its preliminaries, follows:[11]

---

9. *3 Am. Jur. Proof of Facts,* pps. 161-163. Some courts require certainty and some only possibility.

10. *Christastie v. Elmira Water Co.* (3rd Dept. 1922), 202 AD 270-272, 195 N.Y.S. 156, 157, 136 ALR 965, 66 ALR 2d 1082; *Amer. Juris Proof of Facts* 6:159-210.

11. Taken from a hypothetical question used in substantially the same form in an actual case which was recently tried by the writer and in which the jury returned a verdict of $17,709.05 for injuries which were basically musculo-ligamentous sprain of the low back found to be 10-15% permanent by plaintiff's doctors and none by defendant's expert. *Williford, etc. v. Byrd,* Circuit Court for Anne Arundel County, Maryland, Law No. C-1038.

For other forms see *6 Amer. Jur. Proof of Facts,* pps. 167-191.

(a) The Facts

[Assume this state of facts: a female motorist (your client) was proceeding on a four-lane highway with a median grass strip separating them into two lanes going in each direction; two motorists were proceeding in the opposite lanes when the one in the rear tried to pass the one ahead at a high rate of speed and struck the lead motorist's vehicle in the rear, throwing it out of control, causing it to cross the median strip and to strike your client's vehicle; your client was taken to the hospital suffering from cuts and bruises, some tooth damage, two fractured ribs, but primarily from severe low back pains; the doctor you are examining is a general surgeon who is not the treating doctor but who has been called by you as an expert to evaluate her injuries and disability.]

(b) The Doctor's Qualifications

Q. Dr. M. . . . , of what medical school are you a graduate?

A. Graduate of the University of Maryland Medical School in 19 . . .

Q. And what has been your practice since then, Doctor?

A. After graduating from the University of Maryland Medical School, I went to an internship and residency in surgery at Sinai Hospital in Baltimore. After I finished my residency in 1953, I went into the services; in the Air Force, I was the far eastern consultant in surgery for United States Air Force in the Far East; I was stationed at Clarke Field in the Phillippines as Chief of Surgical Services. In 1955 I came back to Baltimore and entered the practice, private practice of surgery. I've been in the practice since then in Baltimore City. I'm on the active surgical staff at Sinai Hospital, Lutheran Hospital, South Baltimore, and North Charles General Hospital in Baltimore City. I'm certified by the American Board of Surgery as a qualified surgeon as of 1952. I'm a member of the Baltimore City Medical Society, the State Medical Society, and the American Medical Association, and a Fellow of the American College of Surgeons and the International College of Surgeons.

Q. Doctor, in becoming a member of these different organizations that you mentioned for surgery, are there—is it necessary to pass examinations?

A. Well, the Board of Surgery is the highest one and in that you have to—after you've finished doing internship and gone through a residency in surgery you have to take three examinations, two of them are written and one of them is practical, where they watch you and you then become qualified for that. The Americal College of Surgeons, if you submit enough number of cases to the American Board of Surgery and go through a personal interview and everything and you qualify, they certify you also.

(c) The Doctor's Familiarity with the Case

Q. Now, Doctor M. . . . , at my request, did you examine for purpose of evaluation Mrs. M.W.?

A. Yes, sir, I did.

Q. When did you examine her?

A. I first saw her on March 23rd, 1970, at my office.

Q. And did you also get and read the hospital report from the North Arundel Hospital and the South Baltimore General Hospital?

A. Yes, sir, I saw them at that time.

Q. And did you see her again after that?

A. Yes, sir, I did.

Q. What date was that?

A. I saw her again on July 16th, 1970, again on June 11th, 1971.

Q. All at my request?

A. That is correct, sir.

Q. Doctor, will you give us your physical findings with regard to Mrs. W. Let's take your first report.

A. When I first examined her on March 23rd, 1970, I found a well-developed, well-nourished 33-year-old white female weighing 135 pounds and measuring 5'4-3/4" in height; movements of her back were within normal limits except for a pulling sensation in her lower back and left hip area in the extremes of movement. In other words, when she bent down, back and forth she could move fully except she complained of a pulling sensation localized in the left hip and the lower back in certain movements of her back. It was noticed a two and a half-inch diagonal slight red scar on the right side just above the knee laterally. In other words, on the outer aspect to the leg, see, this is my knee (indicating) right here on the outer side of her knee was a scar two and a half inches in length. On the outer side, right here, there's a two and a half-inch scar, that's the lateral side of the right knee. There was also noticed a small reddish scar three and a half inches above the right ankle. In other words, three and a half inches above the ankle, the ankle is here (indicating) there's a small reddish scar right here. There was a small scar up here on her forehead.

Q. How long was that one?

A. That was about a half-inch on the left frontal area.

Q. Half-inch long?

A. Uh-huh, small scar there. Movement of the legs were within normal limits and movement of the head and neck, everything else were within normal limits, but it was noticed that the upper left tooth and the one adjacent to it in the left upper jaw had been capped. In other words, she had caps on these two teeth up here. We had X-rays taken at that time of her back, pelvis, and hip, and they failed to reveal any bone abnormalities. As was mentioned before, I also reviewed the records from the hospital and the X-rays of the skull were taken there. ****

Court: You said X-rays of the skull were taken there.

*   *   *   *   *

A. Yes, they were taken at the hospital, I reviewed them also. * * * * I saw the X-rays and found no fractures in the skull. * * * * And the X-rays of the back, which were taken originally, showed some muscle spasm in the back area on X-rays. In other words, the back X-rays, when we took them the bone, the vertebrae were perfectly normal in alignment at the hospital, when I saw those X-rays the bones were not in alignment as normal. They had a reversed curve, which means there was straightening of the curve which is due to what we call muscle spasm in the back, at that time. And the vertebra with this muscle spasm weren't in alignment, they were pushed around a little bit; this came back to normal on subsequent X-rays.

*   *   *   *   *

After some other X-rays were taken, after she got out of one hospital, she was admitted to another hospital and further X-rays at that time confirmed what they found in the lumbar spine, but also we found two non-displaced rib fractures. In other words, the rib fractures, the rib was cracked, but the ribs were in good position alignment and there was no displacement. In other words, the fractures, say, my thumb is one piece, the fracture is in good position.

Q. Will you point out to me, Doctor, the area of the body where the fractures were?

A. The fractures were in the left rib cage.

Q. And there were two ribs?

A. They were the 10th and 11th ribs. There are twelve ribs beginning up here with one, the twelfth rib is the bottom rib that you can see and it was the two ribs above that that were fractured. This is the twelfth rib, 11th, 10th, so these were the two ribs that were cracked and they were in good position, they weren't separated or apart. And again when we X-rayed her in my office the rib fractures had healed and we couldn't pick them up.

Q. Doctor, will you state whether rib fracture is painful or not?

Attorney for Defendant: Object.

Court: Overruled.

A. Yes, rib fractures are usually painful because every time you breathe you tend to move them and it hurts.

* * * * *

Q. Now, will you go to your next examination, your findings then.

A. I saw her again on July 16th, 1970, and—

Q. Tell us what your findings were at that time.

A. Again when we examined her, the spine was essentially the same, the scars were there, the neurological was normal, and she continued to complain of pain discomfort in her lower back and left hip with movement of her lower back and left hip.

Q. And finally, you saw her what other date?

A. I saw her again on June 11th, 1971.

Q. And what were your findings at that time?

A. Findings were essentially the same again.

Q. Did you examine the reports of the treating doctor, Dr. E.H.W.?

A. Yes.

*   *   *   *   *

(d) The Hypothetical Question

Q. Doctor M. . . .will you assume that on November___, 1968, a
hypothetical person was driving a vehicle north on Route 3
near the intersection of Route 648, State of Maryland,
when another vehicle which had been previously struck
went out of control from the opposite lane, came across the
median strip and struck the vehicle in which this hypothetical person was sitting and driving, struck it at or near the
area where the hypothetical person was sitting and driving,
that that person was taken to the North Arundel Hospital
promptly, was there examined and treated and that on the
following day because of intense pain this hypothetical
person entered the South Baltimore General Hospital where
she remained from November 14, 1968 to November 30,
1968, and following that she was treated by Doctor E.H.W.
from about December 6, 1968 to April 1, 1969, and then
was treated by him about May 13, 1970 and June 23, 1970,
and also received some physical therapy treatments in that
period of time. Now, Doctor, assuming all these facts to be
true and assuming further that this hypothetical person was
in reasonably good health before the accident occurred and
combine this with your own examination, which you have
already testified to, and excluding all hearsay, conclusions,
opinions, and inferences in the aforementioned hospital and
medical reports that you referred to, do you have an
opinion that you can express with reasonable medical
certainty, first as to your physical findings?

A. Well, as I said before, on the physical examination my
findings were the scars, the permanent scars, the permanent
teeth damage which has been capped, the fractured ribs of
course had healed and were not bothering her, her only
complaint as far as I could find—

*   *   *   *   *

Q. What did you find, if anything, with regard to her back and
her hip?

A. On certain movements of her back and hips you could feel
the muscles tighten up and she had pain in certain areas of
her back and left hip on certain movements of her body.

Q. Now, Doctor, assuming the hypothetical question that I put to you, do you have an opinion that you can state with reasonable medical certainty whether or not there will be any permanency of these symptoms that you referred to?

Attorney for Defendant: Object.

Court: I think the Doctor can testify as to whether or not the objective findings that he had whether or not they were permanent if he has some basis on which to determine that those objective findings were permanent or not, the objective findings, not again based on complaints.

Q. All right, Doctor, what is your opinion?

Court: To a reasonable medical certainty.

A. Reasonable medical certainty I feel she has a permanent partial disability of her back and hips of about 10 to 15 percent.

Attorney for Defendant: Object and move to strike.

Court: Will overrule the objection.

Q. And Doctor, do you have an opinion that you can express with reasonable medical certainty as to the role that the accident alluded to in the hypothetical question played in respect to these symptoms?

Attorney for Defendant: Objection. [12]

Court: Sustained.

Q. Doctor, do you have an opinion that you can state with reasonable medical certainty whether or not the accident played any role in respect to these permanent symptoms that you just mentioned?

Attorney for Defendant: Objection.

Court: Sustained. Will counsel approach the Bench?

[Bench Conference Held]

Q. Doctor, can you state with reasonable medical certainty whether, based upon the hypothetical question I've given to you, these symptoms that you've described as being permanent could probably have been caused by the facts referred to in the hypothetical question?

Attorney for Defendant: Object.

Court: Court will overrule the objection.

---

12. For a lengthy discussion with authorities on the reasons for the various components of a hypothetical question and how defendant's attorney may attack the question, see *6 Am. Jur. Proof of Facts*, pps. 167-191.

A. Well, from the history in the hypothetical question that you gave me that there's no previous accidents or injuries, what I found on my physical examination could very well have gone along with the hypothetical patient who had this accident.

Q. Now, there's a reference in the North Arundel Hospital report to a slight reverse spondylolisthesis at L-4 in relation to L-5. What does that mean, Doctor?

A. Well, as I said before, the muscle pull is so straight at that point that the vertebrae, instead of being on top of one another in the normal curve, one of them is pulled out from the other.

Q. There's also reference in the North Arundel X-ray Report that there was a marked straightening with a natural reverse in normal Lordotic curve beginning at L-2 and extending through T-12. What does that mean, Doctor?

A. Well, as he said, the normal Lordotic curve has been destroyed and it's reversed the other way. Instead of a curve, let's say, being like this, it's like this because it's been destroyed.

* * * * *

Sec. 4.9 How to Cross-Examine a Medical Expert with Medical Literature

Frequently, it can be anticipated what the opposing medical expert will say, by virtue of discovery proceedings. For example, in the neck or back injury case, the opposing doctors will disagree on causal relation or on permanency of the symptoms, or on both. To avoid a stand-off, it is recommended that medical literature which supports your doctor's position be used in court. This may tip the scales in your favor. There follows an example of such an examination.

[Assume that the plaintiff injured his neck in an accident, but experienced the pain symptoms a few days after the accident. Also assume the defendant's doctor is experienced in litigation and is aware of the text-book method of cross-examination and is prepared to fence with the questions of plaintiff's attorney. Assume, finally, that he has testified that plaintiff suffered a mild neck sprain and that he found no objective symptoms and that there is no disability therefore from the accident and that the complaint of subjective symptoms a few days after the accident is too late to be connected with the accident.][13]

Q. Doctor, as a specialist in orthopedics, I presume that you are familiar with the basic textbooks on the subject?

A. Well, yes—that is, generally. I am familiar with the better known ones.

Q. And you do current reading to keep abreast of the newer knowledge and developments in your field?

A. Yes, I do—that is, within the time allowed me by my practice. Of course, I am not familiar with everything written. No busy doctor could be.

Q. I understand. You are familiar, are you not, with Gartland's "Fundamentals of Orthopedics?" (Counsel holds up the book so the jury can see it).

A. No, I'm not.

Q. You've never heard of it?

A. Oh, I've heard of it. It's not a well-known textbook—at least not in my opinion. In any case, I've not read it and I don't know what's in it.

Q. I see. Well, what about the book by Dr. Lewin entitled "The Back and Its Disc Syndromes?" (Counsel holds it up for exhibition).

A. No, I haven't read that one. Again, I don't consider it to be a well-known or a highly regarded textbook.

Q. Oh, you've discussed it?

A. Well, I've heard about some of Dr. Lewin's statements in that book and I disagree with him.

Q. Are you familiar with its contents then?

A. No.

Q. Very well. Well, let's go to a third textbook. I believe this one is used in our medical schools to teach the students. I am referring to Key and Conwell's "Management of Fractures, Dislocations and Sprains," 7th edition. Are you familiar with it and its contents?

A. Yes, generally.

Q. This is a well-known textbook, is it not?

A. Well, yes.

---

13. This is a composite of a number of such cross-examinations used by the writer in similar cases.

Q. And it is consulted by practicing doctors, as well as by students?

A. Yes.

Q. Now, doctor, I am going to read to you from it at pages 300 and 301 as follows:

> Minor Injuries (Disc Lesions).—These may be termed sprains or subluxations of the cervical vertebrae, but we believe that in most of them the lesion involves an intervertebral disc in this area. They are relatively frequent, may follow sudden turns of the head, falls, and especially automobile accidents in which the car in which the patient is sitting is struck from behind so that the body is forced forward and the head snapped backward (the so-called whiplash injury, Fig. 210). The pain may come on immediately or there may be relatively little pain at the time and symptoms may appear after a few days.

Do you agree with that?

A. Well, I guess I'll have to disagree.

Q. I suppose you are familiar with the well-known textbook, Comroe's "Arthritis?"

A. Yes, I am.

Q. I would like to read this excerpt from Comroe's at page 909:

> "The effect of trauma upon articular structures depends upon the type, severity and duration of the injury, as well as the reaction of the individual. The period between the injury and the production of traumatic joint disease may vary from days to several months. Pain and limitation of motion may persist for years following a single strain or contusion, even without obvious anatomic change."

Do you agree with that eminent writer?

A. No, I don't.

Q. And I suppose you disagree on this point with Dr. . . . . . also, the orthopedist who testified just before you [he is the plaintiff's medical expert].

A. Yes.

Q. Do you consider Dr. . . . . reliable in his field?

A. Certainly. But I'm entitled to my opinion too.

Q. I think that's all, doctor. Thank you.

Sec. 4.10   How to Prove Pain and Suffering
Before Death

In Sec. 1.3 supra, reference is made to the factors to look for in proving pain and suffering in wrongful death cases. However, the most effective method is to present the testimony of the treating doctor. In many such cases, the deceased went into shock before death. The jury is inclined to equate shock with unconsciousness and therefore to conclude that the deceased was without suffering in this critical period. On the contrary, it does not necessarily follow that because a person is in shock, he is out of pain.

Shock is caused by a sharp drop in blood pressure and this is evidenced by a high pulse rate. (It is felt that it is the reduction in the volume of blood which is returned to the heart which causes shock.) Hence, it is wise to discuss this with the treating doctor in advance of trial and to probe for the probability of pain in the picture.

Primary shock does not always cause complete unconsciousness; the patient may be partly unconscious and therefore in some pain. This should be discussed with the treating doctor in an effort to ascertain if there was evidence of pain.

Transfusion is resorted to in order to bring the blood pressure back, and when this occurs consciousness frequently returns, with concomitant pain.

Pain-killing medication is not always resorted to. It depends on the nature of the injury. For example, in chest or head injuries, administering pain-killler is not always recommended because it may aggravate the condition. This inquiry should be gone into with the treating doctor also, in order to combat the anticipated cross-examination by your adversary to the effect that it was automatic for the physician to reduce the pain.[14]

Sec. 4.11   How to Introduce Medical Aids in
the Examination of the Medical Expert

In a preceding chapter, Sec. 1.4 supra, reference is made to the importance of using medical aids, such as medical charts and skeletal exhibits, in examining your medical expert. It not only clarifies the medical phases of the case, but it has a visual and dramatic impact on the jury. There follows a sample of such examination.

---

14. See Speiser's *Recovery for Wrongful Death*, pps. 765-770 for sample examination of the treating physician on shock and pain.

[Assume a low back injury in an accident with evidence of disc rupture and resulting pain in the back and legs. The medical aids sought to be introduced are a medical chart of the skeleton showing the vertebrae involved and a skeleton model of the human spine.]

After the history, examination, and the general findings of the doctor have been testified to, and when the doctor is being questioned about the details of the mechanics of the injury, the medical aids should be introduced as follows:[15]

Q. Doctor, would a medical chart help you to explain the location and the nature of the vertebrae involved?

A. Yes, it would.

Q. Are you familiar with the American Frohse Chart of the Human Skeleton?

A. Yes, I am.

Q. Is it considered a reliable chart to show the nature and dimensions of the male human skeleton?

A. Yes, it is.

Q. At this time I would offer for identification as plaintiff's Exhibit No. 1 the American Frohse Chart of the Human Skeleton (male).

The Court: Hearing no objection, the same will be allowed as plaintiff's Exhibit No. 1 for identification.

(Counsel exhibits the chart at a location where it is visible to judge, jury, witness, and both counsel).

[It is advisable to have a stand on which to hang the chart and the string with which to attach it to the stand. (There are roll-down charts available at dealers.) The stand can be purchased at the sources previously mentioned (see chapter 1, footnote 7, supra). The unfolding of the chart should be practiced in advance of trial. It is embarrassing and disconcerting to experiment in the handling of these mechanical gadgets at the time of trial.]

Q. Now, doctor, have I displayed to you the skeleton model of the spine, which I have here?

A. Yes.

Q. Would this be of assistance to you in explaining the nature of the injury in this case?

A. Yes, it would.

---

15. This is a composite of a number of such examinations used by the writer in similar cases.

Q. Is the model a faithful replica of the spine and vertebrae in the male adult human body?

A. Yes.

Q. I offer this model as plaintiff's Exhibit No. 2 for identification.

Counsel for Defendant: I object to it. It is intended to be exhibited for dramatic effect and to exaggerate the damages in this case.

Court: The doctor has said it will assist him to explain the nature of the injury, so I will allow it.

(Plaintiff's counsel then suspends the spinal model on a stand in full view of judge, jury, the witness and counsel).

Q. Doctor, will you come forward and show us which vertebra is involved in this case?

A. Surely. It is lumbar 2. (Pointing it out.)

Q. Will you show the jury how it is constructed in the spine and what motion, if any, it has, and why?

A. (He demonstrates and explains.)

Q. Now, will you explain where the disc to which you referred is located and what its function is?

A. (He demonstrates and explains.)

Q. Now will you show us what you mean when the disc has ruptured and how it affects the feeling in and the functioning of the legs?

A. (He demonstrates and explains.)

Sec. 4.12   A Full-Scale Examination by Both Sides of Plaintiff's Medical Expert in a Back Sprain Case

As pointed out in Sec. 1.3, supra, there are numerous sources for locating a specimen examination of a medical expert on almost any type of injury. A sample of such a dialogue on a back injury case follows.[16]

[Assume the following facts: plaintiff is a 54-year-old railroad freight conductor; he fell from a defective ladder supplied by the employer during the course of his work; he injured his low back; his condition was aggravation of a pre-existing low back condition by the trauma, complicated by osteoporosis (softening of the bones).]

---

16. This was the testimony of the plaintiff's medical expert in *Ryan v. B. & O.*, Civil No. 18805 (D.C. Md. 1969). It was not necessary to use the hypothetical question. See general discussion at Sec. 4.8, supra.

Direct Examination

Q. Dr. . . . . ,where is your office?

A. . . . . . . (Address)

Q. And what is your specialty in medicine?

A. Orthopedics.

Q. And what is that, Doctor?

A. That is the study of the bones and the joints and the muscles.

Q. And do you perform surgery in this field, too?

A. I did, but no longer do.

Q. All right, sir.

Now, Doctor, of what medical school are you a graduate?

A. University of . . . . in 19. . . . .

Q. And what has been your training and experience since then?

A. I interned at . . . . . . Hospital, thereafter took my orthopedic training at the . . . . . . Hospital, and then went into the United States Army where I did orthopedics, returning in 19 . . . , and have been actively engaged in the practice of orthopedics since.

Q. As I understand it, orthopedics is a speciality of medicine which is devoted to the bones and related conditions of the bones?

A. Yes, sir.

Q. All right. Now, Doctor, do you do any teaching in your field?

A. Yes, sir.

Q. And where is that done?

A. I teach at . . . .

Q. . . . . Medical School?

A. Yes, sir.

Q. And what subject do you teach there?

A. Orthopedics.

Q. And are you associated with any of the medical organizations?

A. Yes, sir. I belong to the American Medical Association, the American Academy of Orthopedic Surgery, the American College of Surgeons, the International College of Surgeons, the Geriatric Society, and the Maryland Orthopedic Society.

Q. Now, these orthopedic organizations that you belong to, Doctor, are there certain qualifications to belong to them?

A. One must be a certified orthopedist, which I am, I passed an examination and then was awarded my certificate as a Diplomate of the American Board of Orthopedic Surgery.

Q. And does that mean that you are qualified, then, to act as an orthopedic specialist?

A. Yes, sir.

Q. All right. Now, are there any other qualifications, Doctor, that you wish to tell us about?

A. No, sir. I belong to the various hospitals here in . . . .

Q. Which hospitals are you associated with in the practice of your specialty?

A. . . . . , ... , ... , ... , ... , ... , and I'm Consultant with the Health, Education and Welfare Department of Social Security.

Q. Of the United States Government?

A. Yes, sir.

Q. Now, Doctor, did you at my request examine Mr. . . . . . . ?

A. Yes, sir.

Q. When did you first see him?

A. On . . . . , 19. . . . .

Q. And what did your examination disclose?

A. I took a history from the gentleman and then examined him.

Q. And what was that?

A. The history revealed that he was 54-years of age, that he was a passenger conductor. His chief complaint was that his low back hurt him. He stated, according to a written personal record which he presented me a copy of, that he was injured on May 13, 1964, and he, apparently, cut his right leg, his left thigh, and twisted his low back.

He was seen and an orthopedic support was prescribed several days later, he apparently continued to have discomfort with his back, and he was seen on numerous occasions by numerous physicians.

Q. Excuse me, Doctor, can the Jury hear him?

A. I'm sorry.

Q. Just raise your voice a little, Doctor.

A. At the present time, that is . . . . , 19 . . . , he continued to complain of pain in his back, but has been working fairly regularly. The pain is said to radiate down both of his legs. It was not aggravated, the pain was not aggravated by coughing or sneezing, but he has avoided lifting.

He is taking medication, Dianabal, which is for osteoporosis, and he told me that in . . . . . . of 19. . ., a blood study was done on him and this proved to be normal.

I examined the patient. He stated that his height was five feet, eight inches tall, and that he weighed 142 pounds.

As he stood, there was an increase in his slouching forward of the upper part of his body.

Q. An increase in what, Doctor?

A. His slouching forward of the upper part of his body; he hunched forward.

His pelvis, or hips, were level. There was no evidence of any fractures of the thoracic vertebrae, which are the portions of the spine between the neck and the waist.

He was sensitive over the joint in the middle of the body about the level of the waist, the lumbosacral joint, and also was sensitive over the right sacro-iliac joint, which is the joint a little bit lower and to the right thereof.

He was also tender over the buttock on the right where the sciatic nerve emerges.

He was not tender over the kidney. He breathed with his abdomen. He was able to bend well, but he did complain.

He removed a support, a corset, for the examination. Reflexes, the bounces that are obtained when you strike the knees and the ankles, were obtained at the knees and ankles.

In a seated position I was able to straighten his knees out without any complaint of pain on his part. His hip motion was good. There were no unusual features noted at the knees or at the ankles.

The left thigh measured thirteen and a quarter inches, and the right measured thirteen inches, which has no real significance as far as I can determine. So there wasn't any true wasting of the muscles of the thighs.

His ability to raise his great toe was good on both sides. This was a test for a disc and showed that there was no real evidence of disc protrusion, and he was able to sit bolt upright on the table with his legs extended out in front of him.

We took an X-ray of his back and the vertebral bodies showed what we refer to as bi-concavity. Ordinarily, the vertebrae, the vertebral bodies, when you look at them, as if a person were standing in front of you sideways, they look like squares, elongated squares, but his vertebrae showed a depression on the

top and bottom, just as though you had taken a marshmallow
and depressed the top surface and the bottom surface together
by squeezing.

Q. Doctor, would it help if I produced at this time a chart so that
you could demonstrate what you're talking about?

A. I would be happy to have it.

*   *   *   *   *

Q. Doctor, where is the pelvis, just point it out?

A. All right, the pelves are the winglike projections that I will now
point out, and that form the hips, and here is the actual joint
down below, this is the lumbo-sacral joint, would be right in
this level.

I felt that this patient had a chronic sprain of the back
secondary to his injury and complicated by the fact that he
probably had osteoporosis, or thinning of the bones of his
lumbar vertebrae.

Q. Will you tell us, Doctor, what you mean by a chronic low back
strain?

A. A chronic low back strain is a weakness of the lower portion of
the back which is present over—well, forever, if you wish,
permanently, that will cause the individual discomforts, perhaps when he overdoes, does too much lifting or too much
walking or pulling or pushing.

It doesn't necessarily incapacitate a person, by that I mean
making him stay in bed, they can carry on, but it does affect
their ability to perform constant, repetitive work over an eight
or ten hour day.

Q. Would you explain, Doctor, the mechanics of a chronic low
back strain, what actually happens to the anatomy?

Counsel for Defendant: Objection, Your Honor.

Counsel for Plaintiff:

Q. As related to this case.

Counsel for Defendant: I withdraw the objection as related to this
case.

Counsel for Plaintiff:

Q. Go ahead.

A. The low back sprain, or any sort of chronic sprain, I guess we
have to be specific, means that under ordinary circumstances
when you bend your back or bend any joint, for that matter,

you can go up to a certain limit. At that point, the ligaments and the muscles and the natural configuration of the joint stops you, just as if you bend your wrist up, it will stop at a certain point, you can't go beyond that, but suppose you fall, or twist, or do something accidental that forces it past the point it would ordinarily go.

When that happens, one of several things is going to occur. The ligaments and the muscles get stretched past their normal stretchability and so they get torn. If the force is continued, then, of course, a fracture occurs, but if the force stops at that point, why then you have a stretching or tearing of the ligaments and the muscles and the tendons, all the soft tissues, which are there to protect the joint and act as check reins to its going past its normal range of motion.

So when this happens, again, you end up with what we call a sprain or a strain. There is usually swelling and tenderness and pain, and then over the course of time, nature will repair this situation.

Now, in the presence of a chronic sprain, or one that hangs on and stays with you over a long period of time, as does happen in some instances, we theorize that the ligaments having been stretched past their normal stretchability now have healed with scar tissue, just as if you cut your skin, say, over your knee where the skin gets stretched, you notice that the scar will heal wide because it doesn't stay together, and we figure that the same thing happens in the ligament that has been stretched or strained and that it heals wide.

So, now, instead of permitting the joint to go through only a certain range of motion, it will, perhaps, give it a little excessive mobility, too much range of motion, there is scar tissue present which can be painful and instead of holding the parts together snugly and nicely, there perhaps is a little extra motion.

And so, now, you have in the presence of a chronic sprain a painful condition which can come and go and which, in the course of time, may get better or may persist.

In this instance, I felt that this gentleman had a chronic back strain and had this strain for a long period of time, he had these symptoms of pain, he has had a history of injury, he has, on top of all this, a thinning of the bone in the back, this so-called osteoporosis.

So, these factors all add up, in my mind, to mean that this man has a permanent disability.

Q. Now, Doctor, you referred to the fact that there are ligaments and muscles covering the bone in that spinal area of the back, is that correct?

A. Yes, sir.

Q. Now, we have another chart here, does this demonstrate this to you?

A. I don't know, I'll look.

The chart shows in some fashion what happens to muscles. Muscles, as they approach home, instead of remaining fleshy, like a nice steak, get to be more fibrous, as demonstrated on this chart by the whitish portions. They become gristly, and that's the part of the meat usually you cut off because you can't chew it, it's too thick to chew through, and too stringy, and this particular aspect, which is the back of the human, shows some of the tendons of the muscles which come over and insert, or tie into, the spinal cord—I beg your pardon—the spinal column, not the cord.

You can see that these ligamentous areas are scattered around wherever muscle ends.

Q. And the spinal column, then, is covered by ligaments and muscles and what else, Doctor, tendons, you say?

A. Oh yes, all of the usual soft tissues, ligaments and muscles, tendons, nerves, and blood vessels.

Q. And the scar tissue that you referred to has formed in relation to these soft tissues around the lower back, is that correct?

A. We can assume this, sir.

Q. Right.

A. I didn't open this man up and look in, but this is, I think, a rather valid assumption, that there is scar tissue present which is painful in this area.

*   *   *   *   *

Q. Now, Doctor, based upon your training and your experience as a specialist in orthopedics, can you state with reasonable medical certainty after examination of this man whether or not this man does have pain in this area and what it's due to?

Counsel for Defendant: Objection, Your Honor.

The Court: What is the basis for your objection?

Counsel for Defendant: As to whether he has pain or not?

The Court: Well, he can relate subjective symptoms, from his medical knowledge.

All right, go on.

Counsel for Plaintiff:

Q. Go ahead, Doctor.

A. Yes, sir, I do have an opinion.

Q. And what, in your opinion, stated with reasonable medical certainty, is that due to?

A. The pain in the man's back is due to his injury plus the presence of a chronic low back strain augmented, I am sure, by the osteoporosis.

Q. And, Doctor, can you state with reasonable medical certainty whether or not this condition will be permanent?

A. Yes, sir.

Q. All right, what is your opinion?

A. He does have a permanent partial disability.

Q. And can you state that, Doctor, in percentage, with reasonable medical certainty?

A. Yes, sir, I would estimate this to be 20 percent of the back.

Q. And what does that mean, Doctor, 20 percent loss of what?

A. Loss of the use of the back. If you asked me more specifically, I'd say, perhaps this man can do things, but he probably doesn't have the lastability that he had, he can't last as long as he did before, and he couldn't lift and shouldn't lift, in my opinion, heavy weights over a persistently long period of time.

Q. How, in your opinion, Doctor, stated with reasonable medical certainty, will this affect his motion, particularly at work?

A. Well, this is a rather broad question. It depends on what you mean by work. If you are referring particularly—

Q. Let's talk, first of all—

Counsel for Defendant: I would object, unless a foundation is laid, Your Honor.

The Court: Yes, sir, you must lay a foundation. Objection sustained.

Counsel for Plaintiff: All right.

Q. Are you familiar with the work of a freight conductor?

A. In a layman's fashion, if you would.

Q. You are generally familiar with the work a freight conductor does on the railroad?

Counsel for Defendant: I object to further questioning on this line, Your Honor, the Doctor already indicated he has only—

The Court: Did the man tell you what work he did, Doctor?

Witness: Yes, sir.

The Court: Did he tell you what he had to do in reference to it?

The Witness: I don't recall whether he, himself, told me, but, in general, shall I tell you what I think—

The Court: I'll permit the answer, go on, answer it.

Objection Overruled.

The Witness: A freight conductor has to walk along the freight car, over track, over rough terrain, on occasion, and has to be able to climb up and down and get on and off cars, has to be able to couple and uncouple, on occasion, on cars, and bend over, and I imagine he looks in at the bearings to see if they have a hot box, or something like that.

Counsel for Plaintiff:

Q. All right. Now, Doctor, can you state with reasonable medical certainty whether he will be limited in any way in doing this work as a result of his injury?

A. I would advise that an individual with this sort of a situation avoid repetitive bending and lifting, that he not lift heavy weights, that he avoid bending over constantly, and that he keep his walking within bounds. I can't say exactly how far he should walk or should not walk, but, in essence, he should protect his back, he's the best judge of the pain in his back, you see, and it depends on the man's motivation; some people give in right off the bat and don't work, and others keep going; this depends on what sort of man he is, that's all.

Q. All right. Now, Doctor, did you see the man the second time?

A. Yes, sir.

Q. When did you see him?

A. On . . . . , 19 . . . . .

Q. That's about a month ago, or less than a month ago, and were your findings substantially the same, or not, at that time?

A. They were substantially the same, yes, sir.

Counsel for Plaintiff: That's all.

Cross-Examination

Q. Doctor, in your report concerning the examination of . . . .

. . . . . ., you indicate that Mr. . . . . submitted a written personal injury file; will you describe that?

A. Yes, sir, I have it here.

Q. Were these papers that he had kept and gave to you at the time of examination?

A. Yes, sir.

Q. Are these in the nature of medical reports, or—

A. No, sir, those were his personal file, the thing that—I guess he kept it like a diary, if you would.

Q. In other words, writing down his complaints?

A. Yes, sir, and the history of his condition, what happened, when, where, and how.

Q. Doctor, you indicate in that report that Mr. . . . . apparently continued to have discomfort following this injury of . . .

. . . .

Of course, in reporting this, you were basing this on what he had told you?

A. Very definitely, this is the man's history, sir, and history is what the patient tells me, I did not observe it.

Q. Doctor, would you describe for the Jury the difference between a subjective complaint and an objective finding?

A. Certainly. A subjective complaint is what the patient tells me that he feels in the way of pain or what he suffers in the way of impairment. For instance, I have a pain in my back, I can't lift 20 pounds. Well, he tells me that, that's subjective.

Now, an objective finding is one which I make when I watch him do certain test motions that I demand of him, his responses to certain pain producing maneuvers, and his ability under my guidance to move his joints and bones to what I would consider a normal range of motion.

Those are things that I see and I can swear that I saw, and I know is the truth insofar as I can tell the truth.

Q. Pain, then, is a subjective complaint?

A. Pain is subjective, yes, sir.

Q. When you report pain, then, you must rely on what the patient tells you, is that correct?

A. The patient—the direct answer, certainly, is yes. I am dependent on what the patient tells me. Do I hurt you when I press you? Yes, you hurt me, Doctor. Therefore, he has pain.

But we always try to verify, particularly in cases of this type where I know I'm going to be sitting in this rather warm seat, by observing, to see how the patient reacts.

If, you know, some people you go up to and you make a—just reach your finger toward them and they jump, and it's pretty obvious, a feigned or hysterical reaction, or something like that; but in the ways of observing a person over the course of twenty years, or twenty-five years, I think it is now, I think we pick up to see whether a person is really having pain in the way they flinch and the way the muscles react to stimulation, so it's sort of a combination.

Q. But still, you must, basically, rely on what you're told?

A. When the patient tells me he has pain, then that is his response, yes, sir.

Q. You can't say he doesn't have it, if he says he does?

A. Oh yes, I have.

Q. Doctor, you indicate that this pain was not aggravated by coughing or sneezing.

What would the significance of this finding be?

A. I was interested in whether or not his symptoms might be caused by a disc protrusion. I don't think, really, he has a disc protrusion.

Do you want me to explain that, or not?

Q. Well, if you feel he doesn't have it, I think—

A. No, I don't think he has.

Q. You indicated, Doctor, that there was a slouching forward in Mr. . . . .'s posture. Would this be caused by what you indicate in your report as thoracic kyphosis?

A. Well, I'm sorry, I used the word slouching forward when I was trying to explain my findings, instead of thoracic kyphosis. I don't think thoracic kyphosis would mean very much, but slouching forward does mean something.

Q. Well, this slouching forward, or thoracic kyphosis, I gather, is the result of degenerative change in this man, is that correct?

A. Well, it can happen, it can be, I don't like to try to avoid the question, but it can be, some people at adolescence slouch forward, and in older people, why there is a degenerative change which does occur and increases the thoracic kyphosis and does cause them to be slouched forward, one of the signs we attribute to the aging processes.

Q. In Mr. . . . . . . , would this not be a degenerative condition brought about by the aging process?

A. Well, he's 54, I believe, at the present moment. He has osteoporosis in his spine, which is a softening of the bone, and it could be a combination of the softening of the bone plus, he is not old by any manner or means, he's too close to me, but—

Q. We'll stipulate.

A. But, certainly, I guess after we got to be 45 or 50, we do have a tendency to lose that very erect carriage unless we work very hard at it.

Q. Well, in no event, you relate this thoracic kyphosis to the accident?

A. Oh no, sir.

Q. I believe, Doctor, that from your report you actually found that Mr. . . . . had good motion of the back?

A. Yes, sir, at the time I examined him, he did well.

Q. You indicate that the straight leg raising test was well performed.

Well, with regard to that particular test, am I correct in assuming that this is an important test used in evaluating a back condition or back disability?

A. This is an important test, yes, sir.

Q. And the fact that a person could well perform this test would be certainly of significance in evaluating any complaints he might have referable to the back, isn't that correct?

A. Yes, sir, it's correct.

Q. Doctor, would you describe for us exactly what osteoporosis is?

A. That's a very difficult question to answer, sir.

Q. Well, as succinctly as possible.

A. Well, I don't know that much about it, I don't think anyone knows that much about it to explain exactly; the type process we're talking about is a thinning of the bone; I'll try to use an example.

If we take a picture, just a regular photograph, of an individual in flesh and blood, you get a certain feeling of density, it looks solid to you; but then suppose this were a spirit, the same individual were a spirit and we took an X-ray—I mean, took a picture of him then, you could sort of see through him a lot easier than you could if he were fully flesh and blood.

Now, when we take X-rays of the average individual's spine, say, 54, and look at it, you get a feeling of a certain density, a certain thickness of the bone, because the bone being thicker and having more mineral content stops the X-rays, and so that on the X-ray it actually looks whiter, but that's a small detail, but in his particular case, the bone did not look as thick as it should be, it didn't stop the X-ray, it looked more like a spirit, if you would, a thinness was there, and this is an X-ray finding of thinness of the bone which we see and see rather frequently in some cases, and in some cases it is not productive of pain and in others there is an associated pain with it.

Q. Well, this depression of the vertebrae to which you referred, Doctor, would be caused by the osteoporosis?

A. Yes, sir, because of the thinness of the bone, we feel that the pads of gristle which are contained between each one of the vertebral bodies, if you will refer to my diagram over there, you will see that I drew the upper vertebra and then there is a space and then there is a lower vertebra.

Well, between those two is a piece of gristle, which is sort of a liquid-like gristle, which is contained in that space.

Now, under ordinary circumstances, over the course of years, those spaces become narrower as these discs, that's what the disc is, become compressed, but in this instance, the bone is, apparently, not as strong, so that instead of becoming compressed, this disc has expanded and pushed up into the body of the vertebra above and the one below.

Q. Doctor, this osteoporosis, or thinning of the bone, would not be caused by accident?

A. No, sir, I don't think that the osteoporosis itself is caused by accident.

Q. Doctor, actually, in this 20 percent permanent disability rating, you are, in some measure, relying on the fact that Mr. . . . . . . had this condition of osteoporosis, are you not?

A. This does figure in, yes, sir.

Q. Now, Doctor, did Mr. . . . . tell you at the time of this . . . . examination, at which time you gave him this permanent partial disability rating, that he had injured his back in 1947?

A. I have—yes, sir, I have the record which he had kept on his previous medical mishap.

Q. This is not reflected in your report.

A. No, sir, I'm sorry, but I didn't want to go through this whole record. There are some individuals who keep this sort of diary and present them to a physician; to incorporate this three-page record into my own three-an-a-half-page record, and my own history, would make it rather bulky.

Q. The reason I asked the question, Doctor, is in your latest report of . . . . , you do indicate that he had sustained back injury in 1947, 1949, and in 1962. However, you do not indicate that in your earlier report where you gave him this percentage rating, is that correct?

A. That is correct.

Q. As a matter of fact, in 1962, he was hospitalized for a pinched nerve in the back, isn't that what he told you?

A. Well, again, I don't remember what he told me, but I have—yes, I'm sorry, I'm referring to the patient's own record here, and he said . . . . , 1962, to . . . . , 1962, he was in the hospital, pinched nerve, upper left side of the back.

Q. In view of these prior accidents, Doctor, isn't it fair to say that you can't really separate what percentage of this 20 percent disability of the back you would attribute to this accident and what percentage would be attributable to prior accidents, or to a pre-existing condition?

A. This certainly brings in questions to the act of trying to give a rating of disability, but one goes, to some extent, by the fact of continued working after those previous accidents, and I think he was active, or, rather, his record shows that he was active after his other injuries, so that even though he may have had injuries, they did not, apparently, impair his disability to the extent that it kept him from working in a very productive fashion.

Q. Here, again, you're relying on what, of course, you were told by Mr. . . . . ?

A. Very definitely.

Q. Doctor, you saw Mr. . . . . again on . . . . , I gather, at the request of plaintiff's counsel?

A. Yes, sir.

Q. Plaintiff's counsel, I don't believe, went into that report, and I'm not going to go into it at great length, but I do have a few questions.

A. Yes, sir.

Q. What was his range of motion at that time, Doctor? Would you describe it?

A. Yes, sir. Let's see, he flexed well.

Q. What is flexion?

A. Bending forward from the hips reaching for the floor.

Q. You indicate extension does not cause pain, will you show us that maneuver?

A. Extension, meaning backwards from the straight upright position.

Q. So, he moves forward well and backward well?

A. Yes, sir; he did complain of pain, however.

Q. Would you then describe his range of motion of the back as good?

A. Oh yes, I'd say he had a good range of motion.

Q. You indicate in that later report of . . . . , that there was no sensitivity over the lumbo-sacral joint.

Now, in your earlier report you indicate there was some sensitivity over the lumbo-sacral joint.

Would this reflect improvement in his condition?

A. No, this represents a more or less normal variation; as I indicated before, this man is not disabled completely, he's going to have days when he feels good, just like all of us, and some days he will feel better than others, and if you happen to catch him on a bad day or after a heavy day's work, you will find more than if you catch him on another day.

So that there is certain variability, has some value to us, and means he's acting like a normal human being.

Q. Doctor, in this . . . . report, you indicate the Trendellenberg is well performed. Would you describe that for us?

A. Trendellenberg is the ability to stand on one leg and when you do so to hike the opposite hip up; it shows that the muscles of the hip are intact.

Q. You also indicate that Mr. . . . . could squat without complaint, is that correct?

A. Oh yes, squatting is a test I use, I remember before I indicated we are, perhaps, a little sly in our examinations—when you squat, you don't use your back muscles, you use your leg muscles, so if a person complains of pain when he's squatting, I wonder what he's talking about.

Q. Well, you indicate that he could stand on his toes and heels?

A. Correct.

Q. This is a significant test, I gather, in evaluating—

A. It shows that the patient's muscles are intact and that he can walk well, and that, again, it's also a sort of thing, when a person is trying to sell you something, why perhaps he puts on too much show and overreacts.

Q. It indicates he can walk well?

A. Oh yes, sir, he can walk, without any question.

Q. You indicated that the reflexes were obtained in knees and ankles, as in your earlier report, and, again, that the straight leg raising test was well performed, as at the time of your earlier examination?

A. Yes, sir.

Q. You found no swelling, I gather, of the legs?

A. No, sir.

Q. Nor any swelling of the back?

A. No, sir.

Q. Actually, a person with osteoarthritis present, Doctor, would present, basically, the same complaints which Mr. . . . . . . has, would they not?

A. He could.

Q. Arthritis is a form of degenerative change?

A. Yes, sir.

Q. Thoracic kyphosis, I think you testified, is a form of degenerative change?

A. Can be, yes, sir.

Q. You indicated that Mr. . . . . could bend and lift if not being done on a constant basis, if not being done on a repetitive basis. I gather that by this you feel that he can bend and squat and make normal movements, if it's done on a somewhat occasional basis?

A. I would tell an individual like this when he comes to me for treatment, don't get a job where you have to be bending and lifting all day long, but get a job where you can rest, where you can sit down if your back hurts you or you feel it coming on, sit down and relax a bit, don't overburden yourself, and as far as lifting a chair or a glass of water, stuff like that, sure, he could do that, but as far as lifting heavy weight, and by heavy in today's market I guess you can say 50 pounds is beginning to be heavy, I'd say, avoid it, because he might hurt himself.

Q. Avoid it on a regular basis?

A. He might do it once or twice and get away with it, but whether he'd get away with it the third time, I don't know.

Q. Doctor, the first time you saw Mr. . . . . on . . . . , was over three and a half years after this accident, so you don't know what his back was like before the accident?

A. Correct.

Q. And you have to rely in large measure on what he told you as to what his back was like between the accident and when you first saw him three and a half years later?

A. Yes, sir.

Q. You never had the opportunity to review X-rays of his back prior to the accident?

A. Prior to the accident, no, sir.

Counsel for Defendant: No further questions.

Redirect Examination

Counsel for Plaintiff:

Q. Doctor, is there anything in your examination when you examined this man clinically and got his history which revealed that the osteoporosis had disabled him before the accident of May 13, 1964?

A. I'm sorry, in my examination, you say?

Q. Yes. In your history you obtained from him and in your clinical examination—strike that. In your examination of the man, particularly, from the history, did you obtain any indication from him that he had been disabled before the May 13, 1964 accident because of the osteoporosis?

Counsel for Defendant: Objection.

The Court: The basis of the objection—
Overruled.

The Witness: I had the man's records, which had been supplied to me, and I don't know that he had any particular osteoporosis episodes that kept him from working, as far as I can tell from the records that were supplied.

Counsel for Plaintiff: All right. Just one further question. Do you state with reasonable medical certainty then that this disability that you've given him, 20 percent permanent partial disability, is due to the accident of May 13, 1964, or not?

A. The medical—I have an opinion.

Q. Yes, I want that.

A. On this, with reasonable medical certainty—

Counsel for Defendant: I object. The doctor already answered this on cross-examination and said he would have difficulty.

The Court: Well, he's going to answer—he answered also on direct. In view of your question on cross-examination, I will permit it.

The Witness: As I have already stated, the osteoporosis does enter into the picture and I cannot really pull it out of the picture, but I do feel that the injury sort of triggered this disability which he has at this time.

Counsel for Plaintiff: All right, that's all. Thank you very much.

Recross Examination

By Counsel for Defendant:

Q. Just one question, Doctor. The records to which you referred were the records given you by Mr. . . . . These were not official hospital records or medical records?

A. Yes, sir, I assume they're official; they are copies of reports from a clinic, from the Blaine Clinic.

Q. Yes, but that would be 1966, I believe, would it not?

A. Yes, sir, 1966.

Q. Right.

A. And then there is the Connellsville State Hospital.

Q. Again, 1964, after the accident, correct?

A. Yes, sir, 1964, sprained left thoracic region, lumbo-sacral region.

Q. Specifically, Doctor, were you given a copy of a record from Sacred Heart Hospital in 1962 for a hospitalization for a pinched nerve in the upper back?

A. I have one here from the Sacred Heart Hospital.

Q. 1967?

A. 1967.

Q. How about 1962?

A. That's what I'm looking for now, I have a little book here. 1966, 1964, 1964. No, sir, I do not have a 1962 record.

Q. So, all of the records to which you have referred, which were furnished by Mr. . . . . . , pertain to examinations he received following this accident of May 13, 1964?

A. Yes, sir, it would appear so. They all refer to the previous accident.

Q. None of them refer to his history prior to this accident?

A. I'm sorry, they do refer to the history prior.

Q. You don't have the Sacred Heart Hospital record from 1962?

A. The actual record itself I do not have, but, for instance, they do say that the patient had been treated before.

Q. I see.

A. For a pinched nerve, and I was aware of this.

Counsel for Defendant: No further questions.

Further Redirect Examination

By Counsel for Plaintiff:

Q. Doctor, the X-ray, does that—that discloses bones, does it not?

A. I beg pardon?

Q. The X-ray will reflect bone?

A. Is that your whole question?

Q. Yes.

A. Yes, sir.

Q. Will it reflect soft tissue?

A. In rare instances.

Q. I beg your pardon?

A. In rare instances.

Q. All right, then, generally, it does not?

A. It does not.

Counsel for Plaintiff: Thank you, Doctor.

Sec. 4.13   How to Prove Medical and Hospital Expenses

Where you use the treating doctor, you may ask him, at the conclusion of his testimony, whether his treatment was necessary and what the reasonable charge was for his services. The burden of proof as to the necessity of treatment and the reasonableness of the charges are on the plaintiff. Generally speaking, these expenses cannot be satisfactorily proven in any other way, over objection.[17] The hospital bills can be proven by sub-poenaing them along with the hospital records. However, to be on the safe side and especially if the bills are large, it is advisable to subpoena the custodian of the records to prove the records, and the bursar of the hospital to prove the bills, since frequently they are kept in two separate depart-

---

17. *3 Am. Jur. Proof of Facts,* pps. 755-759.

ments. Make certain that you question the hospital bursar about the reasonableness of the hospital charges. The usual questions are as follows:[18]

Q. What is your position with the hospital?

A. I am the bursar.

Q. What is your function with reference to the hospital bills for its services and supplies furnished to a patient?

A. I keep those records and I prepare the bills.

Q. Did you have as part of your records the bills charged to John Smith of 10 Alcindor Drive, Baltimore, Maryland, for his hospital stay from January 1, 1970, to March 1, 1970?

A. Yes; they are right here.

Q. I offer these as plaintiff's Exhibit No. 1 for identification. I note that the gross total is $2,000 and that the amount is broken down into the daily charges for room, nurses, drugs, operations, and laboratory tests. Is this a correct statement?

A. Yes.

Q. How do these charges compare with the usual and customary charges made in your locality for the same items?

A. They are about the same.

Q. Are these fair and reasonable charges?

A. Yes.

Q. So far as you know, were these examinations and treatments of the plaintiff required by the doctors in charge necessary in the plaintiff's medical case?

A. Yes.

Q. I offer these bills in evidence.

If a distant doctor and hospital are involved, it may be necessary to take depositions to prove such.

A sample questioning of the doctor as to his bills follows:[19]

Q. Doctor, how much is your overall bill for treating Mr. . . . . ?

A. Five hundred dollars.

Q. This was for office visits only?

A. Yes, and for X-rays and tests.

Q. How many visits?

---

18. See footnote 15, supra. Frequently the other side will stipulate that the bills are reasonable and that they may be admitted into evidence, thus avoiding the necessity of proving them; hence it is wise to contact the opposing counsel to obtain such a stipulation in advance of the trial.

19. See footnote 15, supra.

A. Thirty-five.

Q. How much did you charge for each office visit?

A. Ten dollars—making a total of three hundred and fifty dollars for the visits.

Q. How much for the X-rays?

A. One hundred dollars—there were fourteen different X-ray plates taken.

Q. How much for the laboratory tests?

A. Fifty dollars—this was for urine and blood tests.

Q. Do you consider these charges to be fair and reasonable?

A. I do.

Q. Were these examinations, tests, and treatments necessary in the treatment of plaintiff's condition?

A. Yes, sir

Chapter 5

WHERE TO TRY

YOUR CASE

Sec. 5.1   Should You Use the State or the Federal Court?

It is obviously to the plaintiff's advantage to try his case in the forum where he can get the highest award. Also it is to his advantage to use that forum where he can achieve the maximum discovery of information in preparation for the trial. Another important consideration which may arise, particularly where delay has occurred in filing suit, is where the Statute of Limitations is the most liberal. The defendant's object, of course, would be to locate the case in the locale where the lowest award would be attainable. Ordinarily, the state court alone has jurisdiction—this applies in the usual case of an auto collision within the state involving drivers who are residents of that same state where injuries and damages have resulted. Where the case involved a federal statute and the amount exceeded $10,000[1] or where the parties are from different states and the amount in dispute exceeds $10,000, then the federal courts could assume jurisdiction.[2] It is possible, however, even in such cases, to pick a state court. For example, if your case involves a Jones Act suit on account of injury to a merchant seaman[3] or if it concerns

---

1. *28 U.S.C.A., Section 1331.* There is authority that no jurisdictional amount is required in certain types of tort cases, for example such as Jones Act suits. *Ballard v. Moore-McCormack Lines, Inc.,* (D.C. N.Y. 1968), 285 F.S. 290.

2. *28 U.S.C.A.,* Section 1332.

3. *O'Donnell v. Gt. Lakes Dredge & Dock Co.* (Ill. 1943), 63 S. Ct. 488, 318 U.S. 36, 87 L. Ed. 596.

an F.E.L.A. suit on account of injuries befalling a railroad worker,[4] suit could still be filed in the state court where the defendant does business.[5]

If the suit concerned an accident occurring in Maryland when the plaintiff driver resided in New Jersey and the defendant driver resided in New York, it is possible to bring the suit in the state court of Maryland or of New York, as well as in the federal court.[6]

If the case involves death, the jurisdictional principles closely resemble those applying to personal injuries and it may be brought wherever the defendant may be found, except where the death statute specifically fixes the venue.[7] It must be remembered also that the limitations periods in death cases differ frequently from those in personal injury cases.[8]

So the first decision is whether to sue in the federal or in the state courts. A general observation, but one subject to exceptions, is that if the plaintiff's case is reasonably strong on liability as well as on damages, the federal court is the desirable forum. The reason is that although the federal juries are stricter on liability, they are more liberal on damages. The federal court juries are frequently made up of persons with more business experience who are more accustomed to dealing with higher levels of money than are members of state juries.

Another factor favoring the federal courts as a forum is the liberality of its discovery rules. The new federal discovery rules of July 1, 1970,[9] far outdistance the general run of state courts' discovery procedures. Some of the recent innovations in discovery availability are the following:[10] information as to insurance coverage; only "substantial need" and not "good cause" is required in order to obtain documents and things or entry on land, and this may extend to investigate material prepared by the defendant's agent in the course of his investigation of some cases; discovery may be obtained of

---

4. *Miles v. Ill. Cent. R. Co.* (Tenn. 1942), 62 S. Ct. 827, 315 U.S. 698, 86 L. Ed. 1129.

5. *Kilpatrick v. Texas & P. Ry. Co.* (CCA NY) (1948), 166 F. 2d 788, cert. den. 69 S. Ct. 32 (2 mems), 335 U.S. 814, 93 L. Ed. 369; *Pure Oil Co. v. Suarez* (CA Fla. 1965), 346 F. 2d 890, aff'd 86 S. Ct. 1394, 384 U.S. 202.

6. Maryland would assume jurisdiction because of a statute allowing process against non-residents using Maryland highways Code 1957, Article 66-1/2, *Maryland Code Annotated*, Section 115; *West's Maryland Law Encyclopedia*, Vol. 3, Section 191. Many states have similar provisions. New York would have jurisdiction because that is where the defendant resides. As to the substantive law applicable to the case, this would be that of the state where the accident occurred. *West's Maryland Law Encyclopedia*, Vol. 3, Section 192.

7. Speiser, "Recovery for Wrongful Death," Section 11:2. The law applicable to the jurisdictional removal for a death action can become complicated, as for example when the doctrine of forum non convenius is employed by the defendant. For this problem and other problems affecting when the Statute of Limitations is to begin, i.e. whether at the time of the injury or the time of death or the time when the administrator is appointed, see Speiser "Recovery for Wrongful Death," Section 11:5.

8. See Sec. 2.5, supra.

9. *48 F.R.D.* 487-545; *28 U.S.C.A.*, Rules 26-37 of Federal Rules of Civil Procedure.

10. See "The Impact of the Revised Federal Rules of Discovery" by John J. O'Connor, Jr., Baltimore, Maryland, 24th Annual Convention, American Trial Lawyers Association, 1970.

"facts known" and "opinions held" by experts developed in anticipation of trial; on interrogatories and requests for admissions, matters of opinion may be discoverable; defendants no longer have priority in discovery; liberal inspection of opposing party's documents, even without court orders, is encouraged.

Another bonus feature of federal jurisdiction is the thrust toward settlement of cases. This is initiated usually through the pre-trial conference procedure. The usual federal requirement is the preparation of a pre-trial court order by the plaintiff preparatory to the pre-trial conference in order to expedite the conference and the trial. Among other things, the order capsulizes the contents of the case, the positions of each side, the documents to be produced, and the damages claimed to be proven. By the time the pre-trial confrontation occurs, each side should have the money value of the case in mind and some courts will explore the settlement gap.[11] Some states follow this pattern too and where this occurs, choice of the state court as to the forum should be seriously considered.

This discussion does not mean to exclude the state courts as the preferable place for the trial of your case. There are communities where the plaintiffs' lawyers consider the federal courts as the corporation lawyer's preserve only and where the poor man is treated as an alien. This is unfortunate and certainly should not be so. In such instances, certainly the state tribunals should be utilized. This jaundiced picture of the federal courts is sometimes attributable to the judge who has had a corporation law practice before ascending to the bench and who considers personal injury litigation, particularly of the less serious kind, as of picayune importance and demeaning to the court's dignity. It cannot be too urgently argued that our courts of justice were not intended to be used exclusively for legal contests between money giants, but were intended for the holy search for equity and justice between human beings, whether they be mighty or humble.

Sec. 5.2   What to Do if You Can't Get a Fair Tribunal

In Maryland,[12] as in some other states, a party is entitled to removal of a civil case from the court where it is filed to another court in the state if either of the parties files a form under oath that he cannot get a fair trial. No particulars must be given. This is a salutary procedure and there should be no

---

11. In passing, an accolade should be accorded to the federal courts and to their progressive procedural measures. Their stress is upon free discovery of the facts by both sides so as to achieve an accurate and just presentation of the case. This contrasts dramatically with the techniques of surprise and rhetoric-relics of a by-gone period, but still used in many state courts at the expense of the expeditious and fair administration of justice.

12. Constitution of Maryland, Article IV, Section 8; Maryland Rules, Rule 542.

reluctance to use it. The judge from whom the case is removed may not like it, but he must respect the lawyer for his courage and he may well be persuaded to change his attitude in similar cases in the future. No judge wants to acquire willingly the image of being inequitable or a tyrant. In some cases, the removal petition is not directed at him but at the juries in that county.

The author has frequently used the Petition For Removal and carries the forms with him before every case he tries, ready for use. Examples of cases where such petitions may be used are the following: where the judge is notoriously anti-plaintiff in personal injury actions; where the judge is anti-defendant in suits for damages against labor unions; where the juries in a water resort county are pro-resort owners in cases of personal injuries to patrons in bathing accidents; where the juries are pro-defendant in suits brought against the city fathers on account of personal injuries suffered from falls due to street and sidewalk defects; and where the juries are notorious for their low verdicts generally.

The party asking for the removal takes the risk of removal to even a less favorable forum. It is discretionary with the judge where the case is to go. To counteract this, it is advisable for counsel who is the movant to try to get agreement from his opponent as to the new forum. Frequently, the opposing counsel will agree on a county nearer home which may not be too unfavorable. Usually, the court will accept the forum stipulated to by counsel. Plaintiff's counsel should try to locate the case in the county which has a large city as the county seat. Usually, larger verdicts are obtained here because the population is accustomed to a higher standard of living and more experienced professional experts are available here. However, due consideration must be given now to the current phenomenon of substantial citizens moving from the cities to the suburbs. In such cases, perhaps it is wiser to try your case in the suburbia county because the larger verdict can be obtained there.

If your state does not allow for a statutory right of removal in civil cases and if the case is a serious one, counsel should consider filing a petition for removal, specifically raising federal as well as state constitutional grounds predicated on denial of due process of law. Such a petition should be supported by affidavits spelling out why a fair trial cannot be obtained and testimony should be presented to make a record for appeal. For example, if the juries are illiberal in their awards to members of the black race because they exclude blacks from the petit juries, same should be proven by producing the court clerks and their records showing how the jury panels have been chosen to discriminate against the blacks. In the event of a flagrantly unfavorable verdict on damages, the way should be open for an appeal to the federal courts on the federal constitutional issue raised.

The same can apply in a county where blue collar working persons are deliberately kept off the juries by the court administrators.

Chapter 6

HOW TO PICK
THE JURY

Sec. 6.1   Pre-Trial Investigation of Jurors

In many states, jury investigative services are available to trial attorneys in order to inform on the background and to provide general information about prospective jurors. These should be utilized.

In addition, in many states, the court publishes information about the prospective jurors, such as occupation, education, spouse's occupation, etc. These should be carefully scrutinized.

In many states, the court makes a general statement to the entire jury panel instructing them on the duties of the jurors, the method of a trial, and reminding them not to make up their minds until they have heard both sides of the case, that objections made by counsel are not to be considered obstructive, and that conferences with lawyers at the bench out of earshot of the jurors are necessary to settle points of law raised, etc. Whenever possible, counsel should attend these sessions or get copies of the judge's remarks where possible. This will enable the lawyer to observe the general character of the jury panel and to absorb the atmosphere into which they are introduced just before being chosen for a case. Sometimes, the instructing judge will stress some point out of context, such for example that the jury should not give too much weight to the opening statements and the closing arguments because they are not evidence. Counsel can try to accomodate to this in his opening and closing statements.

Also, there are services which relate the doings in the various courts revealing what verdicts the juries are returning. These should be utilized.

The legal newspaper usually records the verdicts brought in by each court each day. This should be studied.

Sec. 6.2 When to Try Your Case

When to try your case is a question not easy to answer. Certainly, if a jury panel has a record of conservatism and if you have a difficult case, either on liability or damages, a postponement of the trial, if possible, would seem to be in order. On the other hand, if the jury panel has a record of liberality, then the defendant's attorney should consider postponement, if possible.

A new jury would be more desirable to the plaintiff than one which has been sitting a long time. The older jury has a tendency to develop cynicism toward the litigants and their contentions, and this is not helpful to a plaintiff with a difficult case.

As far as the plaintiff is concerned, the sooner he can get his case heard, the more effective it should be because the injuries and the pain and suffering are still fresh, and a stronger appeal can be registered therefore on the jury. Of course, it would be better for the defendant to delay such a trial until the acute stage of pain has passed.

Nevertheless, where plaintiff has a case which is strong on liability and damages, the element of time is not so important. It is the author's feeling that if a case has merit, the average jury will do it justice, regardless of when it is tried.

Sec. 6.3 Preliminary Considerations Before Selection

It is advisable to approach the court in advance of the trial and to request that each juror be required to stand as his name is called so that counsel may observe him or her. Some courts do this as a matter of course.

There are many lawyers who place much store by observation in choosing jurors; they favor those whose appearances they like, because they feel they can mentally communicate with them better during the course of the trial. While much can be said about judging people by their appearances (and many able trial lawyers seem to be gifted with intuition in this respect), there are too many exceptions to make this a safe rule to follow, in the author's opinion. The experiences in a human being's life which shape his predilections in matters such as jury service are not written in his face. Nevertheless, open observation can reveal certain factors in potential jurors, such as age, dress, ethnic group, and, to a lesser extent, manner (whether meek or bold, stern or kindly, leader or follower).

This can be of definite assistance in eliminating some of the prospects. If the person is aged and infirm or hard of hearing, he would not be too helpful. If he is of the same ethnic group as the defendant, he might not be a good risk, although this generalization certainly has its exceptions. If he is obviously a poor and illiterate person, he will be tantamount to a zero figure on the jury. If the prospect is a housewife who has had no previous business or work experience and who feels that she is here to escape her household drudgery, she will be a virtual zero and will simply follow what the leaders propose.

Many lawyers are firm believers in favoring certain ethnic groups and opposing others on juries. For example, many favor the Negro and the Jew because they identify with the underdog, and the plaintiff is frequently in that role. These same lawyers tend to oppose those with backgrounds which are Germanic or Scandinavian because they are supposed to be less warmhearted and therefore less plaintiff-minded. The author finds these generalizations very illusory. However, it cannot be denied that the Negro and the Jew are to be desired because of their greater empathy for the underdog and if they are not of the same ethnic group as the defendant, assuming you are representing the plaintiff.

Some lawyers tend toward those with more humble occupations, such as factory worker, barber, and salesman, who are considered outgoing and extroverts, as contrasted with the business executive, chemist, or engineer, whom they consider as introverts or "loners," less likely to go along with the majority.[1] While there may be some merit to this argument, still there are too many exceptions to it to abide by it strictly. Besides, in a case of serious injury, the author deems it almost essential to have on the jury some persons of business or executive or scientific background, who are more accustomed to dealing in large sums of money and thus to raise the level of damages which the jury will consider.

As to women prospects, it is important to inquire if they have had any previous business or work experience. If they have, they will be more self-reliant when damages, particularly, are being considered, because they can better appreciate the value of a dollar in terms of the limitations placed on the incapacitated plaintiff. All too often women jurors without previous work experience consider jury service as a welcome and exciting vacation from their home chores and simply follow the leaders on the jury.

Serious consideration must now be given to the make-up of juries in the big cities, where the population changes have been so great recently. In cases

---

1. See "Persuasion: The Key To Damages," published by The Institute of Continuing Legal Education, Ann Arbor, Michigan (1969), p. 4. Speeches for the Plaintiff by Murray Sams, Jr., Esquire of Miami, Florida.

of serious injuries, it would seem advisable to get some business or executive type persons on the jury to beef up the amounts of damages the jury will consider.

Careful questioning should be resorted to in order to eliminate the business or executive or white collar type of prospect who has had claim investigative background. This type of person will be conditioned against a plaintiff's verdict, or a large one.

The lawyer should have in his kit the law which states those who are disqualified for jury duty. Mistakes are sometimes made by the clerical staffs in this respect.

The trial lawyer should keep an account of who is chosen for the final jury and who is rejected.[2] This insures compliance with the rules. Also, it enables the lawyer to know what kind of evidence and argument will appeal to each type of juror (i.e. the nurse will be interested in the medical and discomfort phases of the case, the engineer will be interested in the mechanics involved in the accident, etc).

The prospect who is himself obviously crippled or disfigured may not be a good choice as a juror even though the plaintiff has suffered similar disabilities. Instead of empathy, such a person may react with antipathy, feeling that he has survived his disabilities well and without compensation, so why can't the plaintiff do the same?

Sec. 6.4 How to Use Voir Dire Examination

There are many lawyers, particularly in small communities, who advise against the pre-examination of the jury panel by voir dire questions. They are afraid that it will antagonize the judge and the jury panel against the party putting the questions. The author disagrees with this approach. He has found that the prospective jurors are usually eager to serve and are equally eager to show that they wish to be fair, and therefore they do not resent inquiries about their qualifications to serve. Some judges may resent it because it is unusual for their courts and because it takes up additional time, but this is frequently forgotten in the course of the trial.

The ostensible purpose of the voir dire examination is to ascertain which jurors harbor any bias and to eliminate them. It serves another purpose, namely, to inform them what the case is about and to try to subtly persuade them toward your side.[3]

Some states permit counsel to question the prospective jurors directly.

---

2. For a box form to use, see the authority in footnote 1 supra at p. 11 by Jack E. Horsley, Esquire of Mattoon, Illinois.

3. See authority in footnote 1 supra, pps. 3-16.

Others, including the Federal Courts, usually do not but require counsel to submit the questions to the judge, who questions the jurors, usually en banc. Some states employ the latter system but permit counsel to ask some supplementary questions subsequently.

The general law is that it is descretionary with the judge whether to allow certain voir dire questions and that there is reversible error only where there is a showing of abuse of this power of discretion.[4] The same rule applies generally to the exercise of challenges.[5]

It is strategically wise to couch your questions in such a way as to maneuver a biased prospective juror into a case of a challenge for cause. This will protect the limited number of peremptory challenges you have where you can challenge a juror because you generally disapprove of him as a juror. As an example, the following voir dire questions could be coupled in this manner:

Q. Have you or any member of your immediate family ever had a claim or suit made against them on account of alleged injuries and/or damage resulting from an automobile accident?

Q. If so, wouldn't you think it fair to say that you would rather not serve in this case, which does involve a similar type of accident?

Were the prospective juror to answer both questions in the affirmative, he should be disqualifying himself for cause.

Were the usual coupling question put, it would sound like this:

Q. If so, do you feel that you could hear and fairly decide this case on its merits, which is of a similar nature?

The likelihood would be that the prospective juror would answer in the affirmative because he would not like to admit any bias, although it is subconsciously there, and because he is eager to serve. In such a situation, counsel for the plaintiff would have to use one of his few peremptory challenges to get rid of him.

While each case presents its unique problems requiring special voir dire questions, there are certain standard ones applicable to all. These will be discussed later in this chapter under the title "Checklist of Voir Dire Questions."

Again it is stressed that the voir dire will serve primarily to eliminate those who are obviously biased. It cannot make an ideal jury for either side. Neither will any of the other preliminary considerations hereafter discussed.

---

4. *50 C.J.S.*, Section 275.
5. *50 C.J.S.*, Section 249.

Assuming an honest and well intentioned jury and assuming that the case is well presented by both sides, the merits of the case will determine the issue and how much. Sometimes the mistakes or the breaks of the game are decisive, very much as in a professional sports game between evenly matched antagonists. If the plaintiff or defendant or an important witness for either side falters badly, it will make the substantial difference in the case. Usually it is not the selection of the jury which is the decisive factor, if it is selected in the manner described.

Sec. 6.5   Checklist of Voir Dire Questions for Plaintiff[6]

[The following would represent recommended stock voir dire questions to be put by the plaintiff in the average case involving a collision between two automobiles and injuries to the plaintiff-driver[7] of the musculo-ligamentous character to the neck; each party claims to have one eyewitness and each party has a doctor favorable to his side of the case.]

1. Do you know any of the parties to this case, namely, the plaintiff, John Smart, of 1200 Cedona Road, Baltimore, Maryland, and the defendant, Sam Slippery, of 1600 New Falls Road, Baltimore, Maryland?

2. Do you know any of the members of the immediate families of either of the parties?

[If the defendant is a corporation, then substitute for question two the following questions:

a. Do you know any of the immediate family of the plaintiff?

b. Do you know any of the officers, directors, representatives, or employees of the defendant corporation?

c. Do you or any member of your immediate family have any financial interest in the defendant corporation?

d. Do you or any of your immediate family do business with the defendant corporation?]

3. Do you know the plaintiff's attorney, namely John Rogue, 20 W. Baltimore Street, Baltimore, Maryland, and the defendant's attorney, William Slick of the First National Bank Building, Baltimore, Maryland?

4. Have you or any members of your immediate family ever been represented by any of these attorneys?

5. Are you familiar with the event involved, namely, a collision between the automobiles of the parties at Baltimore and Charles Streets, Baltimore,

---

6. The court may not allow all of these questions. See the discussion concerning admissibility under footnotes 4 and 5, supra.

7. Counsel may wish to omit certain of these questions depending on the situation at hand.

Maryland, on May 1, 1970, at about 11:00 a.m., and if so, in what way are you familiar with it?[8]

6. Have you or any members of your immediate faimly ever had a claim or suit made or filed against you or them in any type of accident?

[If the answer to the previous question is in the affirmative, you may wish to put this disqualification question.]

7. If your answer to the previous question is "yes", wouldn't you think it fair to say that you would rather not serve on the jury in the trial of this case?

or

If your answer to the previous question is "yes", don't you feel in all fairness that you could not pass on the issues of this case objectively and impartially?

or

If your answer to the previous question is "yes", do you feel that you could hear and determine the issues in this case objectively and impartially?

8. Have you or any member of your immediate family ever served on a jury before and if so, when and where?

9. Have you or any member of your immediate family ever been involved in a lawsuit? If so, what was the nature of it?

10. Have you or has any member of your immediate family ever given testimony as a witness in a trial, and if so, what was the nature of the case and the nature of your participation in it?

11. Have you or has any member of your immediate family ever been engaged in any kind of investigation or inquiry on account of health or accident claims? If so, please state the nature of it.

12. Do you know Dr. James Minimus, orthopedic doctor, of 1200 N. Charles Street, Baltimore, Maryland, whom the defendant claims he will call to testify for the defendant in this case?

13. If your answer to the previous question is "yes", then in what way do you know him?

14. Do you know Harry Metoo of 13 Patapsco Avenue, Baltimore, Maryland, whom the defendant claims he will call as a witness to this accident, and if so, what is your relationship to him?

15. Do you know Joseph Oger of 1800 S. Hanover Street, Baltimore, Maryland, whom the defendant claims he will call as a witness to this accident, and if so, what is your relationship to him?

16. If you are a woman juror, state if you have ever had any employment or business experience, and if so, what was the nature of it?

---

8. If the prospect answers the question "yes", and then proceeds to describe the accident unfavorably to your side of the case, a motion for mis-trial should be filed promptly.

17. Do you have any feeling of prejudice against the plaintiff in this case for any reason?

18. Do you have any reason which has not been covered by the questioning thus far which you feel would affect your qualification to serve on the jury in this case? If so, please state it now.

Sec. 6.6   Checklist of Voir Dire Questions for Defendant[9]

[Assume the same facts as appear under Plaintiff's Checklist]

1. Do you know any of the parties to this case, namely, the plaintiff, John Smart, of 1200 Cedona Road, Baltimore, Maryland, and the defendant, Sam Slippery of 1600 New Falls Road, Baltimore, Maryland?

2. Do you know any of the members of the immediate families of either of the parties?

[If the defendant is a corporation, then confine the question to the family of the plaintiff.]

3. Do you know the plaintiff's attorney, namely John Rogue, 20 W. Baltimore Street, Baltimore, Maryland, and the defendant's attorney, William Slick, First National Bank Building, Baltimore, Maryland?

4. Have you or any members of your immediate family ever been represented by any of these attorneys?

5. Are you familiar with the event involved, namely a collision between the automobiles of the parties at Baltimore and Charles Streets, Baltimore, Maryland, on May 1, 1970, at about 11:00 a.m., and if so, in what way are you familiar with it?

6. Have you or has any member of your immediate family ever filed a claim or suit against anyone in any type of accident?

[If the answer to the previous question is in the affirmative, then you may wish to put this disqualification question.]

7. If your answer to the previous question is "yes", don't you feel in all fairness that you could not pass on the issues of this case objectively and impartially?

8. Have you or any member of your immediate family ever served on a jury before and if so, when and where?

9. Have you or any member of your immediate family ever been involved in a lawsuit? If so, what was the nature of it?

10. Have you or has any member of your immediate family ever given testimony as a witness in a trial, and if so, what was the nature of the case and the nature of your participation in it?

---

9. See Defendant's Jury Checklist prepared by Jack E. Horsley, Esquire, at p. 15 of the book mentioned in footnote 1, supra.

11. Do you know Dr. Phillip Dogood, general practitioner, of 1200 St. Paul Street, Baltimore, Maryland, whom the plaintiff claims he will call to testify for the plaintiff as his medical witness in this case?

12. If your answer to the previous question is "yes", in what way do you know him?

13. Do you know Louis Seeall of 200 N. Calhoun Street, Baltimore, Maryland, whom the plaintiff claims he will call as a witness to this accident, and if so, what is your relationship with him?

14. Do you have any prejudice against the defendant because the suit was filed against him, and do you feel that the plaintiff is entitled to recover simply because he filed the suit?

15. Will you follow the court's instructions as to the law in this case?

16. Will you determine the facts according to the evidence heard in the case and not on the basis of sympathy?

17. Will you keep an open mind until the case is concluded?

18. Do you have any reason which has not been covered by the questioning thus far which you feel would affect your qualification to serve on the jury in this case? If so, please state it now.

Sec. 6.7   Special Voir Dire Questions

In addition to the aforegoing inquiries, counsel may wish to put other questions which will uniquely apply to the particular case. For example, the author recently was to try a case in which two men who had spent about seven hours in a tavern drinking were struck and seriously injured by a racing motorist as they were crossing the street on their way home. There was a dispute as to who had the green light. One of the plaintiffs was an admitted alcoholic and the record of it appeared in the hospital record. The applicable voir dire questions follow:

1. Assuming that there would be evidence in this case that the two pedestrians involved had been drinking beer for a few hours in a restaurant and bar near the scene of the accident and then were injured when struck by a motorist while crossing the road at an intersection in an unmarked pedestrian's crosswalk near the restaurant and bar, but where there will be testimony and evidence that the pedestrians were sober at the time of the accident, do you feel that under these circumstances you could find in favor of the plaintiffs, assuming further that you were convinced that the defendant negligently ran his automobile into the plaintiffs?

2. Assuming that you were not convinced that the plaintiffs were sober at the time that they were crossing the road near the restaurant and tavern at

the time the accident happened, but that they had the green traffic light in their favor at the intersection when they crossed in the unmarked pedestrian's crosswalk, and were hit by the defendant's automobile which had the red traffic light facing it, do you feel that you could find a verdict in the plaintiffs' favor nevertheless?

3. Assuming that you were convinced that the plaintiffs were not entirely sober at the time the accident happened, would this prevent you from rendering a verdict in favor of the plaintiffs if you felt that based on the evidence and the law, they were otherwise entitled to a verdict?

4. Assuming that there was evidence that either or both of the plaintiffs was an alcoholic prior to the occurrence of the accident, would this prevent you from rendering a fair and impartial verdict in this case?

5. Assuming that one of the plaintiffs in this case had a long history of drinking and alcoholism before this accident occurred and that on the evening of the accident, he spent a number of hours in a restaurant and tavern drinking and then while crossing the road near the tavern was struck and injured by a passing motorist, would this prevent you from finding in favor of this plaintiff, assuming that otherwise you felt he was entitled to a verdict based on the evidence and the law?

Chapter 7

WHAT TO SAY IN
THE OPENING STATEMENT

Sec. 7.1   Know the Stage Setting

Before the jury has been picked, it has already been indoctrinated by the judge in the general rules and what to anticipate in the trial of a case. Therefore, bear in mind that the jury looks to the judge with obeisance and as the symbol of justice which he, the juror, has sworn to uphold.

As the process of selection takes place, each juror feels that his personal life has been somewhat scrutinized in relation to his qualifications and he wishes to vindicate himself well as being a fair juror.

The average prospective juror is eager to be chosen and feels somewhat ostracized if challenged. There are exceptions, of course, particularly those who are indifferent or unwilling jurors and those who have served before.

The average new juror looks with eager anticipation to his experience and expects to have his interest galvanized throughout. Perhaps he also has been overnourished on a diet of television and movie versions of criminal trials. His sense of reality will be sobered up some by the actual trial.

So when the average new juror assumes his place in the jury-box, he is a very curious but dutiful and apprehensive person. He is going to accept the judge's words over those of the lawyers, and he will want to be shown before he believes. Nevertheless, the lawyer will be an important personage in the cast of players confronting him and he will respect the lawyer and what he says. The lawyer will be the first to make real contact between the jury and the case. Before the case will be over, the lawyer will play many roles in the drama—legal spokesman, medical pundit, gladiator, actor, and salesman. If he plays his parts well, the jury will admire him and he will feel the satisfaction of having done a good job. If he wins handsomely, then he will bask in glory, at least until he gets to his next case with its responsibilities and risks. If he loses, he will ruminate over his supposed mistakes and may secretly vow to try an easier way of making a living–until he tackles his next case.

Sec. 7.2   What the Lawyer's Image Should Be

Generally, juries expect the lawyer to look his part, namely, that of a respected professional man. He should be well dressed and groomed. Extremes in dress or grooming will be disapproved, by some of the jurors at least. There still are some lawyers, especially in the smaller communities, who affect the role of a poor country lawyer in order to win the jury's sympathy to his cause, especially when confronting an outside city lawyer. The time has about passed when this kind of ploy is effective any longer. But don't be surprised by it when it happens to you, in which case it might be wise in the closing argument to mention that defendant's counsel is not only able but one of the most financially successful lawyers in the area.

He should impress the jury with the fact that he knows his case well and is fully prepared, and that he is sincere in everything he says and does on behalf of his client's cause.

He should give the impression that he is open and truthful with the court and jury, and is not concealing anything of importance to the case.

While polite and respectful, he must not appear to be abject to the judge, jury, or the other side. The world likes a fighter and not a groveler.

He should constantly remember that the jury is meant to be a cross-section of laymen who do not understand the complexities of law and medicine, or the lexicon of either. Do not address them as an appellate court, but as a group of ordinary human beings. Do not talk down to them but address them always as equals and in their language throughout the trial.

A word or two should be said here about the oratorical manner of delivery. Generally speaking, it is now passé. Juries are too sophisticated today to be taken in by the stentorian-voiced and the table-thumping mouthpiece. It is the facts and their intelligent presentation which the juries seek. However, in some of the smaller, rural communities, demagoguery still is welcomed by juries. In such cases, it may be wise to change the tack of your boat's course to compete with the elements on the scene at the time–at least at some moments in the trial, such as in the closing argument.

In any case, be yourself. If you are not an orator, do not try being one. If you are not a wit, don't try being witty. You may be sure it will come off badly if you do. But you can offset such an advantage which your adversary has by commenting, usually in the closing argument, that you are not blessed with your opponent's gift for rhetoric or wit, but that you are sure the jury will not be blinded by its brilliance in searching for the facts and truth in this case.

Sec. 7.3   What to Do and Not to Do

The opening statement should be well prepared because it essentially embraces your entire case in capsulized form. It must attract the interest of the jury at once and hold it to the end. Find out what preparation technique is best suited to you, whether notes, an outline, or a fully written out opening statement. The author advises rehearsing your opening statement in front of a mirror. You will find that you will want to rid your delivery of certain kinks or bugs, whether in wording or in manner of delivery. But do not memorize your opening remarks. If you do, it will show and you will not be loose and relaxed, as you should at least appear to be.

Set a dignified tone for the trial and show your politeness by opening with "Your Honor, Judge . . . . , Mr. Foreman, and Ladies and Gentlemen of the Jury."

You should only consult your notes periodically in making your opening statement. You should keep your eyes on each juror from time to time as you narrate your case. Impress each juror with the fact that you are interested in his reaction. Try to establish a rapport promptly with each one of them.

It is said that the average juror makes up his mind early in the case and does not change it.[1]

The statement should be brief and not repetitive, to hold the jury's undivided interest. Feel no compunctions about using some oratorical flourishes when the climaxes are reached, as when you describe the impact between the two colliding vehicles and the intense pain experienced by the plaintiff.

Be the first to tell the jury about a weakness in your case, such as a previous injury to the same member of the body. Unless you do this, the defendant's attorney will seize the opportunity and the impression will be conveyed that you are withholding information from the jury.

The author is a firm believer in building up the damage phase of the case early and in the opening statement. For example, do not be content with

---

1. A jury project study conducted at the University of Chicago and led by Professor Harry Kalven showed that 80 percent of jurors made up their minds early in a case and did not change. "Persuasion: The Key To Damages", published by the Institute of Continuing Legal Education, Hutchins Hall, Ann Arbor, Michigan (1969), p. 90.

merely stating that there will be some permanent disability. Expatiate on it. Relate in layman's language what the nature of the disability is and why it will be, describing the physiological mechanics of it. For example, if you are claiming a musculo-ligamentous sprain of the neck resulting in 15 percent permanent disability, state that you will show, through your medical expert, that this sprain constituted a tearing of the soft tissues in the neck area, including muscles, ligaments, nerves, and blood vessels, and that on healing scar tissue formed; because it is less pliable than the natural tissue, the plaintiff will suffer discomfort and pain when he moves his neck in such a way as to pull on the scar tissue.[2]

Throughout your opening statement, use the affirmative words, "I will show", and not the weaker and apologetic words, "we expect to prove" or "we hope to show you", etc., because the weaker language implies doubt that you can prove your case.

Make your statement of proof and contentions as general as possible. Do not tell what you will prove through each witness. It is not unknown for eyewitnesses, for example, to falter in their testimony. If plaintiff's counsel sets out in his opening statement with the assertion that he will corroborate his case by an impartial eyewitness and the latter proves to be a failure, the defendant's counsel surely will make capital of it in the closing argument.

Do not be too specific as to the money amounts you will show were lost as damages. Frequently damage information is excluded, as for example, when you cannot produce the treating doctor to establish the reasonableness of his bill.

While the opening statement should contain only what you intend to prove, there is a certain amount of argument and persuasion in it. To the extent that it is openly and blatantly argument, it is objectionable and the court in its discretion can bar it.[3] Hence, it is wise to couch your statement in the framework of what you will prove or show.

On the other hand, if defendant's counsel resorts to open and flagrant argument in his opening statement, have no hesitancy in objecting. It will not only serve to keep out what amounts to a premature closing argument, but to throw your opposing counsel off stride in making his opening statement.

Sec. 7.4 Hypothetical Case

Let us assume the trial of a rear-end auto collision in which the plaintiff, who was the driver of the first autombile, suffered musculo-ligamentous

---

2. See the examination of a medical expert on this subject in Sec. 4.12, supra.
3. *88 C.J.S.*, Section 161.

sprain of his neck. The plaintiff claims he stopped for a red light. The defendant claims the plaintiff stopped too suddenly and without adequate warning. Assume that each party has an eyewitness who supports his version of the accident and that the police came upon the scene and took statements from the drivers. Assume further that the plaintiff had had a previous injury to his neck.

Since a diagram showing where the accident happened and the location of the traffic lights is important in the presentation of the case, the outset of the opening statement would be an ideal point at which to put it on the blackboard. It serves two purposes at this juncture; it distracts the jury from their tensions and it projects plaintiff's counsel in the role of an instructor.

Now go into your statement. It should be made up of the following topics: the nature of the lawsuit (suit for money damages on account of wrongful personal injuries and for property damage to the automobile); the accident (narrate it as dramatically as possible, telling the place and time, and emphasize the intensity of the impact to account for the severity of the injuries, i.e. the plaintiff's vehicle was driven completely across the intersection and up an embankment); the injuries (plaintiff's head was thrown violently backward and forward, and he felt immediate pain); the arrival of the police (the taking of statements of the drivers); plaintiff's treatment (he was taken by ambulance to the hospital and, after being released, underwent a long regimen of treatment through medication and therapy, and had to use a neck brace); the fault (that of the defendant exclusively because he was not alert in that he did not see the red light promptly enough, did not have his vehicle under proper control, and was following plaintiff's vehicle too closely); no contributory negligence (plaintiff did what the reasonable man would have done under similar circumstances and came to a gradual stop for the red light); if the defendant has clearly indicated in the discovery preceedings that plaintiff caused the accident by stopping too abruptly, this defense should be anticipated and answered at this point; the special or out-of-pocket damages (mention generally that plaintiff incurred substantial damages on account of hospital, medical, therapeutic, drug, and surgical appliance expenses and on account of lost earnings, mentioning generally how much time plaintiff lost from work); the permanent disability (mention the extent and the nature and mechanics of the injury in layman's language, and how it will affect plaintiff in his work and recreation); anticipate the reference to plaintiff's previous neck injury and mention it with the observation that its symptoms had cleared up, if such is the case; the pain and suffering (the first few weeks were acute and intense and there has been more or less chronic pain since); after consideration of all of the evidence and of these items of damage and disability, you will ask the jury to return a substantial verdict in order to do justice to the plaintiff on account of this civil wrong done to him.

Sec. 7.5 Checklist for the Opening Statement

While each case will require its own treatment in an opening statement, depending on its facts, the following represents fundamental or stock factors which should be included in the average case just mentioned (a rear-end auto collision when plaintiff stopped for a red traffic light and in which the plaintiff driver suffered a musculo-ligamentous strain to his neck; the defendant claims plaintiff stopped too abruptly and without giving warning; plaintiff had a previous neck disability):

1. Establish an atmosphere of dignity and decorum in your opening statement by a formal salutation to the court and jury.

2. Draw a diagram on the blackboard showing the location of the accident. Ask the court's permission to do so first.

3. Establish an image of yourself as a knowledgeable and able lawyer who is utterly sincere about the justice of your side of the case, and that you are being truthful and open with the judge and jury.

4. Be polite but not meek, whether with the judge or the jury, or the opposing counsel. Be a fighter, not an apologist for your client.

5. Preface your remarks repeatedly with the words, "We will show" or "We will prove." This will keep your opening statement affirmative in tone and will keep it within the legal perimeter of an opening statement rather than a closing argument.

6. The contents of your opening statement should be carefully prepared in advance, with notes to consult as you deliver it. It is advisable to rehearse it before delivery, but it should not be memorized.

7. Establish immediate rapport with the jury by looking at each one of them from time to time as though you want them to respond in words to your remarks. Do not let your notes distract you from this task.

8. Make your statement brief. Do not be repetitive. Hold the interest of your jury from beginning to end. Appear poised and relaxed.

9. Mention first the nature of the case (i.e, suit for money damages on account of personal injuries and property damage suffered in an automobile accident).

10. Next mention the accident, telling it as dramatically as you can, and referring to the diagram to assist you. Stress the nature of the impact, thus to account for the severity of the injuries.

11. Describe how the injuries occurred (i.e. plaintiff's head was thrown violently backward and forward, and he had the feeling of immediate pain).

12. Mention the treatment (i.e. the period in the hospital and the long regimen of medical treatment thereafter).

13. Discuss fault (i.e. it was exclusively that of the defendant and give the reasons).

14. Negate contributory negligence (i.e. explain that plaintiff acted as the ordinary, reasonable man would have in similar circumstances. In this connection, negate defendant's contention of an abrupt stop before defendant's counsel mentions it as a defense).

15. Mention the special or out-of-pocket expenses(i.e. hospital, medical, drug, therapeutic, surgical appliance, and auto damage expenses, and the lost time and wages). Do not be too specific as to amounts, to allow for gaps in proof which may develop later in the trial.

16. The permanent disability (detail the physiological mechanics of the injury in the manner in which the medical expert will describe it later on the stand, but in layman's language, and mention how it will affect the plaintiff in his work and in his recreation permanently). *This is an important item and the first one in the build-up of the damages in the case, which should get at least as much attention, if not more in this case, than the liability phase.*

17. Mention plaintiff's previous neck injury so the jury will feel you are not hiding any facts from them. Try to relate the effect of the new accident to it, as for example, the plaintiff was symptom-free from the previous accident until the new one.

18. Detail generally the pain and suffering (break it down into periods of intensity, to set a price on it later by periods in your closing argument).

19. Conclude with an itemization of the elements of damage for which you are asking compensation (i.e. hospital, medical, surgical, surgical appliances, physical therapy, lost wages, permanent disability, and pain and suffering). Mention that you are asking for a substantial sum but an amount which the jury considers fair. Do not state a specific amount at this time.

20. Thank the jury for its attention.[4]

---

4. For another specimen checklist, see *5 Am. Jur. Trials*, p. 309; *13 Am. Jur.*, p. 228, 229. For a general discussion on Opening Statement, see *6 Am. Jur. Trials*, pps. 637, 638.

Chapter 8

HOW TO USE

HOSPITAL RECORDS

Sec. 8.1   Trial Purposes of the Hospital Records

The hospital records serve a number of purposes in the trial of a negligence case. First, they constitute an important part of the medical log pertaining to your client's injuries. This will cover the history concerning how the injuries were incurred; it can help to establish that the injuries resulted from an accident. For example, suppose your client's automobile was sideswiped by a hit and run motorist, causing the injuries in a state which has an Unsatisfied Claim and Judgment Fund. Suppose there were no witnesses to the accident except your client. Suppose further that your client went immediately to a hospital and was treated for his injuries. The history as to how he got hurt, which he gave at the hospital, would be significant to establish his story of the offending phantom driver. In fact, in such a case, this would constitute the only confirmation of his story, except for the damage to his automobile.

A second purpose is to narrate the physical and/or mental condition which he suffered and the treatment which he had to undergo to be cured of it. If he underwent an operation, a detailed description of it will appear, albeit in aseptic medical terms (which can be explained by your medical expert at the time of trial). This should enhance the damage value of the case.

A third purpose is to lay a foundation so the medical experts used by either of the parties can render an opinion.

A fourth purpose is to refresh your client's recollection of past painful events in connection with his testimony about his pain and suffering.

The overall effects of the hospital reports should be to impress on the jury the pain and suffering endured by the plaintiff as a result of the accident.

Sec. 8.2   What Records to Ask For

Counsel should request a photostat copy of the *entire* record and the bills incurred for treatment. As previously stated, one of the purposes is to lay a proper foundation for the testimony opinion of the medical expert. To a simple request for a report, the hospital may respond with an abstract or a mere resumé of the hospital record. In such a case, the defendant's counsel may object to the admissibility of the medical expert's opinion on the ground of insufficiency of the medical background information on the case. All too frequently, some adverse material appears in the full hospital record which can be used devastatingly against the plaintiff, if his counsel does not have the full record and is therefore caught by surprise.

In a malpractice case against a hospital, counsel must be ultra-careful to ascertain if he has gotten the full hospital record. It is not unknown for portions of a hospital record to be sequestered. The way to establish the completeness of the record is to depose the records custodian.

Sec. 8.3   What the Hospital Record Consists Of

The forms of the records kept vary from hospital to hospital. Generally, a complete hospital record is made up of the following parts:

1. The Face Sheet (it sets forth mainly the name and address of the patient, his admission and discharge dates, the admitting diagnosis, the personal family data, religion and age of the patient, the referring physician, and the discharge diagnosis and operations performed);

2. Authorization Sheet (it consists of consent to diagnostic or therapeutic procedure, permission to operate and authorization for release of information; it is signed by the patient or by the nearest relative in case of inability of patient to sign, or in case of the patient being a minor);

3. The Discharge Summary (it contains mainly the history, physical examination, laboratory and X-ray data, course in the hospital and disposition, operations, condition on discharge, and the final diagnosis);

4. The Personal History (it consists mainly of family data, chief complaints, past history, and former and subsequent admissions to the hospital);

5. Physical Examination (it contains mainly pulse and respiration counts, and nutrition and physical findings on various parts of the body);

6. Consultant's Notes (it consists mainly of the comments of the specialists called in to examine the patient, i.e. internist, neuro-surgeon, etc.);

7. X-ray Requisition and Report (it consists of the X-rays taken of specific portions of the body and the clinical diagnosis or suspected pathology);

8. Miscellaneous Reports (it consists mainly of the laboratory, reports of the hematology (study of the blood), routine blood chemistry, spinal fluid, feces, special chemistry, urine analysis, serology, (antigen-antibody reactions), bacteriology, etc.);

9. Electrocardiograms (it consists of tests or traces made of the heart);

10. Operative Record (it consists of the pre-operative diagnosis, postoperative diagnosis, the nature of the operation, and the details of the operation, including the procedure used);

11. Doctor's Clinical Notes On Progress of the Patient (it consists of the condition of the wound, drainage, removal of stitches, consultations, change in diagnosis, complications, condition on discharge, and instructions to patient);

12. Doctor's Order Sheet (it consists of directions in respect to the patient, i.e. diet, prescriptions, X-rays, pathology examinations, etc.);

13. Nurse's Notes (it consists of medication and treatments, and remarks on the progress of the patient at numerous intervals on a daily basis, including complaints of pain, sleeplessness, depression, lack of appetite, etc.).

Additional sheets may appear in a hospital record when the case involves an emergency admittance and/or a serious or critical case. Such sheets are the following:

1. Emergency Sheet (if the patient were brought in as an emergency case, the sheet so indicates and contains patient information, financial information, nature and circumstances of the emergency, medical history, i.e. pulse, temperature, blood pressure and respiration, condition on admission, and medication and treatment);

2. Anesthesia Record (it consists mainly of pre-operative medication, the time when administered, the nature and quantity of the drugs administered, the drugs used at the operation, the methods employed (i.e. intravenous), the nature of the operation, the names of the surgeons, the anesthetists, the sponge count and drains, the course of the patient before, during, and after the operation);

3. Recovery Room Record;

4. Blood pressure sheet;

5. Temperature charts;

6. Intake (nourishment) and output (waste) charts.

Sec. 8.4   How to Read and Understand the Hospital Report

It is advisable to make at least two photocopies of the report. One should be for your own use. You may anticipate that the hospital original will be subpoenaed by you or by the other side for introduction in evidence at the trial. The other copy should be sent to your medical expert for his use in advance of trial.

When you are ready to study the report, it is suggested that you have a medical dictionary[1] at one elbow and a help-aid on medical abbreviations and symbols at the other elbow.[2] Also, it is advisable to have nearby for quick reference The Merck Manual.[3] It is a handy, compact little book on general medicine covering, among other things, etiology (cause), pathology, symptoms, diagnosis, prognosis, and treatment. Armed with these aids and with access to a friendly doctor by phone when you get stuck, you are ready to attack the hospital record.

When you find a term which baffles you, write it down on a paper entitled "Medical Terms" and enter its definition alongside it, first in medical language and then in language which you can understand; i.e. edema—the presence of abnormally large amounts of fluid in the intercellular tissue spaces of the body (swelling). To be more expeditious, write on the record page itself the understandable definition in the margin nearest the word. When you re-read it later in preparation for trial, you will not have to look it up again. As you write down the medical term, practice its pronunciation aloud, and then place a stress mark over the syllable which should be stressed. This will enable you to use the term authoritatively in court. The judge and jury are not impressed by the lawyer who stumbles over medical terms; they want to be enlightened and not confused. Besides, the opposing

---

1. Recommended medical dictionaries are: Dorland's Illustrated Medical Dictionary, 24th ed., published by W.B. Saunders & Co., Philadelphia, Pennsylvania; Stedman's Medical Dictionary Illustrated, published by The Williams & Wilkins Company, Baltimore, Maryland.

2. Recommended aids are: "The Doctor's Shorthand" by Dr. Frank Cole, published by W.B. Saunders Company, Philadelphia, London and Toronto (1970); "Medical Abbreviations" by Dr. Edwin D. Steen, published by J.A. Davis Company, 3rd ed. (1971), London, England; "Abbreviations in Medical Records" by Edward R. Pinckney, M.D., Beverly Hills, California; "Understanding Medical Terminology", 3rd ed., by Sister Mary Agnes Clare Frenay, S.S.M., 1964, published by The Catholic Hospital Association, St. Louis, Missouri; "Colson's Hospital Record Summary", published by Lawyers and Judges Publishing Company Inc., 4156 E. Grant Road, Tucson, Arizona 85716; Medical Abbreviations Cross Reference Dictionary compiled and published by the Special Studies Committee of the Michigan Occupational Therapy Association, Department of Physical Medicine and Rehabilitation, University Hospital, Ann Arbor, Michigan 48104.

3. *The Merck Manual*, 9th ed., published by Merck & Company Inc., Rahway, New Jersey.

doctor on cross-examination becomes convinced that you are unfamiliar with the subject and will become encouraged; frequently, he will correct you openly before the jury, thus to demonstrate his superiority over his adversary interrogator.

A particularly aggravating factor is the illegibility of the writing in many a hospital record. The worst offenders are the busy doctors. Frequently, these are interns or resident doctors with foreign backgrounds who have difficulties with the English language. In such cases, it is suggested that your secretary communicate with the secretary of the records custodian at the hospital and elicit her help in deciphering it. Caution: do not write down a meaning you do not understand; it will be of no help to you and may embarrass you if you mistake its true meaning at the trial.

Besides medical terminology, there is the problem of medical symbols appearing in the hospiital record, i.e. □　♂ =male. Also, there are medical abbreviations used, i.e. R/O = rule out. Unfortunately, all hospital records do not use uniform symbols and abbreviations. Fairly common symbols used follow:

L	left	$\pm$	not definite
R	right	$\downarrow$	decreased depression
□	male		
♂	male	$\uparrow$	elevation increased
O	female	$<-$	is due to
♀	female	$>$	greater than
†	death	$<$	less than
$\bar{p}$	after	℥	ounce
$\bar{a}$	before	𝒰	urine
$\bar{c}$	with	·/.	defecation
$\bar{s}$	without	*	birth
?	question of questionable possible		
$\tilde{v}$	approximate		

Fairly common abbreviations used follow:

A	area
	or
	anterior
Ad	admitting diagnosis
	or
	right ear (auris dextra)
Adm	admission
A & D	ascending and descending
alcho.	alcohol
anesth	anesthesia
ANT	anterior
ANTE	before
A & P	anterior and posterior
	or
	auscultation and palpation
AR	alarm reaction
	or
	artificial respiration
ARD	acute respiratory disease
A & W	alive and well
BF	blood flow
bk	back
BL	blood loss
blad.	bladder
bld.	blood
BM	bowel movement
BR	bed rest
BS	blood sugar
	or
	breath sounds
BX	biopsy
$\bar{c}$	with
CA	cancer
	or

CA	carcinoma
	or
	cardiac arrest
ca	about (circa)
Card.	cardiac
Cath.	cathartic
	or
	catheter
cc	cubic centimeter
CC	chief complaint
	or
	critical condition
	or
	current complaint
C.D.	contagious disease
C/D	cigarettes per day
C & D	cystoscopy and dilatation
Cent.	centigrade
Cerv.	cervix
	or
	cervical
cent.	centimeter
CL	chest and left arm (cardiology)
	or
	critical list
CIB	food (cibus)
Clin	clinic
	or
	clinical
cm	centimeter
cm³	cubic centimeter
CO	carbon monoxide
	or
	cardiac output
C/O	complains of
Contrib.	contributory

CV	cardiovascular
	or
	cerebrovascular
CVA	cardiovascular accident
	or
	cerebrovascular accident
CVD	cardiovascular disease
Cysto	cystoscopy
DB	date of birth
	or
	disability
D & C	dilation curettement
DD	died of the disease
	or
	differential diagnosis
D & E	dilation and evacuation
DEC	deceased
DI	diabetes insipidus
DIG	diagnosis
	or
	diagnostic
DIS	disease
DM	diabetes mellitus
	or
	diabetic mother
	or
	diastolic murmur
DNT	did not test
DOA	dead on arrival
DOB	date of birth
DP	dementia praecox
	or
	diastolic pressure
DL	danger list
EA	each
ECG	electrocardiogram
EEA	electroencephalic audiometry

EEG	electroencephalogram
EENT	eye, ear, nose and throat
EGM	electrogram
EKG	electrocardiogram
EOD	entry on duty
	or
	every other day
EOM	extra-oscular movements
EST	electroshock therapy
ET	and
	or
	etiology
	or
	eustachian tube
Et Al	and others (et alii)
Etiol	etiology
Ext	exterior
	or
	external
F	Fahrenheit
	or
	father
	or
	female
	or
	finger
Fem	Female
FIB	fibrillation
FH	family history
ft	foot
Fr. or frx.	fracture
FU	follow-up
FX	fracture
g	gram
GB	gall bladder
GE	gastroemotional
	or
	gastroenterology
	or

GE	gastroenterostomy
GEN	general
genit	genitalia
GI	gastrointestinal
gm	gram
GP	general paralysis
	or
	general paresis
	or
	general practitioner
gr	grains
gtt	drops
GU	gastric ulcer
	or
	genitourinary
GYN	gynaecology
HB	heart block
	or
	hemoglobin
H & C	hot and cold
HD	head
	or
	hearing distance
	or
	heart disease
	or
	high dosage
HG	hemoglobin
HIP	health insurance plan
hist.	history
HL	hearing level
	or
	hearing loss
H & L	heart and lungs
H-L-K	heart, liver, kidney
HN	head nurse

H/O	history of
Hosp.	hospital
H & P	history and physical
HPE	history and physical examination
HR	heart rate
	or
	hospital record
	or
	hospital report
HT	heart
	or
	height
	or
	hypertension
HYG	hygiene
HYP	hypertrophy
HYPN	hypertension
HYS	hysterical
	or
	hysterectomy
HV	hospital visit
HX	history
IC	intensive care
	or
	intercostal
	or
	intermediate care
	or
	irritable colon
ICF	intensive care facility
ICU	intensive care unit
ID	identification
	or
	infant deaths
IMP	impression
	or
	improved

In	inch
INF	inferior
	or
	infusion
Info	information
Intox	intoxicated
INJ	inject
	or
	injured
INT	internal
I & O	in and out
	or
	intake and output
IQ	intelligence quotient
irreg	irregular
IT	inhalation therapy
	or
	intratracheal tube
IV	intravenous
IVD	intervertebral disc
IVP	intravenous pyelogram
K	kidney
KJ	knee jerk
KK	knee kick
KUB	kidney, ureter, bladder
L	liver or left
L & A	light and accomodation
Lab.	laboratory
Lac.	laceration
Lam.	laminectomy
LBM	lean body mass
LBP	low back pain
	or
	low blood pressure
LCM	left coital margin

LE	left eye
	or
	lower extremity
LG	large
LH	lower half
LIQ	liquid
	or
	lower inner quadrant
LK	left kidney
LL	left leg
	or
	left lower
	or
	left lung
	or
	lower lobe
LE	left eye
	or
	left lower
	or
	left lung
	or
	lower lobe
LMD	local medical doctor
LMP	last menstrual period
LOM	limitation of motion
	or
	loss of motion
LP	lumbar puncture
L & R	left and right
L R	left to right
LS	left side
	or
	lumbosacral
LSK	liver, spleen and kidneys
LT	left or left thigh
	or
	long term

LUE	left upper extremity
LW	lacerating wound
L/W	living & well
M.D.	doctor of medicine
	or
	manic depressive
	or
	medium dosage
	or
	muscular dystrophy
	or
	myocardial damage
MM	millimeter
	or
	muscles
M & N	morning and night
MP	as directed
	or
	menstrual period
M.S.	multiple sclerosis
N	nasal
	or
	nerve
	or
	normal
Neg.	negative
N/C	no complaints
NCD	not considered disabling
NF	Negro female
NG	nasogastric
	or
	no good
Noc.	night
Norm.	normal
NM	Negro male
NP	nasopharyngeal

NP	or
	not performed
	or
	nursing procedure
	or
	neuropsychiatry
NPO	nothing per mouth
NS	nervous system
NSC	no significant change
O	eye
	or
	none
	or
	obstetrics
	or
	oral
	or
	orderly
OA	old age
	or
	osteoarthritis
O_2	both eyes
	or
	oxygen
OB	obstetrics
Occip.	occipital (head)
O.D.	right eye
O_2 CAP	oxygen capacity
O.M.	every morning
O.N.	every night
OBS	obstetrical service
OC	office call
	or
	on call
	or
	oral contraceptive
OP	operation

OPS or	
OPD	outpatient service
OPT	outpatient
OR	operating room
ORS	orthopedic surgery
ORT	operating room technician
Orth.	orthopedic
OS	bone or mouth
	or
	oral surgery
Oz.	ounce
PA	posterior-anterior
P & A	percussion and auscultation
Para	number of pregnancies
Path.	pathology
P.E.	physical examination
Ped.	pediatrics
PEG	pneumoencephalogram
Pen.	penicillin
Pent.	pentathal
Per	by
	or
	period
	or
	person
Per Os	by mouth
PH	past history
	or
	personal history
	or
	public health
PI	present illness
	or
	pulmonary infarction
PM	night
	or
	postmortem

Pneu.	pneumonia
PO	by mouth
	or
	parieto-occipital
	or
	period of onset
	or
	phone order
	or
	posterior
	or
	post-operative
POC	post-operative care
Pos.	positive
Post	posterior
	or
	post-mortem
Postop	Post-operative
PR	far point
Preg.	pregnant
Preop.	preoperative
Prep.	prepare
Pros.	prostatic
Psy.	psychiatry
PT	paroxysmal tachycardia
	or
	patient
	or
	permanent & total
	or
	physical therapy
	or
	pint
PX	prognosis
	or
	past history
q,q̄	every
q.d.	every day

q.n.	every night
q.2 h.	every two hours
q.i.d.	four times a day
R	rectal temperature
R.A.	repeat action
	or
	rheumatoid arthritis
	or
	right atrium
	or
	right auricle
RAO	right anterior oblique
RBC	red blood cell
	or
	red blood count
RC	red cell
	or
	red cell casts
RDA	recommended daily dose
	or
	recommended dietary allowance
REG	radioencephalogram
Rehab.	rehabilitation
R-L	right to left
R–>L	right to left
R/O	rule out
ROM	range of motion
RN	registered nurse
ROS	review of systems
ROT	rotating
Rt.	right
RX	take (recipe)
	or
	treatment
	or
	prescription
$\overline{s}$	without

SB	single breath
	or
	still birth
sig.	take on prescription
sec.	second
semi	half
seq.	sequela
SI	sacro-iliac
	or
	self-inflicted
	or
	seriously ill
sibs.	siblings
skel.	skeletal
SLR	straight leg raising test
SOB	short of breath
S.O.S.	when necessary
sp. gr.	specific gravity
SS	side to side
	or
	signs and symptoms
Supp.	suppository
Syph.	syphilis
	or
	syphilogist
T	temperature
	or
	thoracic
T & A	tonsillectomy and adenoidectomy
	or
	tonsils and adenoids
T.A.T.	tetanus antitoxin
TB	tuberculosis
TE	tetanus
	or
	tooth extracted
	or

TE	tracheo-esophageal
Thromb.	thrombosis
TLC	tender loving care
TPR	temperature, pulse, respiration
Upper G.I.	upper gastrointestinal
U	unit
	or
	unknown
	or
	upper
	or
	urology
UK	unknown
UO	under observation for
UR	upper respiratory
	or
	urine
UQ	upper quadrant
URD	upper respiratory disease
V	see
	or
	vein
	or
	vision
	or
	voice
	or
	volume
Vag.	vaginal
VD	venereal disease
VDG	venereal disease—gonorrhea
	or
	voiding
VDRL	serologic test for venereal disease
vent.	ventral
VH	vaginal hysterectomy
VIP	very important patient

VOD	vision, right eye
VOL	volume
VOS	vision, left eye
VRBC	red blood cell volume
VR & E	vocational rehabilitation and education
VS	against
	or
	vaccination scar
	or
	vital signs
W	water
	or
	Weber (test)
	or
	week
	or
	weight
	or
	widowed
	or
	wife
	or
	with
WB	weight bearing
	or
	whole body
WBC	white blood cell
	or
	white blood count
WF	white female
WH	well-healed
WM	white male
	or
	whole milk
WMF	white, middle-aged female
WMM	white, middle-aged male

WN	well-nourished
WNF	well-nourished female
WNL	within normal limits
WNM	well-nourished male
WO	without
	or
	written order
WT	weight
	or
	white
Y	year
YOB	year of birth
Z	zero

Sec. 8.5 How to Prepare the Hospital Record for the Trial

The plan should be to have the hospital record in such shape that you can refer to it quickly for any purpose—whether for examination, cross-examination, for reading portions of it to the court and jury, or for final argument.

There are numerous methods to achieve this. One is to have a tab or record summary system in which each part of the record is compartmentalized.[4] Another is to check-mark the pages of your copy of the hospital record from which you intend to read or which you intend to refer to in the examination or cross-examination. Another is to make your own tabs and to place them at the pages to which you wish to refer.

Sec. 8.6 How to Use It Effectively

It is important to remember that an important purpose is to impress on the court and jury the pain and anguish which your client endured. To effectuate this, look carefully at the doctor's clinical notes on the progress of the patient, and at the nurse's notes. The doctor's notes should record the condition of the patient periodically, the complications and setbacks, and the consultations with other doctors pointing up the treating doctor's concerns about the patient's condition. The nurse's notes should record the condition of the patient on a periodical basis each day—usually every few hours. His bleeding, vomiting, fevers, sleeplessness, lack of appetite, and

---

4. This method is used in "Colson's Hospital Record Summary," see footnote 2, supra.

pains, among other things, are recorded here in a sterilized but dramatic way. These portions should be read to the jury after the entire record is offered in evidence. They should be available instantly in final argument to the jury, to remind the hearers of what the patient endured.

Chapter 9

HOW TO PROVE PECUNIARY LOSSES

SCIENTIFICALLY

Sec. 9.1   Why an Expert to Prove Pecuniary Losses?

For some time the courts have been permitting experts to be used to prove property values, as for example, in condemnation cases. In the past generation, the courts have commenced to extend the same rule of evidence in serious personal injury and death cases.[1] If personal rights are to be treated as equal to, if not superior to, property rights, then the extension of the rule is inevitable. Although belatedly, the courts are recognizing this step forward in negligence cases.

The underlying reasons for the use of experts in wrongful injury and death cases are: (1) the proof of such damages has become complex and there is a need for specialists in the field; (2) the use of the expert brings a more accurate measure of compensation and in many cases a higher award.

The general rule of evidence is that testimony of an expert is admissible if it will assist the court and jury in arriving at a verdict.[2] A new type of expert has appeared on the scene to unravel the complexities of economic facts surrounding serious wrongful disability and death cases, and to present the

---

1. *16 Am. Jur.–Proof of Facts*, p. 701.

Reference in this chapter will be made often to *Am. Jur., Am. Jur.–Trials, Am. Jur.–Proof of Facts,* Speiser's *Recovery For Wrongful Death,* and Speiser's *Economic Handbook,* because these sources are pioneers and are very complete in the field of proving pecuniary losses scientifically.

Other references to prove scientific pecuniary losses appear in an extensive bibliography in an article entitled "Economist Testimony: Proof of Economic Loss Suffered by Youth Severely Injured by Diving" by Philip H. Corboy, and published in *Trial Lawyers Guide* (May, 1969, Volume 13, No. 2, pps. 55-76) by Callaghan and Company, 165 N. Archer Avenue, Mundelein, Illinois 60060.

2. *Jones on Evidence,* Section 412.

losses sustained by the survivors on a clear and logical basis. The figures presented favor neither the plaintiff nor the defendant; and, whether the expert is produced by either or both of the parties, the results should be similar.

Sec. 9.2   Scientific Proof Versus Speculation

The United States Government, represented particularly through the Department of Labor and the Department of Health, Education and Welfare, has issued many valuable and reliable tables, charts, and statistical studies affecting our entire population. These are important fact-finders and are of immeasurable help in projecting future earning losses in wrongful injury and death cases for members of practically all sectors of our society.

For example, the government has issued mortality and work-career tables, earnings trends, and price trends tables and charts covering many recent decades and up to the present. It furnishes statistics on the likely earnings for almost any class of persons of any age. The data is available according to the level of education, age, sex, and geographic location of the person.[3]

These statistics show what has been the trend of earnings for American workers in manufacturing industries, and what has been the trend for consumer prices and of medical care costs.[4]

These items can be and are utilized by the economist-statistician as the basis for projecting future pecuniary losses in a specific case.

Fringe benefits in union contracts of which a wrongfully injured or killed worker could have benefited, had he not met with the misfortune, can be evaluated in terms of future dollars. For example, health and welfare insurance provided for the sick worker can be measured in value by the amount which the employer contributed for the premiums in a plan where the employer paid the full premiums. Another method for establishing its money value is by ascertaining the cost of comparable benefits on the open insurance market. The same yardsticks apply to fixing the money value of pension benefits provided in union contracts. Fringe benefits should be taken into consideration in estimating pecuniary losses.[5]

---

3. *16 Am. Jur.—Proof of Facts*, Section 16.

4. *16 Am. Jur.—Proof of Facts*, Section 14. These statistics indicate that the trend of earnings for American workers since 1909 has been an increase of about 4 percent per year, that the trend for consumer prices has been an increase of about 1-1/2 percent per year since 1950, and that medical care costs have been going up even faster.

5. *Bryant v. Woodlief* (1960), 252 N.C. 488, 114 S.E. 2d 241, 81 A.L.R. 2d 939 (railroad retirement benefits were being drawn at the time of death), noted in 27 NACCA L.J. 205 (1961); 39 N.C.L. Rev. 107 (1960).

Heskamp v. Bradshaws Adm. (1943), 294 Ky. 618, 172 S.W. 2d 447 (railroad employee was receiving nothing but railroad retirement benefits at time of death).

The courts have ruled in favor of the admissibility of mortality tables[6] and work-life tables,[7] the present value of loss or impairment of an injured person's general earning capacity,[8] and proof of present worth of future loss.[9]

The discount rates vary in appraising the present value of future losses.[10]

Statistics are available to show personal consumption expenditures—that is, the victim's daily or weekly living expenses, which are to be deducted in computing future losses. These are arrived at by the process of bracketing the victim according to his income and the number of persons in his family. Armed with this information, an average can be reliably struck.

The expert can project future earnings based on the past record of earnings and hourly rate and hours worked of the subject. He can strike an average of wage increases and hours worked per year in the past and apply this pattern to the future.

The arguments that such projections are speculation and conjecture are readily overcome because there is less guessing in this way of proof than to allow the jury to make conclusions based on the lawyer's concluding arguments and from a mass of seemingly unrelated and confusing facts.[11]

The courts of our land are not yet uniform in allowing this kind of future appraisal of lost earnings by expert testimony, namely by incremental or

---

Wands v. Cauble (1967), 270 N.C. 311, 154 S.E. 2d 425.

Brooks v. U.S. (1967) (D.C.S.C.), 273 F.S. 619.

Fringe benefits of various kinds should be taken into consideration in estimating pecuniary losses. Eden "For More Adequate Measurement of Impaired Earning Capacity and Medical Care Costs of the Injured"—*Trial & Tort Trends*—1962, Belli Seminar, p. 297; Speiser's *Recovery for Wrongful Death*, Section 3:21.

Speiser in his *Economic Handbook*, at p. 132, lists the following as being fringe benefits and which should be considered as additions to appraisals of earnings (for production workers in manufacturing as of the year 1962):

Social security	2.6%
Private pension & retirement plans	2.4
Savings and thrift plans	.1
Life, accident, health insurance	1.3
(dependents' coverage assumed to	
be about one-half of the 2.7%)	
Total	6.4%

The basic source for information on fringe benefits is "Employer Expenditures for Selected Supplementary Compensation Practices For Production and Related Work Areas", issued by Bureau of Labor Statistics, U.S. Department of Labor, Bulletin No. 1428.

6. *50 A.L.R. 2d 419* (depends on showing of permanency of injury).

7. *Dixon v. U.S.* (1954, D.C. N.Y.), 120 F.S. 747 (mod. on other grounds) 219 F. 2d 10.

8. *79 A.L.R. 2d 275*

9. *79 A.L.R. 2d 259*

10. *16 Am. Jur.—Proof of Facts,* Sections 19 and 20. In the 1960s, a frequent range for discount rates was between 3 percent and 5 percent. However, in 1971, some experts used a 5-1/4 percent and even 5-1/2 percent rate.

11. *Krohmer v. Dahl* (1965 Mont.), 402 P. 2d 979.

augmented projections as distinguished from flat projections. Still, it is important to get into evidence the past records to show even the conservative estimate, which is based on the flat projections, in order to argue future losses.

Sec. 9.3   How It Helps Settlements

The defendant is concerned about the extent of its damage exposure in any case. Defendant's counsel usually will estimate the maximum amount of damages which an adverse verdict might impose on his client. Then, usually, he will reduce it proportionately, depending on the weakness of the plaintiff's case in proving liability.

For example, if defendant's counsel estimates that the maximum verdict which the jury might bring in a wrongful death case is $100,000, he will then reduce it by 25 percent if he feels that there is that much of a chance that the jury might bring in a verdict for the defendant. Then his valuation of the case for purposes of achieving a settlement might range up to a maximum of $75,000 or less.

So, it is important and helpful to plaintiff's counsel in the discussion of settlement to show convincingly that there is a high exposure. To achieve this, a settlement brochure prepared on the scientific approach can be very useful. This is a carefully prepared document specifying each item of damage and the amount thereof which the plaintiff is prepared to prove. The assistance of the economist in its preparation is important in a serious case of good liability. In other cases, the scientific approach can be utilized by counsel without the benefit of the economist's services.

Many lawyers do not believe in the brochure, because it means divulging the plaintiff's case beforehand and alerts the defendant in the event the case goes to trial. Such practitioners present their figures orally, instead, at the settlement conference. There is another advantage to this method. In case it is necessary to make any changes in the figures, this can be done without serious embarrassment. However, whether the settlement figures are presented in writing or orally, the scientific approach should be used.

The defendant's argument that certain items of damage (i.e. projected future lost wage increases) have not been previously allowed in the local jurisdiction should not be insurmountable. Generally speaking, the law of damages is judge-made law, and that law is constantly changing.

Sec. 9.4   Admissibility of the Economic Expert's Opinion

The tendency of the courts is to permit the opinion of an economist or statistician to show pecuniary losses due to serious disability or death.[12] In the case of *Krohmer v. Dahl,*[13] it was held that it was not an abuse of the court's discretion to permit the testimony of an economist-statistician to prove the future earning capacity of an 18-year-old college student who was wrongfully killed. An earlier decision held that it was not an abuse of the court's discretion to refuse to admit such testimony. *Barnes v. Smith* (1962 CA 10, N.M.), 305 F.2d 226. In *Krohmer,* the court reasoned that the expert's testimony and opinion enabled the jury to estimate the probable future earnings of the decedent. In *Merrill v. United Air Lines, Inc.* (1959 D.C. N.Y.), 177 F.S. 704, such testimony was allowed. In the Maryland trial courts, such expert testimony is being admitted.[14] This is true in other state trial courts, also.[15]

It has been held that the prospects in life of a decedent before he was killed or even his reasonable expectation as of the time of his death of earning more in the future may be considered, whether the monies go to the statutory beneficiaries[16] or to the decedent's estate.[17]

It has been held that it is proper for the court to consider the decedent's chances for promotion if there was a reasonable likelihood of it at the time of his death.[18] However, it is necessary to lay a foundation by putting on evidence, as, for example, the testimony of his employer that the decedent was about to be promoted or that he had a good chance of it in the future.

On the other hand, some courts allow testimony relative to the probable

---

12. Speiser's *Recovery for Wrongful Death,* Section 3:18.

13. (1965 Mont.), 402 P. 2d 979.

14. *Plant, et al. v. Simmons Company, et al.* (D.C. Md.), Civil Nos. 17326, 17373 and 17374 (1971).

In *Hall v. Lutheran Hospital* (Sup. Ct. of Baltimore City, No. 40100), where an eight year old girl suffered serious permanent injury, the economist was allowed to testify as to the probable earnings that she would have enjoyed if she had been able to continue in school, graduate and move into the job market. Verdict was $294,000.

See "Loss of Earning Capacity in Personal Injury and Wrongful Death Cases"—Francis N. Iglehart—*Daily Record* July 6, 1970, Baltimore, Maryland.

15. For example: N.Y.—*Zaninovich v. American Air Lines Inc.* (1965), 47 Misc. 2d 584, 262 N.Y.S. 2d 854.

16. Pa.—*Johns v. Baltimore & Ohio R. Co.* (1956, D.C. Pa.), 143 F. Supp. 15, aff'd per curiam (C.A. 3) 239 F. 2d 385 (applying Pennsylvania law).

See Speiser's *Recovery for Wrongful Death,* Section 3:1.

17. Speiser's *Recovery for Wrongful Death,* Section 3:1, citing:

Florida East Coast R. Co. v. Hayes (1914), 67 Fla. 101, 64 So. 504, 7 ALR 1310.

Annotation: 7 ALR 1328, 26 ALR 595, 163 ALR 257.

18. Okla.—*National Valve & Mfg. Co. v. Wright* (1951), 205 Okla. 565, 240 P. 2d 769 (testimony of a former employer that he had offered decedent a job which would pay him a better salary with more chances of advancement and that decedent had agreed to take position, held properly admitted).

Pa.—*Johns v. Baltimore & Ohio R. Co.* (1956) (D.C. Pa.), 143 F. Supp. 15, aff'd per curiam (C.A. 3) 239 F. 2d 385 (applying Pennsylvania law; supervisor working for decedent's employer testified that decedent was regarded as an outstanding man from the start, had shown outstanding traits as a sales type person, and definitely would have progressed in his work).

See Speiser's *Recovery for Wrongful Death,* Section 3:01.

diminution of the decedent's capacity to earn, as for example, on account of age and infirmities.[19]

Sec. 9.5   How to Lay a Foundation for the Economist's Opinion

The first plank in laying the foundation for the admissibility of the economist's opinion is his qualifications. The two most important supports for this plank are that he be an economist and that he has had experience in testifying as such in the appraisal of earnings. The opponent's challenge to this new type of expert can be expected to be sharp and exhaustive. Therefore, one should be very careful in looking to the proper qualifications.

A person may be qualified if he has employment in a similar field, especially in government service or as a consultant (a college degree would be desirable, even if a Bachelor of Arts or Science, but better still if in economics); likewise, if his specialty is economics, especially on a university level, and if he has had experience in this kind of appraisal and in court work relative to it; affiliation with the American Economics Association would be helpful; it would be of assistance if he is a writer on economics, especially in this field.[20] An actuary who has had experience in making such appraisals and who has had court experience in this area would be qualified.

The next plank is the establishment of the authenticity of the charts and statistical tables which the economist will use. Since this will be U.S. government issued data, for the most part, request should be made of the specific department of government for a certified copy of the particular data used. This will make it admissible in evidence.

The other planks are the following: the liability; the medically proved disability; the earnings before death or disability proved through the proper custodian of the records (i.e. employer) and through the management-union contracts under which the subject worked; the fringe benefits to which the subject was entitled in the job; the amounts contributed by the subject to his family; previous condition of health and habits; the subject's age; the subject's opportunities for promotion;[21] the subject's education; the subject's personal consumption expenditures; the personal services rendered by the subject about the house.

Generally speaking, these planks should lay a solid foundation upon which the economist can appraise lost earnings and for the admissibility of his expert opinion into evidence.

---

19. Ark.—*Missouri Pac. R. Co. v. Gilbert* (1944), 206 Ark. 683, 178 S.W. 2d 73 (remarking that decedent at 30 years of age was at the peak of his earning capacity as a common laborer, and that his ability to earn would grow less throughout the remaining years of his expectancy).
See Speiser's *Recovery for Wrongful Death*, Section 3:01.
20. See Speiser's *Economic Handbook*, Section 13:2, p. 208.
21. This should be proved through his employer or through an employment expert.

There are special types of cases which will require different prerequisites of proof. For example, the wrongful death of a wife and mother,[22] of the high school graduate,[23] of the business man,[24] of the wealthy person,[25] of the professional person,[26] of the retired person,[27] of the civil service employee,[28] and of the seaman.[29]

As to inflation and the depreciated value of the dollar, courts generally will take judicial notice of it and should allow argument to the jury about it.[30] However, this is an area where the economist should be permitted to testify to establish scientifically what the future depreciation of the dollar will be, based on the records of the past.

Funeral expenses, where same were paid out or obligated for, are allowed by some states and disallowed by others.[31]

It may be mentioned in passing that diminishing prospects on account of age and bad health may be considered also.[32]

Sec. 9.6   Checklist of Data for Making Appraisal

A succinct reminder of what to furnish the economist in order to assist him in making his appraisal of pecuniary losses follows.[33]

    1. The nature and date of the accident and whether it was a fatal case or not.

---

22. If the subject was a wrongfully killed wife and mother, then the widower should prove the value of a "substitute mother" through a home economist or through an officer of a public or private employment agency. Also, it can be shown what is the prevailing cost of a live-in housekeeper. See: *Sarvis v. Seaboard Air Line Railroad Company* (Dade County, Florida—unreported); Speiser's *Economic Handbook,* p. 304.

23. Special consideration should be given to the probability of the high school student attending college. Testimony should be offered about the intentions of the student as shown by applications by him to college and his scholastic standing and his field of interest. There are government statistics showing the probable income of the high school student and of the college student. The economist will make good use of these to project lost earnings. See: *Krohmer v. Dahl,* 402 P. 2d 979; Speiser's *Economic Handbook,* p. 329; see also *Re Consolidation Coal Co.* (1968, D.C. Pa.), 296 F.S. 837, *Putnam v. Pollei* (1969 Mont.), 457 P. 2d 776 and *Leavitt v. Gillaspie* (1968 Alaska), 443 P. 2d 61.

24. It is the losses from decedent's labor and services and not from the profits lost from the capital invested which is the standard used. *Chic. I. & L.R. Co. v. Ellis* (1925), 83 Ind. App. 701, 149 N.E. 909. Hence, proof should be made to establish such losses as by the books and records and income tax returns.

25. It is not alone the amount he left but it is important to show also what he gave his survivors and, therefore, what they would have probably received had he survived. See: *English v. So. P. Co.* (1896), 13 Utah 407, 45 P. 37, 35 L.R.A. 155 (proof of wealth).

26. For elements of proof, see *16 Am. Jur.—Proof of Facts,* Section 25.

27. For elements of proof, see *16 Am. Jur.—Proof of Facts,* Section 27.

28. For elements of proof, see *16 Am. Jur.—Proof of Facts,* Section 26; Speiser's *Economic Handbook,* Section 4:41.

29. For elements of proof, see *16 Am. Jur.,* Section 26.

30. *12 A.L.R. 2d* 643-645.

31. Speiser's *Recovery for Wrongful Death,* Section 3:49, citing law in the various states.

32. *Central Foundry Co. v. Bennett* (1906), 144 Ala. 184, 39 So. 574.

33. For another sample checklist, see *16 Am. Jur.—Proof of Facts,* Section 21, p. 720, 721.

2. Subject's name, address, birth date, sex, race, education, occupation, work career, social security number, name and address of labor union to which affiliated, if any, and union book number.

3. Similar data on subject's spouse and children, including date of marriage, except for union data.

4. If non-fatal, the medical history and report indicating the permanent disability and nature thereof.

5. Evidence of past and current income, such as income tax returns and W-2 forms for a reasonable period before and the period after the accident.

6. Supplementary data, including important discovery proceedings items bearing on the case and about subject's income and fringe benefits. Produce union contract before and after the accident and copies of all private benefit plans such as health, welfare, and pension.

7. Whether subject performed household services (i.e. upkeep, repairs and maintenance of home), and nature and value thereof annually.

8. Subject's consumption expenses annually (i.e. for clothes, food, and pin money).

9. Authorizations properly executed to obtain the aforesaid information (i.e. to labor unions, welfare and pension fund agencies, employers, etc.).

10. If case involves serious disability of a minor, supply data pertaining to economic and social background of the parents and plans for a college education that may have been thwarted.

11. If case involves a business or professional man, supply data concerning the details of his assets and the chances of future augmentation of income from same.

12. If case involves serious disability which required medical, surgical, hospital, and therapeutic care and attention, and which will require such in the future, supply details and amounts.

Sec. 9.7   The Hypothetical Question to Be Put to the Economist

An example of a hypothetical question to be put to an economist to elicit his opinion as to pecuniary losses follows.[34]

---

34. Taken from *Trial Lawyers Guide*, May 1969, Vol. 13, No. 2, pps. 55-76; question prepared and put by attorney Philip H. Corboy, 33 N. Dearborn Street, Suite 1230, Chicago, Illinois 60602.

The forms for the hypothetical question to be put in other types of cases may be found as follows:

   —for the electrician (*16 Am. Jur.—Proof of Facts*, Section 23, pps. 724-741).

[Assume that a 15-year-old boy suffered a quadriplegia condition (paralysis in all four extremities) as a result of a diving accident.]

Background

Q. Tell us your name, please.

A. Melvin Lurie.

Q. How do you spell your last name?

A. L-u-r-i-e.

Q. And what is your address?

A. 3032 North Summit Avenue, Milwaukee, Wisconsin.

Q. What is your profession?

A. I am a professor of economics.

Q. What are your background studies and your education, sir, with reference to preparing you for the profession of professor of economics?

A. I have a Bachelor's Degree from the Pennsylvania State University in Economics, 1948; a Master's Degree from the University of Chicago in Economics, 1951; and a Ph.D. Degree, also from the University of Chicago, in 1958. That is my educational background. I have worked for the federal government as an economist, the United States Wage Stabilization Board, from 1951 to 1953. I have been an editor of a business review for two years, from 1964 to 1966, the *Rhode Island Business Quarterly*. I have been teaching since 1954. I taught from '54 to '60 at the University of Connecticut; from 1960 to 1966, with the exception of one year, at the University of Rhode Island; and one year I was visiting professor at Wesleyan University in Connecticut.

Q. What have you been teaching?

A. I have been teaching labor economics, statistics, principles of economics.

Q. What professional societies do you belong to?

—for the professional man (*16 Am. Jur.—Proof of Facts*, Section 25; Speiser's *Recovery for Wrongful Death*, Section 4:40, pps. 390-396).

—for the seaman (*16 Am. Jur.—Proof of Facts*, Section 26; Speiser's *Recovery for Wrongful Death*, Section 4:39, pps. 381-390).

—for the civil service employee (*16 Am. Jur.—Proof of Facts*, Section 26; Speiser's *Recovery for Wrongful Death*, Section 4:41, pps. 396-401).

—for the retired person (*16 Am. Jur.—Proof of Facts*, Section 27; Speiser's *Recovery for Wrongful Death*, Section 4:42, pps. 401-407).

—for the student (Speiser's *Recovery for Wrongful Death*, Section 3:19, p. 134).

A. I belong to the American Economist Association, the Industrial Relations Research Association, the Associated Appraisers of Earning Capacity.

Q. What is the Associated Appraisers of Earning Capacity?

A. This is a group of 25 economists throughout the country. Twenty-three of them are university professors who, on a part-time basis, make appraisals of loss of earning capacity and of medical and custodial costs.

Terminology

Q. What does the term 'economics' mean?

A. By 'economics', we mean the study of the American economy. This field deals with the study of banking institutions, tax policy, wages, employment, inflation; all aspects of the study of what makes this economy work.

Q. And in addition to economics, is there a subspecialty in economics called labor economics?

A. Labor economics is a subspecialty in economics.

Q. What is the subspecialty of labor economics?

A. Labor economists train specifically to study how working people make money; they also study employment, wages, fringe benefits, trade unions, and things dealing specifically with working people.

Q. And what experience have you had in labor economics?

A. Well, I have taught labor economics, and my job with the federal government was as a wage analyst, as a labor economist, and I have done a lot of writing and research in labor economics.

Field of Statistics

Q. What is the difference between an economist and a statistician?

A. A statistician is trained in the science of numbers. There are different kinds of economists and there are different kinds of statisticians. For the most part, statisticians try to represent figures so that they are meaningful. Statisticians also sample population and collect statistics. If I may give an example of this: The statisticians collect data for the consumer price index and ascertain employment rates. This data is based on a very small sampling of people, individuals and families, and is published by the United States Government.

Q. In addition to being an economist and a specialist in labor economics, what experience have you had with statistics?

A. I have taught statistics and I use statistics continually in my research.

Fringe Benefits.

Q. What are fringe benefits?

A. Well, fringe benefits are usually defined as income, or income in kind, in addition to regular wages. Fringe benefits may include a pension, as a health and welfare plan, or other insurance plans, or the employer's contribution to Social Security. All of those items are fringe benefits.

Q. Now, have you written any articles with regard to wages and fringe benefits in regard to both the present and the future?

A. Yes, I have.

Q. Explain those, please.

A. Part of my job as a professor of economics at the university involves research and writing, so I have researched and written about twenty articles on labor economics, including wages, and several of these have dealt specifically with the problem of measuring wages in the present and in the future.

Determination of Life Expectancy
and Work Expectancy of Plaintiff

Q. Now, in your field, do you distinguish between reasonable economic certainty and a mere possibility?

A. Yes.

Q. Which do you use?

A. Well, we use reasonable economic certainty. If you just deal with possibility, anything is possible.

Q. With regard to certain information and materials about the plaintiff, David McGrady, which I gave you this morning, are you going to predict the life earnings of David McGrady?

A. No.

Q. What are you about to do?

A. I am trying to predict the work-life earnings of the statistical group that David McGrady belongs to; that is, people of the same sex, age, and same residence in the Chicago area.

Q. Professor Lurie, what are life expenctancy tables?

A. Life expectancy tables are published by the United States

Department of Health, Education and Welfare, the Division of Vital Statistics, and they show the average life expectancy for all persons of different ages and sexes.

Q. What are work-life expectancy tables?

A. Work-life expectancy tables are published by the United States Department of Labor and they show, also on the average, the work-life expectancy of people by age and by sex.

Q. You have been told, have you not, that David McGrady was born on March 7, 1948?

A. Yes, I have.

Q. What is his life expectancy?

A. His life expectancy, as of the date of trial, is 50.1 years.

Q. And what is his work-life expectancy?

A. His work-life expectancy, as of the date of the accident, is 43.3 years.

Q. If I can understand it, then, a person, according to these statistics, does not work to the end of his life.

A. That is correct.

Q. Now, in reaching the figures that you are about to reach, did you rely on some official data?

A. All of the data I have used is from official sources of the United States Government. Most of the data I used is collected by the United States Census, and some of the data I used has been collected by the United States Department of Labor, Bureau of Labor Statistics.

Q. And are these authoritative sources?

A. Yes, they are.

Q. Are these sources accepted by economists, statisticians, and labor economists in this country?

A. Yes, they are.

Q. And are they utilized in determining the loss of earning capacity of any given group of people?

A. Yes, they are utilized in that way as well as in many other ways.

Q. Now, in order to supply this jury with the projected loss of earning capacity of a person in David McGrady's status, do you need certain facts?

A. Yes, I do.

Q. And what facts do you need?

A. Well, I need his date of birth, as has been given to me. I also need the statistics of earnings of people of his age and sex in the Chicago area, which I have obtained from the U.S. Census. I need data on fringe benefits of working people in this area, which I have obtained from the United States Department of Labor.

Hypothetical Question

Q. Professor Lurie, please assume a male person whose date of birth is March 7, 1948, who was injured on July 31st, 1963, and who before that time had reached the eighth grade in grammar school; this person was not employed and intended to enter high school in the Fall of 1963, and intended to graduate from high school some four years later; he had two older brothers, both of whom graduated from high school, a younger sister who is graduating from high school this June; as a result of an injury on July 31, 1963, this person has been permanently disabled and is unemployable because of those injuries. Before the accident, he was in good health and had an I.Q. of somewhere between 94 and 105. This person was regarded as average by a psychologist and probably would have graduated from high school, as I said, some four years later. Is that enough information at this time for you to give an opinion as to the loss of earning capacity of this type of person in the labor market?

A. Yes, that is sufficient.

Q. Do you have an opinion, then, based upon a reasonable degree of economic certainty, as to the loss of earning capacity of such a person?

A. Yes, I do.

Answer to Hypothetical Question

Q. In giving your opinion, are there any materials you would like to refer to?

A. Yes.

Q. What are they?

A. Specifically, a series of charts based upon data published by the United States Department of Health, Education and Welfare, which is in charge of census statistics.

Mr. Corboy: With the Court's permission, as Professor Lurie uses these charts, I will mark them as exhibits for identification purposes. This first page will be Plaintiff's Exhibit No. 51.

The Court: Is there any objection to these, Mr. Sweeney?

Mr. Sweeney: May we reserve it at this time, Your Honor, until after cross-examination, if any?

The Court: All right.

Q. What does the first chart, Plaintiff's Exhibit No. 51, show?

A. This is a summary chart showing loss of earning capacity of persons in the same group as David McGrady.

Q. What earnings are included in the loss of earning capacity?

A. Well, this chart shows loss of earnings and loss of value of fringe benefits.

Q. All right. What in your opinion is the loss of earnings of the hypothetical person in the same group as David McGrady?

A. In my opinion, the loss of earnings is $305,122, and loss of fringe benefits is $45,768.

Q. And that would be a total of what?

A. A total of $350,890.

Q. Now, what materials did you use in making these computations?

A. The basic figures are acquired originally from the United States Census, the decennial census in the country in which everybody was counted, and this census was taken in 1960, but the actual census was taken the year before, in 1959. That is the last complete census taken in the United States. In the chart which is Exhibit No. 51-B, I put in the dates that will describe the work-life expectancy of persons like the plaintiff. These dates are in decimals. So, for example, I have the date of the trial, which is 1968.3. This is actually the fourth month of the year, but in decimals, it will be three tenths of a year—1968.3.

Similarly, the date of the accident is 1963.6; the date the plaintiff would have graduated from high school is June of 1967, or 1967.4. This chart, Exhibit No. 51-C, continues until the end of his work-life expectancy, which would be almost to the end of the year 2010.

Nature of Computations

Q. Did you use the raw data from the Census Bureau?

A. I used them only originally.

Q. All right. Did you either add or subtract from those figures?

A. Yes. I took the census data from the 1960 census and I did three things:

First of all, I reduced them to include all people, whether they were working or whether they were in the armed forces or not.

The second thing I did was to take out of these figures any kind of income that was due to interest, dividends, or non-earnings income.

Q. Specifically, then, is this just working earnings that you have relied upon for these charts?

A. As I have defined them, these are now working earnings; that is, monies a person can earn through his personal services or efforts, rather than through investments or something of that type.

Q. All right, sir, please continue.

A. And the third thing I did was to bring the 1960 census figures up to 1968, up to the date of the trial, and I did this by increasing them at the rate of four percent per year.

Q. And why did you increase them at the rate of four percent per year?

A. Well, as I show, labor wages have been going up on the average of five percent per year.

Q. If they go up five percent, why did you use four percent?

A. Well, I thought I would be conservative in increasing them, so I increased them at the rate of four percent per year.

Plaintiff's Projected Periodic
Earning Loss Following Date
of Injury

Q. Please explain the nature of your computations as shown on the charts identified as Plaintiff's Exhibits No. 51-A and 51-B.

A. These charts show plaintiff's assumed earnings for various periods following the date of his injury. In other words, what a healthy person in plaintiff's group would have earned. For example, for the period from March, 1963, when plaintiff was 15.3 years of age and was injured, until he was age 19.2, I have shown no earnings since it is assumed that plaintiff would have been in high school during that period. The next project period is between age 19.2, when plaintiff would have graduated from high school and entered the labor force, and age 20.1, which is plaintiff's age now.

Q. Does that labor force refer to all people who would be

employed, including those people in the armed services and those who are unemployed?

A. That is correct.

Q. Go ahead, sir.

A. From age 19.2 to 20.1 is nine-tenths of a year. The earnings after the adjustment would have been on an annual basis of $680. So, I took nine-tenths of 680. In that period of time, loss of earning capacity was $612.

Q. What would be the next period?

A. The next period is from the date of the trial until he would have been age 25, and the reason I stopped at 25 is because this is the way the census data is given, 25 to 35, up to 55.

Q. That in effect would be the next five years of his life?

A. Almost five years, 4.9 years. And the adjusted earnings for that period is $4,283. So, I multiply 4.9 times $4,283, and I obtained for this period a loss of earning capacity of $20,897.

Q. Thank you, sir. Would you now go to the next page of your exhibit, and look at the figures between the ages of 25 to 35, from 1973 to 1983.

A. This is a period of ten years. Earnings at this level would be $7,181 per year. This times ten gives $71,810 as the loss of earning capacity for that period. Then continuing down here, from age 35 to 45, another ten-year period, the earnings for that period per year are $8,095, and the total loss of earnings for the ten-year period is $80,950.

Q. Incidentally, if we can stop right there, based upon these statistics and counting everybody in the country, servicemen, professional men, non-professional men, blue collar workers, white collar workers, unemployed people, what is the age group where a person reaches his height of earning capacity?

A. It is in this period of 35 to 45 years of age. You will notice that these annual figures reach a peak of $8,095, and then start declining as a person gets older.

Q. Now, what would he have earned between the ages of 45 and 55, which years would have been 1993.2 to 2003.2, a ten-year period?

A. The annual earnings would be $7,899, multiplied by ten gives you $78,990.

Q. Let me interrupt again. Plaintiff's life expectancy would have brought him over 70 years of age?

A. That is correct.

Q. You did not use his life expectancy in making these computations?

A. That is correct. I did not use his life expectancy, but I used his work-life expectancy.

Q. I see, now. When would the plaintiff, along with other people in the country, have been expected to quit working, according to the tables you are relying upon?

A. Based on the data supplied by the Labor Department, he would have quit working at the age of 62.5 years.

Q. What would be his earnings during that last period?

A. For the last seven and half years, annual earnings would be $6,903, and by multiplying we get $51,773. This completes the work-life expectancy of persons like David McGrady with a total of 43.3 years, and adds up to the total loss of regular earnings over this period in the amount of $305,122.

Amount of Fringe Benefits Lost

Q. Now, in addition to the term "earning capacity," is there also a term called "fringe benefits?"

A. Yes. In addition to regular earnings, working people are paid a larger and larger fraction of their pay now in the form of what is called "fringe benefits." At one time, this was a small portion of their pay, but now it is almost 25 percent of regular earnings paid workers. These fringe benefits consist of pension, health and welfare plans, guaranteed annual wages, contributions to Social Security, and items of that kind.

Q. Did you also rely on United States Census Department figures in determining plaintiff's loss of fringe benefits?

A. No, I didn't. The Census Department does not publish statistics on fringe benefits, just on earnings. But the United States Department of Labor, Bureau of Labor Statistics, does publish data on fringe benefits.

Q. All right. Is this data from the department you just mentioned an authoritative source?

A. Yes, it is.

Q. Is it relied upon by economists, labor economists, and statisticians in reaching the figures you are about to read?

A. Yes, sir.

Q. What would that percentage figure be?

A. The percentage figure varies between 20 and 25 percent of regular earnings.

Q. Did you use that figure?

A. No, I did not.

Q. What figure did you use?

A. I used 15 percent.

Q. Why did you not use the 20 to 25 percent and instead use 15 percent?

A. Some of the fringe benefit data is contained in this Census figure; for example, premium pay and overtime pay are contained in a person's earnings. So I cut those out. They amount to about five percent. Then to be on the conservative side, I decided on 15 percent of regular earnings as a sound estimate of the loss of value of fringe benefits.

Q. What did you compute plaintiff's loss of fringe benefits to be?

A. I took 15 percent of $305,122, and I got $45,768, which is the work-life loss of the value of fringe benefits for persons like the plaintiff in this statistical group.

Q. And that is a total of what, sir?

A. $350,890.

[The witness, during this period of the examination, had been standing in front of the jury next to enlarged versions of his charts, to which he referred during the course of his testimony. He then returned to the witness box.]

Inflationary Spiral of Wages and Prices

Q. In making these estimates, have you assumed wages will remain unchanged?

A. Wages have been going up for as long as we have been collecting data, which is back to 1910. Historically, wages in the United States have gone up at a rate of five percent a year.

Q. What have been the causes of these wage increases?

A. The wage increases that we have had are dependent upon two factors. One is inflation. As prices go up, wages go up. The other factor raising wages is increased productivity and work force, and the machinery employees work with. Exhibit 51-D explains the effect of inflation in this respect. This exhibit shows you what has happened to $100,000 in purchasing power if you had that amount of money in 1940. Because of price increases, this sum is reduced in purchasing power. From

1940 to 1950, it was reduced from $100,000 to $58,000. Then to 1960, we see a further reduction of that $100,000 to $47,412. Then from 1960 to 1966, which is the last data I have available, we witness a further reduction of purchasing power to only $43,213.

Q. Does that mean if I had $100,000 in 1940, it would buy $100,000 worth of goods?

A. That's right.

Q. And that same $100,000 in 1966 would buy $43,213 worth of goods?

A. That is correct.

Q. What is Exhibit 51-C?

A. This Exhibit shows the official statistics of the United States Department of Labor of the consumer price index.

Q. What is the consumer price index?

A. The consumer price index is a statistic which shows the average price consumers would pay to buy a certain bundle of goods and services. It would include rents, food, medical care, automobiles, television sets. All of these are put together and the government publishes every month a consumer price index. This black line on the exhibit shows what has happened to that consumer price index from 1913 up to 1968. You can see in the 1920s how it grows and then drops in the '30s. But since 1933, which was the depths of depression, it has continued to rise. At this rate of increase, if you drew a trend line through this, the rate of increase in retail prices is an average of about three percent per year over this period of time.

Q. How much have they increased in the last two years?

A. Prices have increased a little over three percent each year in the last two years.

Q. Have you an opinion, based upon a reasonable degree of economic certainty, as to how much they will increase this year?

A. Yes.

Q. What is your opinion?

A. Prices up to now are increasing at the rate of four percent per year.

Q. And the bases for your opinion, sir, are what?

A. The commerce statistics as they are reported each month.

Meaning of "Present Cash Value"

Q. What does the term "present cash value" mean?

A. If you have, say, $95.15 today and you put it in the bank at four percent per year, at the end of one year you will have a hundred dollars, and that is a case of interest being added because you are putting the money in the bank and you are taking it a year later.

Now, what we are talking about is the reverse. We are seeking to determine the present value of a hundred dollars given to you a year from now. To find the present value of that, you have to take away the interest. So if I reduce that hundred dollars one year from now to present value, the present value would be the $95.15.

In cases like this, where there is a large amount of money to be given in the future, all of this has to be brought back to the present; it has to be reduced to present value by taking the interest out.

Q. All right. If a person is untrained in financial matters and invests a sum of money now in high grade corporate bonds or stocks, or deposits money in a bank or a savings and loan association, what rate of interest can he expect to receive over the person's remaining life expectancy?

A. About four percent.

Q. Is it a fact, sir, that in certain savings and loan associations today you get five, five and a quarter, and five and three-quarters?

A. Right.

Q. Why do you then say only four percent?

A. Well, we are talking about long periods of time. In this particular case we are talking about the future, 40, 50 years. The interest rate, we must consider, is the long-term interest rate, not the interest rate today or a year ago. Therefore, the question we have to answer is, "What has been the long-term interest rate in this country over the past 40 years?"

The chart, identified as Exhibit 51-G, shows the interest rates from about 1900 up to the present time of different types of possible investments: U.S. Government Bonds; Commercial Bank Time Deposits; Corporate Bonds, twenty years to maturity; net rates of interest for all life insurance companies; interest of savings and loan associations—they're all marked up.

Q. And based upon these basic recent statistics, have you reached an opinion as to what the interest rate would be for a person uninitiated in finances with reference to earning ability of a dollar in the future?

A. In my opinion it is four percent. You can see a period of very high interest rates from 1900 to 1920. Then, for about twenty-odd years, interest rates fell and only recently started to go up again. If you draw a line across here, you can see the rough average here over a long-term trend is four percent.

Relationship of Inflationary Wage
Trend and Present Cash Value
Concept

Q. How are wage trends and reduction of present cash value related to each other?

A. Wage trends and reduction of present cash value offset each other.

Q. What do you mean by that?

A. Wage trends, future wage trends, are almost always up. In this case, you can see they're up about five percent. So this is a factor increasing the future earning capacity of an individual.

Q. Specifically, then, does plaintiff's estimated wage loss of $350,890 in any way include the five percent inflationary trend in wages going on in this country for the last half century?

A. It does not include inflation wage increases.

Q. Have you reduced the projected earnings of $350,890 to present cash value using the four percent interest factor you previously described?

A. No, I have not.

Q. Why have you not included these two factors in determining plaintiff's projected wage loss?

A. The two factors affect each other. On the one hand you have the factor of wages going up; on the other hand, you have the factor involving the reduction to present cash value. One works against the other. If you assume that wages went up, say four percent, and you reduce to present value by using a four percent interest rate, why then they completely offset each other.

Q. Would that mean if you were to earn one dollar one year from now, then in order to have the value of that dollar today, you have to reduce it to present cash value, using a four percent interest factor, and bring it down to 96 cents?

However, in order to allow for the inflationary wage trend of five percent, you just go right back to that one dollar, is that right?

A. That is right.

Q. Isn't there a disparity between the five percent figure and four percent?

A. There is a slight disparity. Again, I think they're close enough to offset each other. True, wages have gone up five percent. If I assume a four percent wage increase, I can offset against that the four percent interest rate.

Q. So we understand each other, on which side of the calculated figure of loss of projected earnings would this disparity be, on which side of the ledger?

A. Well, if I computed the wage increase at five and discounted the interest rate at four, then that would have the effect of raising the $350,000 projected wage loss.

Q. In effect, you take a conservative view in offsetting future earnings due to wage inflation against reducing to present cash value?

A. Right, sir.

Q. What is the effect, then, on the $350,000 projected wage loss by having wage inflation offset present cash value reduction?

A. The sum remains at $350,0000.

Effect of High School Education on Wage Rates

Q. Now, sir, when you were figuring out this loss of earnings of a person in David McGrady's status, did you take into consideration that he would have graduated from high school?

A. No, I did not. I took him from a statistical group that included all males in his age category living in Chicago.

Q. Is there a relationship between a person's education and his earnings throughout the rest of his life?

A. Yes, there is. It is generally true that the more education you have, the higher your earnings are on the average.

Q. Are there statistics available from the same authoritative sources that you previously presented which would indicate his median income at the 1968 level if he had finished high school?

A. Yes, but by educational level, not by age. Chart 51-D shows
median income at 1968 levels from the United States Census
data.

Q. What does "median" mean, sir?

A. Median is a figure which has 50 percent of the figures above
and 50 percent below. It is the middle figure. So for all people
who graduated from grammar school or primary school, the
median income would be $6,634; one to three years of high
school, $7,606; four years of high school, $8,273.

Q. Is this figure of $8,273, which is the median income for people
with four years of high school in the Chicago area, greater or
less than the figures you used in reaching your opinion that
David would have lost $305,122 in regular earnings?

A. It is greater. The highest figure I relied on for a person of
David's status was $8,095 for ages 35 to 45, which is less than
if I had figured on his having graduated from high school.

Q. So, again, were your figures on the conservative side?

A. Yes, sir.

Inflationary Trend of Medical Costs

[Proof offered through other witnesses established that plaintiff would
require continuous medical attention and nursing care for the remainder of his life. This line of questioning established that these costs and
therefore plaintiff's damages in this regard would continue to increase.]

Q. What does plaintiff's exhibit 51-E represent?

A. This represents the Consumer Price Index, which consists of
certain commodities which the Department of Labor considers
an average working family would buy. This index has increased
at the rate of three percent.

Q. Now, do average working families also undergo and assume
medical responsibilities?

A. Yes. Part of the consumer price index has a medical component. It is made up of different parts: housing, food, transportation, and there is a medical component.

Q. And is there a medical care index?

A. Yes. The medical care component of the consumer price index
is indicated by these red dots.

Q. All right. Now, with reference to the medical care index, what
is the relationship between that specific item and the general
increase in the consumer price index?

A. You can see what has happened for a period of time. The medical care index hasn't been collected as far back as the consumer price index. That was brought in the 1940's. But in the early period, medical care prices went up just about in the same way as general consumer prices. In the past ten years, medical care prices have increased at a much faster rate than the general consumer price index.

Q. Based upon a reasonable degree of economic certainty, do you have an opinion as to whether this increase in the uptrend of medical care expenses is expected to go up, is expected to go down, or is it expected to remain at its present status?

A. It has been going up so rapidly, all the expectations are it will continue to rise at this rapid rate.

Projected Cost of Future Custodial Care for Plaintiff

Q. Professor Lurie, from June of 1964 until the present time, Mr. and Mrs. Swaggerty have been taking care of their son and have been giving him custodial medical care. From an economist's viewpoint, what does that entail?

A. Well, that entails taking care of all aspects of the patient. It is providing a medical home, the food, and the actual medical care of the patient.

Q. All right. From June of 1964 up to and including the present time, have you made two charts with reference to the fair, reasonable, and customary charges for the custodial care that plaintiff has received from his parents since 1964?

A. I have made these two charts based on two figures.

Q. What two figures did you use?

A. This first chart assumes medical care cost of $50 per day for two eight-hour shifts. This second chart assumes medical care cost at $60 per day.

Q. All right. Let's first of all do it at $50 per day. From June of 1964 to April of 1968, how many years is that?

A. Well, from the date plaintiff left the hospital to the date of the trial is 3.8 years.

Q. Now, at a cost of $50 per day, what would the annual medical custodial costs be per year?

A. Well, $50 a day times 365 days per year would give you an annual cost of $18,250.

Q. Now, from June of 1964 up to and including the present time, what would then be the fair, reasonable, and customary charge for custodial medical care up to today's date at the rate of $50 a day?

A. Under the assumption it is 3.8 times $18,250, or total medical cost of $69,350.

Q. Now, sir, let's go into the future. You told us that David McGrady has a life expectancy of 50.1 years.

A. As of the date of the trial.

Q. Assuming, now, no increase of any kind in medical expenses, what would the future custodial care be for David McGrady at the rate of $50 per day with a life expectancy of 50.1 years?

A. Well, again, it is just multiplying 50.1 times the annual medical care cost in this case, and multiplying those two equals $914,325.

Q. So, at the rate of $50 per day, what would be the fair, reasonable, and customary charge for medical care from the date of the accident in June of 1964 up to and including the terminal point of David McGrady's life expectancy?

A. A total of $983,675.

Q. All right, sir. Go to the next chart, Plaintiff's Exhibit 51-I, which is at the rate of $60 per day. Now, looking at Exhibit 51-I, there was a disparity in the testimony of two of the previous medical witnesses regarding the cost of the medical care plaintiff will require. One doctor testified $30 per day times two, another doctor testified $25 per day times two. Now, looking at these figures, using the figure of $60 per day without any projection of increase in cost from June of 1964 until the time of trial, which would have been 3.8 years, what would the annual cost be at $60 per day?

A. Well, at $60 per day multiplied by 365, the annual cost would come to $21,900 per year. Then if you take the annual cost, multiplied by the number of years, the time period from the date he left the hospital to date of trial, you get $83,220. Then from date of trial to end of life expectancy, 50.1 years, you get $1,097,190.

Q. At $21,900 per year using $60 per day figure, not including increase in medical expenses of any kind, what would be his fair, reasonable, and customary medical care or custodial-type cost throughout his lifetime?

A. $1,180,410.

Q. Now, again, using either one of these charts, plaintiff's Exhibit 51-H or 51-I, have you in any way increased the value of future medical costs by taking into consideration not only inflation as it affects all commodities, but the increased inflation in medical expenses?

A. No, I have not.

Q. And have you taken into consideration that these figures of $983,675 and $1,180,410 should be reduced to present cash value?

A. I have not.

Q. If you were to use this same formula that you used before in reducing future loss of earnings to present cash value as offset by inflation, which you said would then even the figures out, if you were to use that same formula for future medical care or costs, would these figures then, again, remain the same?

A. Yes, they would. In other words, if reduction to present cash value were offset by the anticipated increase in medical expenses, the basic figure of $983,675 and $1,180,410 would remain the same.

Q. You told us that medical expenses have been increasing at the rate of eight percent a year in the last couple of years?

A. Just the last two years.

Q. Assuming that trend were to continue, would the figures of $983,675 and $1,180,410 be accurate or would they be much more?

A. Well, if medical costs continue to rise at eight percent per year, then the increase in medical cost would be much greater than the discount, the reduction of present value, and that would make these figures even substantially higher.

Q. In any one of these medical care costs for the future, did you include costs for suppositories, skin band urine bottles, or hoses that must be placed in plaintiff's stomach?

A. No.

Q. Did you include the cost for the pills he takes at $5.25 per week?

A. No, I did not.

Q. Did you include the cost of a new electric chair, electric wheel chair, when this one becomes outmoded or outdated?

A. No, I did not.

Q. Did you include the cost of a new hospital bed?

A. No, I did not.

Q. Did you include the cost for hospitalization that has been testified that he needs every year for an annual checkup?

A. No, I did not.

Q. Did you include the cost for doctors' bills which he will need to pay every year for his annual checkup?

A. No, I did not.

Q. Did you include the cost for either X-rays or other types of scientific methods for the purpose of determining whether his kidneys and his bladder are uninfected, which should be done every year?

A. No, I did not.

Q. So that these costs are the raw expenses of custodial care and do not include surgical or medical care that might be required by a doctor?

A. That is correct.

Mr. Corboy: I have no further questions, Your Honor.

The Court: Cross-examination.

The basic items to be included in a hypothetical question, showing the losses to the widow and dependents, involving a deceased wage earner, are the following:[35]

1. Qualifications of the economic expert.

2. Evidence showing yearly earnings income of the subject for a reasonable period of time (about six years) before his death.

3. Evidence showing for the same period of time the hourly wage rate and employer's contributions, expressed in percentage of that hourly wage rate, in fringe benefits, i.e. health and welfare, pension, and vacation.

4. Evidence showing rate of wage increases for the average wage-earner in the country generally from 1910 to 1960 [obtainable from the U.S. Government (see Sec. 9.2, supra)] and the ratio of wage increases of the deceased over the six years preceding his death (to lay a foundation for allowance of lost increase future earnings).

---

35. See *16 Am. Jur.—Proof of Facts,* Section 23, pps. 724-741 for the form of such a hypothetical question.

5. Evidence showing a computation of the equivalent of hours (estimated at straight time) worked in the said six year period (computed by dividing the yearly earnings by the hourly straight time rate—to lay a foundation for projecting future lost earnings).

6. Evidence projecting the earnings of the subject from the date of his death to the end of the period covered by the union contract under which he worked, if any.

7. Estimate of the lost earnings from the date of death to the date of trial. (This is not subject to discounting because it was never received.)

8. Estimate of loss of earnings from date of trial to end of union contract.

9. Work-life expectancies (based on U.S. Government Tables—see Appendix B, infra).

10. An estimate of the loss of earnings during work-life expectancy from the end of the union contract at the rate when the union contract expired, increased by the ratio mentioned in item 4 of this paragraph.

11. An estimate of the value of the household services which would have been rendered by the deceased had he lived. This is to be added to the aggregate losses.

12. An estimate of the personal consumption expenditures of the deceased for the period of his life expectancy had he lived. This is to be deducted from the aggregate losses.

13. The appropriate discount rate and how it is arrived at. A government table is available, which may be used as an exhibit, showing trends of interest rates in the U.S.A. since 1900 to support the rate used. (See Sec. 9.2, supra, and Appendix C, infra.)

14. Evidence made graphic and visible by a blown-up exhibit showing the summary of losses. It would be made up of the following items:

(a) Loss of earnings (inclusive of fringe benefits):
  1. From date of death to date of trial (not discounted)
  2. From trial date to end of union contract period (discounted)
  3. From end of union contract period to end of work-life expectancy period (discounted)
(b) Value of household services (to be added to the overall losses and discounted)

(c) Personal consumption expenses (to be deducted from the overall losses)

(d) Net loss after totalling the above items.

Some economists do not include the rate of wage increases projected into the future (about 5 percent), nor do they include any discount rate (about 4 percent), since one tends to equate and to cancel out the other.

Sec. 9.8   Where to Locate an Economist-Statistician

It may be mentioned that because of the novelty of this kind of expert, he is not easy to locate and obtain. Perhaps the most expeditious way to locate an economist-statistician is to inquire of your fellow lawyers trying serious damage cases. They will be able to inform you not only who is qualified, but what kind of witness he will make in court.

The economics department of metropolitan universities or colleges nearest you may be consulted for such experts. It is advisable to inquire of an economist who is willing to testify if he has had experience in court in such cases. If not, it may prove embarrassing to both of you to use him, unless he is very familiar with this field and with the applicable charts and statistics, and will spend time with you in going over the hypothetical question.

Employees in the federal government are a source for such experts. In point of fact, these persons are most conversant with the sources for government statistics, charts, and tables which are to be used. These people will not testify if the government is a party. Such persons can be located by inquiring of various federal government departments, particularly of the following:

U.S. Department of Health, Education & Welfare, Public Health Service, National Center for Health and Statistics, Washington 25, D.C.

Division of the Actuary, U.S. Department of Health, Education and Welfare, Social Security Administration, Washington, D.C.

Chief, Division of Manpower and Employment, Department of Labor, Washington, D.C.

There are organized societies of such experts, where inquiry can be made for a person nearest to your locality. Such are:

Associated Appraisers of Impaired Earning Capacity, P.O. Box 7131, Berkeley, California, 94707

American Statistical Association, 1757 K Street, N.W., Washington 6, D.C.

There are professional services which can refer a lawyer to such experts.[36] There are other miscellaneous sources.[37]

Sec. 9.9   What an Economist Costs as an Expert Witness

In the late 1960s, the cost of a full appraisal before trial ran in the neighborhood of $600-$1,000. Sometimes, the economist may agree to accept less—perhaps $300-$500—for a settlement negotiation appraisal, which is less thorough than the full or formal appraisal. The expert may agree to allow this cost to be merged with that of a full appraisal for court if the settlement negotiations fall through.[38] In addition, the expert will charge about $500 plus expenses for his court appearance, depending on the number of days he must be in court. Another cost factor may be the time which counsel must spend going over the appraisal with the expert in preparation for trial; some experts do not make a charge for this item.

Sec. 9.10   When to Use An Economist

It is not practical or advisable to use an economist in every case of serious disability and wrongful death. The touchstone is whether his employment will pay off by way of settlement or trial. To make the correct judgment is not always easy. There are some factors which should be considered in arriving at your conclusion. For example, is your case strong or weak on liability? Is the life expectancy involved long or short? Are the lost yearly earnings small or large? Are the fringe benefits large or small? Can dependency be proven on the part of the survivors?

A concrete example will best serve here. Suppose that the deceased was a 55-year-old railroad worker, who was found dead on the tracks, having been run over by a train he was assisting in assembling, but that no one witnessed the accident or knew what caused him to get run over. Suppose he earned about $10,000 per year at the time of his death and that he had some moderate fringe benefits, such as welfare and pension benefits. Suppose he

---

36. *2 Am. Jur. Trials*, pps. 361-369. For publications in the special fields of medicine which may be consulted for leads as to experts, see pps. 371-407 of *2 Am. Jur. Trials.*

37. *2 Am. Jur. Trials*, pps. 293, 585.

Paul J. Garfield, V. Pres. of Foster Association, Inc., Washington, D.C., author of article on Wrongful Death (1967 Law Journal 654).

Philip Eden, Pres. of Associated Appraisers of Impaired Earnings Capacity, P.O. Box 7131, Berkeley, California 94707, author of the article "The Use of Economists and Statisticians in Impaired Earning Capacity Cases" (*The Practical Lawyer*, March 1964), economist and U.S. government statistician.

38. Compare cost estimated in Speiser's *Economic Handbook*, Section 13:4.

left a widow of 53 years who was only partly dependent on him. We would be dealing with a work-life expectancy of about ten years, plus additional earnings thereafter on a sharply diminishing basis. We would be talking about $100,000 of gross earnings which, when discounted at say 4 percent, would amount to about $81,000. The fringe benefits, plus the value of his home services, would be roughly cancelled out by his personal consumption expenditures. If the weak liability is computed at a 50 percent chance of victory, we find ourselves talking about approximately $40,000. This case would hardly merit the services of an economist, especially if it can be settled around that figure.

On the other hand, take for example a 17-year-old high school graduate about to enter college, who is permanently and totally disabled in an accident, where there is good liability and where there will be expensive costs for future care. We would be talking about a long life-span, extensive lost earnings expectations, and big anticipated medical and therapeutic expenses. Here the use of the expert is highly advisable, particularly if the defendant is capable of satisfying a big judgment. If the defendant cannot meet a big judgment, it would be wise to learn from the other side what his insurance limits and assets are, if possible, before calling in the expert.

Chapter 10

WHAT TO SAY IN

THE CLOSING ARGUMENT

Sec. 10.1   Preliminary Observations

Each lawyer has his own style of delivering a closing argument. Some adopt a quiet, clinical approach; some use a flamboyant, oratorical manner; some use freely flowing sentimentality to appeal to the jurors' emotions; some use wit and sarcasm. The master would be capable of applying all of these ingredients in the proper portions and at the appropriate times to concoct a perfect closing argument. Few, if any of us, have such virtuosity. The object of the individual lawyer should be to cover the ground in his own natural manner and style. As was said in the chapter entitled "What To Say In The Opening Statement" (Sec. 7.2), be yourself. Do not try to imitate someone else's style. It will not come off naturally if you do and the jury will be unfavorably impressed. You will be most convincing if you act naturally in your delivery and "pour it on" when you are moved to do it. But above all, be sincere in your position that your client should win, else the jury will hear the hollow tone of your voice and respond accordingly.

In most states, the plaintiff speaks first in making the closing argument, and then the defendant's counsel answers and the plaintiff has a rebuttal. The judge may instruct the jury on the law either before or after the closing arguments. In many states, the judge instructs them before the closing arguments are made.

The prevailing trend of the courts is to limit the time of closing argument for each side, much in the style of the ancient Greeks who limited the period of a trial by use of a sand glass time-piece.[1] The courts feel that the jurors' minds are made up before the closing arguments are reached. A recent Chicago survey shows that about 80 percent of the jurors polled did not change their vote after the opening statement.[2]

The author feels that the closing arguments can change jurors' minds. This applies particularly to the amount of damages to award.

The author believes also that counsel are inclined to speak too long in their closing arguments and to bore the jury unless limited; an exception should be made in the serious injury cases, however, because there is more ground to cover. It is important for plaintiff's counsel to apportion his time between his closing argument and his rebuttal, with the lion's share of his time given over to the closing argument.

As was previously pointed out in Sec. 2.8, have your requests for instructions prepared in advance of the trial. Frequently, the judge will ask for them before the evidence is completed so he may study and prepare his charge in advance of the closing arguments. He will probably discuss his intended charge with counsel after the close of the evidence and indicate what he intends to say. This will enable counsel to argue law to the jury within the proper confines and when counsel wishes to stress some salient point. For example, in the usual rear-end collision case, the legal point should be emphasized that it was the duty of the defendant to be alert, to keep his automobile under proper control and not to follow too closely.

The writer feels that the closing argument should not be prepared in advance, except perhaps for a breakdown of the damages which plaintiff's counsel will ask for; and even this may be altered as the tide of the legal battle rises and falls. Usually, counsel will have some time to reflect on the contents of his closing argument because a hiatus occurs between the completion of the evidence and the commencement of the closing arguments. This period is probably the most soul-searching of the whole trial for the lawyer. He must digest the entire evidence already presented and as objectively as possible consider where his case is strong and where it is weak, and how he can shore it up in the concluding argument; and he must develop a feel as to what is the maximum which the jury is willing to allow for the damages. Also, he must use this precious period to study how he can effectively project to the jurors his appeal and why his client is entitled to the amount he requests. This tests his mettle not only as a lawyer but as an actor and a salesman.

He should avoid engaging in personalities with the opposing lawyer. It must be remembered that it is not the lawyers who are on trial and that

---

1. Aristotle–"Government of Athens", translated by Kenyon, Atkeniesium Respublica, pp. 63-69 (Oxford, 1920); Belli–"Modern Trials," Vol. 4, pp. 64-107 (Bobbs-Merrill, Indianapolis).
2. "Persuasion, The Key To Damages," published by The Institute of Continuing Legal Education, Ann Arbor, Michigan (1969), p. 374, edited by Grace W. Holmes.

often a wily defense lawyer will deliberately bait the plaintiff's lawyer in order to distract him from the issues of the case.

He should appear loose, relaxed, and poised, and should never reveal his apprehensions about his case because if he panics, the jury will sense it at once and act accordingly.

Sec. 10.2   The Hypothetical Case

In the chapter entitled "What To Say In The Opening Statement" (Sec. 7.5) we postulated in the checklist subtitle a set of facts involving a rear-end auto collision when the plaintiff stopped for a red traffic light and in which the plaintiff driver suffered a musculo-ligamentous strain to his neck, in which the defendant claimed a defense that the plaintiff stopped abruptly and without adequate warning, where the police made an investigation, where both sides had a favorable eyewitness, and where plaintiff had had a previous neck injury.

The usual sequence of treatment in the closing argument should be as follows. The plaintiff's lawyer should use the same dignified and respectful salutation to the judge by name, and to the foreman and ladies and gentlemen of the jury (not by name), which was used in his opening statement. He should then carry through with his original plan and theory of the case, but highlighting only certain aspects of each portion, i.e. the accident, the injuries, the treatment, the negligence of the defendant, and the freedom from contributory negligence of the plaintiff. For example, he should refer to the disinterested witness who saw the accident and to the police report which tended to corroborate it by showing the measurements of defendant's skid marks and the place where the debris was found on the road, indicating that the defendant was going too fast and that he hit the plaintiff's automobile before the intersection. He should refer to the hospital report to confirm that the plaintiff was complaining of neck pain on the date of the accident.

In discussing negligence, plaintiff's counsel should remind the jury of the defendant's legal duties in the circumstances and how he violated them. He should show that the plaintiff acted as the ordinary, reasonable man should have under the circumstances, and so was free of contributory negligence.

Now he should talk about damages. He should approach the blackboard and assume now the role of the instructor and the salesman. He should write down each item of damage and the value of each, and should explain how he has arrived at it. This would cover the special or out-of-pocket expenses first. Then he should record the permanent disability and before writing down the value placed on it, he should repeat his medical expert's diagnosis and prognosis (i.e. 15 percent loss of use of the neck), and the nature of the physiological damage done (i.e. tearing of the soft tissue in the neck by the overstretching caused by the accident and the replacement of the torn tissue by the scar tissue which will pull on movement, causing discomfort and pain).

At this point mention the previous neck injury. Explain that the plaintiff was symptom free before the current accident or that plaintiff had only slight symptoms from the previous accident. Explain that the defendant takes the plaintiff as he finds him and is responsible at law for lighting up a pre-existing or dormant condition, and therefore for the full results caused by the last accident.[3] This should be one of your requested instructions.

Then he should discuss the pain and suffering. He should separate it into periods. The first period would be the first few weeks, when the pain was acute and intense. The next would be the recuperative period when the pain was less intense but when he was receiving medication for his pain and was undergoing therapeutic care, and wearing perhaps a surgical neck collar. The last period is the chronic one covering the present, when the pain and discomfort comes and goes with use and changes in the weather. There is also the future pain he will have to endure. On a per diem basis,[4] place a value on each period.

Then total up the items and ask for that figure.

The blackboard entries then would look as follows:

Special Damages:

Sinai Hospital	$ 350.00	
Dr. A.B. (treatment)	$ 200.00	
Drugs	$ 20.00	
Lost wages (1/6/70-2/6/70, 4 weeks @ $150.00)	$ 600.00	
		$ 1,170.00

Permanent Disability:

10% loss of use of back	$10,000.00-$15,000.00

Pain and Suffering:

First 2 weeks @ $50.00 per day	$ 700.00	
Last 2 weeks @ $25.00 per day	$ 350.00	
	$1,050.00	
Future pain and suffering	$1,500.00	$2,550.00
		$13,720.00-$18,720.00

---

3. See Sec. 12.6, infra.

4. The valuation of pain on a per diem basis is now accepted by the courts. See: 60 ALR 2d 1333 and discussion in Sec. 13.8, infra.

Use the rebuttal period to answer the defendant lawyer's arguments. Do not feel constrained to answer every point which he makes, but only the salient ones.

In this connection, it is wise strategy to have the court stenographer write up for you the night before the closing argument certain portions of the testimony, particularly statements made by the defendant or by his witness which are contradictory, and then read these to the jury. Memories do fade and this is an effective weapon to jog the jurors' memory on an important item of evidence.

Be prepared for the blackboard reversal maneuver by the defendant's lawyer. Invariably, he will turn the blackboard around, ostensibly to put some diagram on it, but really in order to remove your damage figures from the juror's view. When you arise for your rebuttal, find a pretext for turning the blackboard around to its original position so that, as the jurors leave for their deliberations, your figures will be fresh in their minds.

It is advisable to ask the judge in advance of the trial or before the closing argument to make paper and pencils available to the jurors so they can make such notes as they wish. This will enable them to record and thereby to remember your figures.

Be sure to make your rebuttal very brief because at this point in the trial, the jurors' attention span is short. Do not bore or weary them.

Sec. 10.3   Sample Closing Argument on Pain and Suffering

There are many able and eloquent lawyers in our profession who have made very effective appeals to juries which have brought substantial awards. Specimens of such addresses appear in various sources.[5] Some of these are available in record form.[6] Samples will be supplied now of brief arguments made by lawyers in cases of lesser magnitude, which tend to represent the more average cases lawyers encounter daily.

Recently at a legal seminar held at the University of Michigan, Mr. Craig Spangenberg[7] delivered a closing argument for the plaintiff in a hypothetical case involving a woman who injured her throat in a rear-end-type of collision. She was an amateur singer, participating primarily in church-type singing. Although physically no cause could be found for it, she no longer

---

5. "Persuasion, The Key To Damages," supra; Stein's *Closing Argument*, published by Callaghan & Co., Chicago, Illinois; 6 *Am. Jur. Trials*, p. 666 et seq.

6. For example, closing arguments by Melvin M. Belli, Esquire, Los Angeles, California, and Moe Levine, Esquire, New York City, New York.

7. Craig Spangenberg of Hasenflue, Shibley & Traci, Cleveland, Ohio. See footnote at pp. 393-395, in "Persuasion, The Key To Damages", supra.

could carry on her singing. This is the way Mr. Spangenberg appealed to the jury on the damages for this injury.

"I want to talk about what I think is really the issue in the case. I want to forget the blackboard and the numbers and talk to you as people. You are not 12 individuals right now; you are a jury. You are part of the government of the United States. You enforce the law of this land. If any people in this country are to receive justice, it must come from you. Otherwise it's just talk. There are no rights that exist in a vacuum. A right is something that people will do something about. I want to talk about her rights as a human being. Judge Quinn will direct you to give her compensation for the injury she has really had. You know that if you knocked over a truck and spilled a load on the street, and the load was tomatoes, you would pay for the tomatoes. You wouldn't say, 'If they had been golf balls they wouldn't have been hurt, so we won't pay for that.' If you hit an egg and destroy the egg, you have destroyed that egg. If you hit a strong man and don't destroy him, you don't pay for that. We look to the actual result to the actual person. You are here to judge Marjorie Dolan, and on this point it makes no difference whether you like singing in choirs. It really doesn't affect me if she can't sing Handel's 'Messiah.' Someone else will sing it. It affects her, if she can't sing Handel's 'Messiah.' And she had the right to sing it. She had a right to achieve something in her life. She had the right to do what she wanted to do.

I don't know what your hobby is. Do you like to bowl? Fish? Hunt? My hangup is golf, you know—hit the ball down the fairway. This is a very unimportant occupation, but it gives me a tremendous amount of pleasure. Those weekends when I can get out and walk on grass and hit the ball, and once in a while hit a great shot or come out of a trap like a pro, it is a great day. That gives life real meaning to me. If all you are going to live for is to get some wages to buy some clothes, eat some food, have a roof over your head and a bed to sleep in, you are saying, 'I'll settle to be a slave.' We do that for slaves—food, clothing, shelter—but none of you would think that is much of a life. What you value is the ability as a free American to do what you want to do. To have the pleasure that you want to have, provided it's pleasure that doesn't hurt other people, of course. And what is Mrs. Dolan's pleasure? Her pleasure is singing—not on the concert stage but to sing better than most, to sing lead, to sing every Sunday, to be head of the section and soloist. What did it mean to her? You will know that by only one sentence in the whole examination, when Mr. Sams said to Marjorie, 'Did you want to sing that Christmas? Did you want to try?' And she said, 'I certainly would have sung if I could.' Just by her tone of voice, which you can't find in print, you knew that this meant everything to her. I don't say this is life itself, but this is a great part of her life; and it is clearly, demonstrably gone because of terror, fear of suffocation, fear of death, imposed on her by this crash. Understandable. I hope you won't go into the jury room and say, 'Well, I'm so brave it wouldn't have happened to me,' because any psychologist will tell you that every man has some point at which he breaks under stress. You don't know how brave you are until you have broken. Then you know what will break you. We know what broke her. Whether she is a golf ball, a tomato, or an egg, she is broken, and broken by this defendant. Her life is changed and destroyed, with the pain she has while doing her housework, the sleeping on a bedboard, and using a heat lamp. No one has suggested when or how she is going to be cured. Although we can cut out cancer and we can cut out tumors, we can't patch up minds. There is no spare part. That's what this case is about. That's what her damage is, and what puts a money value on it. We ask for $25,000. How you react to that depends on what you think of living. If you think your whole life isn't worth $10,000, you won't give her much. If you think your life is the most precious thing you have, then we haven't asked for enough. In that sense, you will go into the jury room and value yourselves. I hope you think highly of yourself. I hope you think highly of every human being in this room, because we are all worthwhile."

In a case involving a permanent knee injury, Mr. Samuel Langerman[8] narrated how he made an appealing argument.

"Ladies and gentlemen, last night when you left here His Honor took care of a few legal matters with us and then told us that tomorrow morning, this morning at 9:00, I would be called upon to sum up the case for you. As I drove home up Central Avenue I was thinking about it and trying in my mind to think of the words that I would use. I had no problem finding the words I would use to describe to you how the collision had occurred. It is simple to visualize my client coming down his own side of the road on his motorcycle. He is going at a rate of speed that everybody can see

---

8. Samuel Langerman of Began & Lewis, Phoenix, Arizona. See footnote 1 at pps. 379-380 of "Persuasion, The Key To Damages," supra.

is within the speed limit. He is looking where he's going. He is doing nothing wrong. A lady comes out of a used car lot in the middle of the block, and coming across the highway she just creates a barrier, a wall in front of him. What could he do? Absolutely nothing. So that was easy to visualize in my mind, but then I tried to visualize what you say to a jury when your client is 21 years old and looks and is in vigorous, glowing health. All of his life he has been able to do everything he wanted to do. He has never had to stop to think about it or to say, 'This I can't do.' Now he has had a broken leg which has healed uneventfully, but it has left him with a knee that doesn't work quite right. His doctor says it will do most of the things he wants, as long as he walks on even ground and doesn't go up and down steps and doesn't try to run or kneel or squat. He can do essentially everything. So you try to find the words to make the jury understand what a stiff knee must mean to him, because that's what we must find out. I couldn't find the words. I got to my house and got out of the car and I did as I do every night. I slammed the door and opened the side door to my house, and the thing that happens every night happened that night. My little four-year-old daughter Amy heard the sound of the door, and she came running from her end of the house yelling, 'Mama, Mama, Daddy's home, Daddy's home.' And I did what I do every night."

At that point I demonstrated to the jury. I took my briefcase in one hand, and I knelt down to show them how I had greeted Amy. Then I arose and said:

"As I did this last night, I knew that my mind had found the right words: You know, Jimmy will never be able to do that, because if he forgets and tries it once, he's going to fall on his face on top of his little girl while she's hugging him and kissing him."

The tone of my voice was sad and regretful because at that mo ent I was Jimmy, and I was sorry for myself because I would never again be able to bend down and catch my little girl in my arms and embrace her and kiss her. I think the jury felt my anguish and I think their verdict reflected it.

The eminent trial lawyer Francis H. Hare[9] relates how he got a large award from a country jury in a case involving a railroad worker who had suffered an injury which disabled him from working further on a regular basis. He asked the jury to relive with his client an average day in his client's life from the time he arose in the morning to the time he retired at night. He

---

9. Francis H. Hare Sr., Birmingham, Alabama.

noted the pain and disability as he arose from his bed, as he washed and shaved, as he sat down and arose from breakfast; his need to lie down in the morning after reading the morning paper because of fatigue and discomfort; his aversion to company because of his fatigue and pain; the self-denial of hunting and fishing that he used to engage in with such delight; the denial of a night out with his wife, and his necessary early retirement, all because of the accident.

Sec. 10.4 Checklist for Plaintiff's Closing Argument

[Assume the rear-end collision with musculo-ligamentous injury to the neck of the plaintiff driver who had a previous neck injury]

1. Reserve final preparation of closing argument until the evidence has been completed, so you will know what the strengths and weaknesses of your case are and so you can shape your argument accordingly.

2. Prepare in advance an itemization of the damages you will ask, but be prepared to alter it in accordance with the way the evidence shapes up.

3. Make your argument as brief as possible and do not repeat. If you are under a time limit fixed by the court, apportion it so the rebuttal gets the least time of your closing argument.

4. As you start your closing argument, address the judge by name, and the foreman and ladies and gentlemen of the jury (not by name). Maintain the high tone of dignity with which you started in your opening statement.

5. Pursue your original plan and theory of the case, but touching only on the highlights of the evidence to support your case. For example, mention your version of the accident but show its corroboration by a disinterested witness and by the police investigation; mention also the hospital report to show plaintiff was treated the same day for an injury to the neck to substantiate the plaintiff actually injured his neck in the accident.

6. Discuss the law of negligence and how the defendant violated it.

7. Discuss the law of contributory negligence and how the plaintiff observed the law.

8. Present damages in detail, preferably on the blackboard, writing down each item and explaining how it is arrived at, and then placing a value on it. Included should be the special or out-of-pocket damages, lost wages, permanent disability, and pain and suffering, past, present, and future. The permanent disability should be repeated as to your medical expert's diagnosis and prognosis, and physiological damage—all in layman's language. The manner in which the plaintiff will be disabled in his work and play should be carefully delineated.

9. Divide the pain and suffering into the periods of intensity and place a per diem value on it.

10. Mention the previous disability of the neck and how the new accident has lit up a dormant condition and has worsened it.

11. Total up the items and ask for it as the damages.

12. In rebuttal, be very brief and touch only on the salient arguments made.[10]

---

10. For another specimen checklist, see *11 Am. Jur. Trials*, pp. 663, 664.

Chapter 11

FUNDAMENTALS ABOUT
JURY INSTRUCTIONS
ON DAMAGES

Sec. 11.1 Damages Have Become More Complex

In recent years, the gamut covered by damage instructions has broadened, necessitating more than the request for the general or stock instruction about permanency vel non, lost wages, medical and hospital expenses, and pain and suffering. This reflects the economic and social advances made by the wage and salary earners in our nation. Also, fatal plane crashes involving wealthy persons have added sophistication to the damage prayer.

For example, suppose your client who, while on a mission of his own, was seriously injured in an automobile collision with another motorist; suppose further that he received his regular salary while recuperating under a private welfare plan prevailing between his union and his employer. Is the defendant excused from paying for the wages which would have been lost to the plaintiff otherwise? The weight of authority says no. (See Sec. 12.8, infra, and footnote 15 thereunder).

Another example. Suppose a young, promising business executive was killed in a plane crash. Is his widow entitled to damages in anticipation of the expected promotions he would have received had he lived? The answer is yes. See Sec. 12.10, and footnote 22 and 23 thereunder, infra.

In order to meet with these problems in the trial, it is necessary to prepare special damage prayers.

Sec. 11.2   Handy Ground Rules You Should Know

Before the request for the court's instruction on damages, counsel should present the prayers for instructions on liability. The basic principles governing the method of drafting each type are very similar. It is desirable, therefore, to discuss the fundamentals of jury instructions before going to the next chapter, which presents the sample or stock requests for instructions for plaintiffs in the general run of personal injury cases. The chapter following that contains stock requests for defendants in such cases.

It is the duty of the court to instruct the jury on the legal principles applicable to the pleadings and evidence.[1] Questions of law (i.e. construction of a city ordinance) are to be decided by the court, but questions of fact (i.e. whether plaintiff came through a stop sign) are for the jury to decide. Mixed questions of fact and law (i.e. whether certain items constitute infant's necessaries) are to be decided by the jury on proper instructions from the court.

When the instructions are to be given rests in the sound discretion of the court. Generally, the court instructs at the conclusion of the evidence and before the argument is made.

The instructions are intended to enlighten the jury as to what the law is in the case before it, and to define the issues and to guide it in the steps and the processes in arriving at a verdict.

The charges should be clear, precise, and impartial.[2] The fact that the instruction was a direct quotation from an opinion in an appellate court or of a statute will not save it from being erroneous if it is not clear.[3]

Repetition of a point in the charge should be avoided because it will serve to confuse and mislead the jury[4] or to place undue emphasis on a particular point.[5]

Another function of the charge is to spotlight the trial judge's view of the issues and of the law, and thus to provide the basis for review on appeal, if the trial court misled the jury by erroneous or biased instructions.

Instructions to the jury are usually prepared by the attorneys in the case but, when given to the jury, they become the court's instructions.

---

1. *Taylor v. Commonwealth,* 186 Va. 587, 592, 42 S.E. 2nd 906, 909; *Williams v. Lynchbury Traction & Light Co.,* 142 Va. 425, 432, 128 S.E. 732, 734; *Pietorycka v. Simolan,* 98 Conn. 490, 499 (1923).

2. *Stryzinski v. Arnold,* 285 A.D. 780, 783, 141 N.Y. S. 2nd 11, 14; *Daubmann v. Metropolitan St. R. Co.,* 180 N.Y. 384, 386, 73 N.E. 59.

3. *Stryzinski v. Arnold,* supra.

4. *Greear v. Noland Co.,* 197 Va. 233, 235, 89 S.E. 2nd 49, 51.

5. *Koehler v. Grace Line Inc.,* 285 A.D. 154, 136 N.Y.S. 2nd 87.

Generally, it is the duty of counsel to assist the court in instructing the jury. It has been held that counsel must be given the opportunity to present requests to charge.[6]

The court does not have to adopt the exact language of the requested instructions, even though they are correct, but may phrase it in its own way so long as the substance is incorporated and the ground is covered.[7]

The primary purpose of requested instructions is to assure that the jury is fully informed as to all of the law applicable and to enable the court to correct any mistakes made in its intended charge.

However, if the court's charge does not cover all phases of a case, or if the charge is incorrect or improper in any respect, counsel should direct the court's attention to it or, generally speaking, he is barred from claiming it as reversible error on appeal.[8] The procedure to criticize the error made by the court is to take an exception to the instruction.[9] However, it is wise to elaborate on the exception by detailing why counsel believes the court to be in error and, if necessary, to cite authorities in support of his position, thus to make it clear to the trial judge what his error is and to provide the court with an opportunity to amend.[10]

Usually, requests to instruct are presented to the trial judge out of the presence of the jury, and frequently in chambers at the conclusion of the evidence in the case being tried.

Sec. 11.3 Why You Should Prepare Requests for Instructions Reasonably in Advance of Trial

It is recommended that the requests for instructions be submitted before trial with a memorandum of law supporting them, if necessary, so the court has the benefit of the law prevailing in the case. Never presume that the judge knows all the law in a particular case; the gamut of legal knowledge is so extensive and is so changeable that no human being can be so omniscient. This will enable the court to better rule on what evidence is admissible. Also, by this method of preparation, counsel's theory of the case is developed before trial, as it should be, and the evidence required to prove a case can be better gauged.

---

6. *Chapman v. McCormick,* 86 N.Y. 479.

7. *Pannill v. Com.,* 185 Va. 244, 256, 38 S.E. 2nd 457, 463; *Mullins v. Siegel-Cooper Co.,* 183 N.Y. 129, 75 N.E. 1112.

8. *Brown v. DuFrey,* 1 N.Y. 2nd 190, 195-196; 151 N.Y. 2nd 649, 654; 134 N.E. 2nd 469. *Gabbard v. Knight,* 202 Va. 40, 46, 116 S.E. 2nd 73, 77.

9. *Brown v. DuFrey,* supra.

10. *Brown v. DuFrey, supra; Read v. Nichols,* 118 N.Y. 224, 231, 23 N.E. 468. *Smith v. Com.,* 165 Va. 776, 781, 182 S.E. 124, 127.

For example, suppose your client got seriously burned when, while driving on a highway, he came to the rescue of a fellow motorist whose truck caught afire. Suppose further that his burns were caused by exploding gasoline cans in the bed of the truck while your client was trying to put out the fire. In such a state of facts, it would be advisable to show that the plaintiff was not foolishly reckless in the circumstances, since the law bars recovery even to a Good Samaritan if he undertakes a rescue when such action would be suicidal in effect. Hence, knowledge of the law in advance of trial from preparing prayers for instructions should cause counsel for plaintiff to inquire if his client saw and recognized the gasoline cans in the burning truck before he attempted to rescue. If the plaintiff did notice the gasoline cans there before he tried to make the rescue, it would come perilously close to a directed verdict for the defendant, because plaintiff would have been acting recklessly with his own safety, mounting up to contributory negligence. On the other hand, if he could not see the gasoline cans because of the thick smoke, then his close approach to the burning truck to effectuate the rescue would bring him well within the Good Samaritan rule, justifying consideration by the jury without interference from the court.

Another example—this one bearing on damages. Let us assume in this same Good Samaritan case that the plaintiff was an employee of the federal government and that he got his medical and hospital care following the accident from the Veterans Hospital in his area, and that same was without charge to him because he was entitled to them under the terms of his employment as a fringe benefit. Is the defendant excused from this item of damage? The defendant is not exempted from these damages under the theory of the collateral source rule. (See Sec. 12.8, infra.) Your recognition of this problem in advance of trial would prompt you to research it and to have a separate damage prayer on it supported by authorities. This could add many dollars to the amount of the verdict.

It is obvious that counsel can prepare requests for instructions more properly and thoroughly if he does so reasonably in advance of trial rather than to wait for the eve of trial, when he will be hard pressed for time.

Without presenting sufficient facts to prove a case, you will never reach the point where you can argue damages, no matter how serious and meritorious they may be.

Sec. 11.4   How to Write a Requested Instruction

Each request for instruction should be precise, should contain a pertinent principle of law, and should conform to the evidence.

The prayer should have appended to it at the bottom citations to the legal authorities which support it. If it is an unusual type of case, i.e. injury to a railroad worker (F.E.L.A.) or to a merchant seaman (Jones Act), then it is recommended that in addition to the citations, a brief memorandum of law be submitted with it elaborating on the authorities.

Ordinarily there should not be more than six to eight instructions altogether, inclusive of the damage prayer. However, in a more complicated case, do not hesitate to prepare more, so as to cover the ground thoroughly.

Avoid argumentativeness and obvious partisanship in the verbiage of a requested instruction. Remember that counsel is asking the judge to read his prayer to the jury, and the judge must be impartial. Furthermore, do not permit zeal of counsel to win his case to furnish grounds for reversal on appeal because of error in framing the instructions.

The general form of the damage prayer should start with the language:

> "If the jury shall find for the plaintiff, then in estimating the damages, it shall, etc."

A more formally typed beginning is:

> "The plaintiff prays the court to instruct the jury that if it shall find in favor of the plaintiff, then in estimating the damages, it shall, etc."

Each prayer should be on a separate sheet of legal-sized paper and typed.[11] This is more desirable than lumping them all together because, if quick changes are desired, only one sheet need be changed rather than the whole set of prayers.

Sec. 11.5   Where to Look for Forms of Instruction Requests

While the cases of the highest appellate court in a state are the best source for the law and the basis for prayers in that state, there is great similarity in the instructions in the various states of the United States. This is understandable because the instructions stem from the settled cases which are common law in origin; even in states where the law has been codified, it reflects the common law. In recent years, many states have prepared stock form jury instructions. These are frequently the result of team research by the respective state judiciaries, and are generally reliable and transferable from state to state. However, they are not sacrosanct and there should be no hesitation about changing them to conform to the facts in your particular case or to some departure from the general law in your state.

---

11. The federal rules specifically require that requests for instructions be in writing. *Swiderski v. Mordenbaugh,* 143 F. 2nd 219 (9C.A.). But see *Downie v. Powers,* 193 F. 2nd 760 (10 C.A.)

Sources for pattern jury instructions are as follows:

California Jury Instructions (Civil)—B.A.J.I. Published in 1943, with 1950 supplement, by West Publishing Company, St. Paul, Minnesota. A fifth edition was published in 1969.

*Connecticut Jury Instructions—*By Wright. Published in 1960 by The Atlantic Law Book Company, Hartford 3, Connecticut. A second edition was published recently.

*Federal Jury Practice and Instructions—Civil and Criminal—*By Mathes and Devitt. Published in 1965 by West Publishing Company, St. Paul, Minnesota. A second edition was recently published (1970).

Illinois Pattern Jury Instructions—Civil—I.P.I. Published in 1961 by Burdette Smith Company, Chicago, Illinois. A second edition was recently published by West Publishing Co., St. Paul, Minn.

Minnesota Jury Instruction Guides. Published in 1963 by West Publishing Company, St. Paul, Minnesota.

New York Pattern Jury Instructions—Civil. Published in 1965 by Baker, Voorhis & Co. Inc., Mt. Kisco, New York. The Lawyers Cooperative Publishing Company, Rochester, New York.

Raymond's Missouri Jury Instructions. Published in 1942 by West Publishing Company, St. Paul, Minnesota.

*Virginia Practice—*By Doubles, Emroch, Merhige. Published in 1965 by West Publishing Company, St. Paul, Minnesota, and Washington Law Book Company, Washington, D.C.

Besides these, there are other sources for standardized jury instructions.[12]

---

12. i.e. *Speiser's, Negligence Jury Charges.* Published in 1961 by Central Book Company, Inc., Boooklyn, New York; *Jury Instructions on Medical Issues—*By Alexander. Published in 1966 by Allen Smith Co., Indianapolis, Indiana; *Standardized Jury Instructions for D.C.*

Chapter 12

HOW PLAINTIFF SHOULD WORD

REQUESTS FOR INSTRUCTIONS

ON DAMAGES

Sec. 12.1   Guideline to the Use of This Chapter

It is important to read the Comment when it appears at the beginning of a topic in this chapter because the general law incorporated in the prayer for instruction is capsulized there.

The footnotes are very important in this chapter because they mention diverse holdings in different states.

Reference to West Key Number Digest System and to Corpus Juris Secundum will appear at the end of each request for instruction for authorities to support the request.

Except where otherwise indicated, these instructions represent a composite form from those appearing in the books of pattern instructions referred to in the preceding chapter.

For case authorities to cite in support, see those cites in the pattern instruction books, and in the West Key Number Digest System and in Corpus Juris Secundum. Frequently, the cases cited merely express the principal of law incorporated in the prayer rather than the actual wording of the instruction.

It is always advisable to consult the cases in your own state for authorities in support of prayers because the local courts will be most persuaded by them. In this connection, you may get a lead to the cases in your own jurisdiction by tracing the key number cited at the end of the sample instruction, supra, into the West Key Digest applicable to your own state (i.e. Maryland Digest for Maryland), and in the footnotes of the Corpus Juris Secundum reference.

Only the generally accepted prayers for instructions appear herein. This should not discourage the lawyer from modifying or enlarging on them if the law of his particular state supports it. This has particular application to the requests for instructions in wrongful death cases where the law is undergoing change.

The author has attempted to supply requests for instructions to fit special cases where the law is not entirely settled; these are undocumented and are placed in the footnotes pertaining to the particular subject (i.e. inflationary dimunition of values).

Sec. 12.2   Personal Injuries (General Prayer)[1]

Sample Instruction

If you shall find that the plaintiff is entitled to a verdict, then in arriving at the amount of the award, you should include the following items:

(1) his physical condition before the accident as compared with his present physical condition following the accident, and whether the same is permanent in nature and any disfigurement which he has sustained from the accident; and

(2) the physical pain and mental suffering which he has suffered and may suffer in the future; and

(3) the expenses for medical, hospital, nursing, and physical therapy care and attention, and for drugs and surgical appliances, and for transportation to obtain medical treatment, all of which he has incurred and may incur in the future; and

(4) the monies which he has lost and may lose in the future by way of wages, salaries, or other earnings.

---

1. You should omit those items from the prayer which do not apply to your case. For example, if there was no disfigurement, then reference to it should be omitted from item 1.

It has been held that allowance may be made "for past and future loss of enjoyment of the usual or familiar things of life." *Culley v. Pa. R. Co.*, 244 F.S. 710, 715 (1965, D.C. Del.) [applied Maryland law]; *McAlister v. Carl*, 233 Md. 446, 197 A. 2d 140, 146 (1964).

There is authority that discounting (present value of lost future earnings and medical and hospital expenses) does not apply to personal injury as contra-distinguished from death cases. *Hutzell v. Boyer*, 252 Md. 227, 249 A. 2d 449.

The majority of the states allow monies for pain and suffering on a daily basis. For the applicable law, see discussion in Sec. 13.8, infra.

All must result from the accident, and you should allow such a sum as will reasonably compensate the plaintiff for his injuries and damages.

See: *West Key Number System on*
Damages, Section 216 (6-10);
Corpus Juris Secundum on
Damages, Section 185 (4-8).

Sec. 12.3   Loss of Consortium[2]

Sample Instruction

If you shall find for the plaintiff (husband), then you may award to him the reasonable value of the society, companionship, and conjugal relationship with his wife, of which he has been deprived, and the present cash value of the society, companionship, and conjugal relationship with his wife of which he is reasonably certain to be deprived in the future.

See: *West Key Number System on*
Damages, Section 99; *Corpus*
Juris Secundum on Damages,
Section 1.

Sec. 12.4   Personal Property (Damages to Automobile)[3]

Sample Instruction

If you shall find a verdict for the plaintiff, in estimating the amount of money to which he is entitled on account of the damage to his automobile, you may consider the reasonable cost of repairs necessary to restore the property to the condition it was in immediately before the damage, and the reasonable value of loss of use pending repairs.

On the other hand, if you shall find that it is impossible or impractical to restore the damaged property to a condition equally as good as the condition existing immediately prior to the damage, the measure of damages is the

---

2. Taken from *Illinois Pattern Jury Instructions Civil I.P.I.,* Sec. 32.04, p. 171, citing: *Blair v. Bloomington & Normal Ry. Elec., etc.,* 131 Ill. App. 400 (3 Dist.) (1906). (Recently I.P.I. Second was published by West Publishing Company; the above reference and all future references herein are to the original edition).

Wife also may recover for loss of consortium due to injuries to husband. *Dini v. Naiditch,* 20 Ill. 2d 406, 170 N.E. 2d 881 (1960).

Some states require that the suit for loss of consortium be brought jointly by husband and wife, i.e. Maryland: *Deems v. Western Md. Ry. Co.,* 231 A. 2d 514, 247 Md. 95.

3. Based on form used in *Federal Jury Practice and Instructions* by Mathes & Devitt, Sec. 77.01 and 77.02, pps. 435, 436; *Restatement of Torts,* Sec. 928 (1939); *Taylor v. King,* 241 Md. 50, 213 A. 2d 504 (damages may include reasonable allowance for loss of use of vehicle).

difference between the market value of the property immediately before the damage and the market value immediately after the damage, plus the reasonable value of any necessary loss of use pending replacement of the property.

See: *West Key Number System on*
         Damages, Section 113; *Corpus*
         Juris Secundum on Damages,
         Sections 83 and 88.

Alternate Sample Instruction

If you shall find a verdict for the plaintiff, then as to the property damage to the automobile, you may award the lesser of two figures only, which are arrived at as follows:

One figure is the reasonable expense of necessary repair of the property plus the difference in the fair market value of the property immediately before the occurrence and its fair market value after the property is repaired.

The other figure is the difference between the fair market value of the property immediately before the occurrence and the fair market value of the unrepaired property immediately after the occurrence.

You may award as damages the lesser of these two figures only.

Sec. 12.5   Loss of Profits[4]

Sample Instruction

If you shall find for the plaintiff, in estimating the damages which he has sustained, you should take into consideration the value of the net earnings or profits lost from his business and the loss of net earnings or profits from his business reasonably certain to be lost in the future, all as a direct consequence of his injuries.

See: *West Key Number System on*
         Damages, Sections 95 and 99
         and other applicable sections;
         Corpus Juris Secundum on
         Damages, Sections 1, 71 and
         other applicable sections.

---

4. Based on *Illinois Pattern Jury Instruction–Civil,* Sec. 30.07, (original edition)/citing: *Douk Bros. Coal & Coke Co. v. Thil,* 228 Ill. 233, 241, 81 N.E. 857, 860 (1907); *Sprickerhoff v. B. & O. Railroad Co.,* 323 Ill. App. 340, 351, 55 N.E. 2d 532, 537-38 (4th Dist., 1944).

The present cash value of future losses of earnings and profits may be considered by the jury. See the authorities in this footnote supra. See also: *Federal Jury Practice and Instructions* by Mathes & Devitt, Sec. 76.12, pps. 433-34.

Sec. 12.6   Aggravation of Injuries

Comment

Aggravation means any circumstances or conduct accompanying or following an injury which increases its consequences but which is not an essential element of the injury itself.[5] Plaintiff is entitled to recover for aggravation of a pre-existing disease or disability.[6] The recovery may include only those effects which are directly traceable to the injury.[7] However, the fact that plaintiff had a tendency or predisposition toward a certain disease will not bar recovery for it if the accident triggered its maturation,[8] and the fact that plaintiff was weaker than the normal person and therefore more vulnerable to the injury should not lessen the amount of the verdict.[9]

Sample Instruction

If you shall find in favor of the plaintiff, in estimating the damages to which he may be entitled on account of his injuries, you are instructed that the defendant is not excused because the plaintiff may have had a pre-existing condition which made him peculiarly susceptible to the injury and disability of which he complains in this action due to the accident of April 9, 1965; and in arriving at your verdict, you are instructed that the defendant takes the plaintiff as he finds him at the time of the accident and you are not to deduct anything from the damages to which the plaintiff is entitled because of his pre-existing condition.[10]

Alternate Sample Instruction

If you shall find for the plaintiff, you are instructed that the defendant is liable for all of the ill effects which, considering the condition of health in which the plaintiff was when he received the injury, naturally and necessarily followed such injury. Defendant's liability is in no way lessened or affected by reason of the fact that the injuries would not have resulted had the

---

5. "Damages to Persons and Property" by Oleck, Part I, Sec. 186, p. 303.

6. *Starrett v. E. Tex. M. Fr. Lines,* 150 Tex. 12, 236 S.W. 2d 776; *U.S. v. Fotoponlas,* 180 F. 2d 631 (C.A. 9, Calif.).

7. Annot. 48 LRA (N.S.) 120, 121, 124, 125.

8. *Peterson v. Goodyear Tire & Rubber Co.* (Md., 1969), 254 Md. 137, 254 A. 2d 198; *Coca Cola Bottling Works v. Catron,* 186 Md. 156, 46 A. 2d 303.

9. *Watford v. Morse,* 202 Va. 605, 608, 118 S.E. 2d 681, 683. See also: *Corpus Juris Secundum,* Damages, Sec. 21 page 658, citing: *Griswald v. Chic. Ry. Co.,* 170 N.E. 845, 339 Ill. 911; and *Armour & Co. v Tomlin,* 60 S.W. 2d 204.

10. Based on: *Peterson v. Goodyear Tire & Rubber Co.* (Md., 1969), 254 A. 2d 198, 254 Md. 137, citing: *Baltimore City Passenger Railway Company v. Kemp,* 61 Md. 74, 81 (1883); *Coca Cola Bottling Works v. Catron,* 46 A. 2d 303, 186 Md. 156.

plaintiff been in good health, or that they were aggravated and rendered more difficult to cure by reason of the fact that he was not in good health.

And if the jury believes from the preponderance of the evidence that the plaintiff, at the time of the accident, was not in good health, or if he was suffering from a pre-existing disability, and that this condition, if any, made any injuries he may have received in the accident more severe, or more aggravated, or more difficult to cure, then, if he is entitled to recover in this action, he may recover for such additional aggravation and difficulty resulting from the accident, but not for any pre-existing disability.[11]

> See: *West Key Number System on*
> *Damages,* Sections 33 and 213;
> *Corpus Juris Secundum on*
> *Damages,* Sections 21, 58 and
> 184.

Sec. 12.6A   Psychiatric and Emotional Damage

Comment

Generally speaking, there is legal authority to support psychiatric and emotional injuries as a factor to be considered in assessing damages in torts. 13 Buffalo L.R. 339-353 (1964); *Ferrara v. Galluchio,* 5 N.Y. 2d 16, 21, 152 N.E. 2d 249, 252, 176 N.Y.S. 2d 996 (1958). See also *Knierim v. Izzo,* 22 Ill. 2d 73, 174 N.E. 2d 157 (1961); *Restatement of Torts,* Sec. 47 (b) (1934). The older authorities required that the mental anguish be accompanied by physical manifestations, *Orlo v. Conn. Co.,* 218 Conn. 231, 21 A. 2d 402, 405 (1941), and by physical impact, even though slight *20 Mich. L.R.* 497, 504 (1922); *Comstock v. Wilson,* 257 N.Y. 231, 237, 177 N.E. 431, 433 (1931). The new trend seems to favor liberalization of coverage, even in a case of fright without impact. *Battala v. State,* 10 N.Y. 2d 237, 176 N.E. 2d 729, 219 N.Y.S. 2d 34 (1961). See *Zeigler v. The F Street Corp.,* 248 Md. 223, 235 A. 2d 703 (1967). But see *Kalina v. General Hospital,* 31 Misc. 2d 18, 220 N.Y.S. 2d 773 (Sup. Ct. N.Y. 1967), aff'd. 18 A.D. 757, 235 N.Y. 2d 808, aff'd. 13 N.Y. 2d 1023, 195 N.E. 2d 303, which limits this new theory.

A sample request for such an instruction appears in this footnote.[11a]

---

11. Based on sample instruction in *Virginia Practice,* Volume 1, by Doubles, Emrich & Merhige, Sec. 23.04, page 151, which cites: *Watford v. Morse,* 202 Va. 605, 608, 118 S.E. 2d 681, 683; and *Ragsdale v. Jones,* 202 Va. 278, 282, 117 S.E. 2d 114, 118.

11a.   Sample Instruction

If you shall find for the plaintiff, then in estimating the damages to which he may be entitled, you may consider the permanent psychiatric and emotional injuries which he

Sec. 12.7   Mathematical Certainty Not Required.[12]

Sample Instruction

If you shall find for the plaintiff, in estimating the damages, you are instructed that the burden is on the plaintiff to prove his damages by a preponderance of the evidence or with reasonable certainty, but he is not required to prove with mathematical precision the exact sum of his damage, but only that he furnish evidence of sufficient facts and circumstances to permit an intelligible and probable estimate thereof.

> See: *West Key Number System on*
> *Damages,* Section 163 (4) and
> Section 184; *Corpus Juris*
> *Secundum on Damages,* Sections
> 144 and 162.

Sec. 12.8   Collateral Benefits Received by Plaintiff Not Deductible

Comment

This subject involves the collateral source doctrine.[13] Defined, it means that a benefit from any source (i.e. weekly disability payments from a private insurance policy owned by the plaintiff), which is received by a plaintiff on account of an injury, with which benefit the defendant has no connection, will not mitigate the amount of damages plaintiff can recover against the defendant in a negligence suit. While there is a spirited conflict between legal scholars on the subject, a majority rule in the United States appears to have emerged favoring the application of the doctrine. The effect is to bar the admission into evidence and to bar consideration by the court

---

has sustained as a direct consequence of the accident and award him such a sum as you shall find to be fair and reasonable for such injuries.

12. Based on *Virginia Practice,* Volume 1, by Doubles, Emrich & Merhige, Sec. 23.02, citing: *Gwaltney v. Reed,* 196 Va. 505, 84 S.E. 2d 101, 102; and *Barnes v. Graham Va. Quarries Inc.,* 204 Va. 414, 420, 132 S.E. 2d 395, 398.

13. For a brief but current discussion on the subject, see "Personal Injury Damages," Practising Law Institute, New York City (1970), at pages 187-200 on "The Collateral Source Doctrine" by Dorsey, Powell, Goldstein, Frazer & Murphy, Atlanta, Georgia.

For a general discussion see: *Harper & James Law of Torts,* Volume 2, Sec. 25.22, page 1343; *McCormick on Damages,* Sec. 310 (1935); *Damages In Personal Injury And Wrongful Death Cases*—Schreiber, Practising Law Institute (1935).

or jury of collateral benefits to mitigate damages which may be assessed against the defendant on account of his tort.[14]

Sample Instruction

In estimating the damages to which plaintiff is entitled, you may award him the full damages to which he has suffered without deduction on account of receipt by him during his disability of salary or pension, or medical or hospital expenses, or of employment benefits, or of social legislation benefits, or of insurance proceeds from a policy or policies which he owned.[15]

Sec. 12.9   Punitive Damages

Comment

Punitive damages, also known as exemplary damages, are awarded over and above the compensatory damages to which the plaintiff is entitled for his injuries and losses, as a punishment to the defendant.[16] Such is awarded where the injury was caused by willfulness, wantonness, oppression, malice, or violence, which is deemed to aggravate plaintiff's injury.[17] It is

---

14. It has been held to constitute prejudicial error if such evidence is allowed in, either by testimony or argument. *Sinovich v. Erie R. Co.*, 230 F. 2d 658 (3 C.A., 1956); *Kickam v. Carter*, 335 S.W. 2d 83 (Mo., 1960). However, there are "back-door" devices used to usher in such evidence (i.e. inconsistent statements made by plaintiff in obtaining private insurance benefits). Courts have discretion and must weigh the admissibility of such evidence against the potential prejudice to plaintiff's case. *77 Harvard Law Review*, 741, 746.

15. Based on the following cases:

(a) As to salary:—*Campbell v. Sutliff*, 193 Wis. 370, 214 N.W. 374. This represents the weight of authority, but not he universal rule. See e.g. *Ephland v. Mo. Pac. Ry. Co.*, 57 Mo. App. 147 (1894). See *Harper & James "The Law of Torts"*, Sec. 25.22.

(b) As to pension:—*Wachtel v. Leonard*, 45 Ga. App. 14, 163 S.E. 512 (1932). See Harper & James, supra, Sec. 25.22.

(c) As to medical and hospital expenses:—*Plank v. Summers*, 203 Md. 552, 102 A. 2d 262; *Denver & R.G.R. Co. v. Lorentzen*, 79 F. 291 (8 C.A., 1897). There is not uniformity on this rule. See e.g. *31 Yale Law Journal*, 776, note 31 (1922) and *Restatement of Torts*, Sec. 920 (e), 924 (c), (f) (1939). See Harper & James, supra, Sec. 25.22.

(d) As to employment benefits:—*Nashville C & St. Louis Ry. v Miller*, 120 Ga. 453, 47 S.E. 959 (1904); *128 A.L.R.* 686 (1940); *McCormick on Damages*, Sec. 87 (1935). There is not uniformity. See e.g. *Drinkwater v. Dinsinore*, 80 N.Y. 390 (1880). But if reimbursement to employer occurs, then the doctrine does apply. *Landon v. U.S.*, 197 F. 2d 128, 131 (2 C.A., 1952).

(e) As to Social Legislation benefits:—*U.S. v. Price*, 288 F. 2d 448 (4 C.A., 1961). There is sharp disagreement whether this type of benefit should be included in the collateral benefit doctrine. See e.g. *Restatement of Torts*, Sec. 924, comment f. at p. 637 (1939); *DeLeo v. Dolinsky*, 129 Conn. 203, 27 A. 2d 126 (1942).

(f) As to insurance proceeds:—*Bradburn v. G. & W.R. Co.*, LR 10 Ex. 1 (1874); *Roth v. Chaltos*, 97 Conn. 282, 116 A. 332 (1922); *Perrott v. Shearer*, 17 Mich. 47, 56 (1868). See Harper & James, supra, Sec. 25.22.

16. See "Damages To Persons and Property" by Oleck, Part I, Sec. 29, page 27, citing: *Zedd v. Jenkins*, 194 Va. 704, 74 S.E. 2d 791.

17. *Gila Water Co. v. Gila Land & Cattle Co.*, 30 Ariz. 569, 249 P. 751.

considered as a deterrent to prospective offenders.[18] Before there can be an award for punitive damages, the jury must first find that the plaintiff is entitled to compensatory damages.[19]

Sample Instruction

If the jury shall find from a preponderance of the evidence that the plaintiff is entitled to a verdict for actual or compensatory damages and should further find that the act or omission of the defendant, which proximately caused actual injury or damage to the plaintiff, was maliciously, or wantonly, or oppressively done, then the jury may, if in the exercise of discretion they unanimously choose to so do, add to the award of actual damages such amount as the jury shall unanimously agree to be proper, as punitive or exemplary damages.

Maliciously done means prompted by ill will or spite or grudge.

Wantonly done means done in reckless or callous disregard of or indifference to the rights of others.

Oppressively done means done in a way or manner which injures or damages or otherwise violates the rights of another person with unnecessary harshness or severity, as by misuse or abuse of authority or power, or by taking advantage of some weakness, or disability, or misfortune of another person.[20]

> See: *West Key Number System on Damages,*
> Sections 87 (1) and 91 (1); *Corpus*
> *Juris Secundum on Damages,* Sections
> 117 and 123.

Sec. 12.10   Wrongful Death of Husband

Comment

The various states have a statute providing for pecuniary loss of benefits by the surviving beneficiaries, i.e. spouse (Lord Campbell's Act—Fatal Accidents Act, 1846 9 & 10 Vict. Chap. 93). Provision is made also, frequently by a separate statute, for recovery on account of out-of-pocket expenses caused by the death (i.e. hospital, medical, funeral and burial), and for pain and suffering endured between the accident and death; this suit is usually brought in the name of the personal representative of the estate, who

---

18. *Scott v. Donald,* 165 U.S. 58, 17 S. Ct. 265, 41 L. Ed. 632.
19. *Federal Jury Practice and Instructions* by Mathes & Devitt, Sec. 76.11, pages 430 and 431 [original edition].
20. Based on sample instruction in *Federal Jury Practice and Instructions,* by Mathes & Devitt, Sec. 76.11, page 430 [original edition].

is appointed by the court.[21] It is particularly important to study your own state's survival death statute, not only to conform your suit to its demands, but to comply with its time limit in filing the suit. Instructions for recovery covering both actions follow.

In proving pecuniary losses adequately, it is frequently advisable to employ the services of an economic expert. A discussion of this subject and of the admissibility of such evidence appears in Sec. 9.1 et seq., supra.

There is authority that the value of deceased's services about the home may be considered in arriving at an award. Speiser's "Recovery For Wrongful Death," Section 3:36, citing: *Pennell v. Baltimore & Ohio Railroad Company* (1957), 13 Ill. App. 2nd 433, 142 N.E. 2nd 497 (decedent's handiness as a workman around the house; F.E.L.A.), overruled on other grounds. *Smith v. Ill. Central R. Co.* (1960), 29 Ill. App. 2nd 168, 172 N.E. 2nd 803. *Kroger v. Safranek* (1957), 165 Neb. 636, 87 N.W. 2nd 221 (value of services in tending the garden, maintaining the home, etc., even though there is no evidence of their monetary value in the record). *Baker v. Salvation Army* (1940), 91 N.H. 1, 12 A. 2nd 514 (66-year-old had attended to all household duties). This has particular application to the loss of use of a wife's or mother's services. *Merrill v. United Air Lines Inc.* (1959, D.C. N.Y.), 177 F.S. 704; *Lithgow v. Hamilton* (1954, Fla.), 69 So. 2nd 776. See Speiser's "Recovery for Wrongful Death," Sec. 9:8.

The probabilities of future increases in earnings may be considered also (see footnotes 22 and 23 of this chapter).

There is authority that inflationary values in the future may be considered in increasing the amount of the award. See Sec. 13.9, footnote 13, infra.

The value of the loss of the spouse's companionship, comfort, and protection is allowed in some states (see footnote 22 of this chapter).

For further discussion, including discounting and consumption expenses as deductions, see Secs. 12.15 and 13.9, infra.

A. Widow's Pecuniary Loss for Death of Husband

Sample Instruction

If you shall find a verdict in favor of the widow, in estimating the damages to be allowed to the widow for benefits lost as a consequence of the death of her husband in the accident, you may consider the pecuniary loss or the loss in money which she has sustained and will sustain in the future by reason of

---

21. For a detailed discussion on survival-death act statutes and their interpretations in the different states, see Speiser's *Recovery for Wrongful Death,* published by The Lawyers Cooperative Publishing Company, Rochester, New York, Sec. 3:1 et seq. Speiser points out that there are sharp differences in these statutues in the various states.

the negligent killing of her husband and, in this connection, you may consider what would have been the reasonable possibilities of the continuance of the joint lives of the decedent and his widow but for his untimely death in this accident.[22]

> See: *West Key Number System on*
> *Death,* Section 104 (6); *Corpus*
> *Juris Secundum on Death,*
> Section 90.

B. Accumulations and Augmentations in Earnings, Savings, and Investments

Comment

There is legal authority that the beneficiaries are entitled to the benefit of

---

22. Based on holdings in *Chesapeake & Potomac Telephone Company of Baltimore City v. State T/U Carry,* 124 Md. 527, 93 A. 11; *Jennings v. U.S.* (4 C.A.), 178 F.S. 516, 291 F. 2d 880, 207 F.S. 143, 318 F. 2d 718. See also: *Illinois Pattern Jury Instructions,* Sec. 31.01 [original edition].

The jury should be allowed to consider the loss of future pension and social security retirement benefits. *Gillard v. Lancashire & yorkshire Ry. Co.,* (1948 Eng.), 12 L.T. 356, Speiser's *Recovery for Wrongful Death,* Sec. 3:14.

The jury should be allowed to consider the increased earnings and promotions the deceased would have enjoyed had he lived. See: *Jennings v. U.S.,* supra; *15 Am. Jur., Damages,* Sec. 93 and 315; *22 Am. Jur. 2nd Damages,* Sec. 298; "Loss of Earning Capacity in Personal Injury and Wrongful Death Cases" by Iglehart, Daily Record Newspaper, Baltimore, Maryland, July 6, 1970. On the other hand, it has been held that the jury may consider the normal diminution in earnings with aging *25 C.J.S.,* Sec. 87, n. 967.

In addition to pecuniary loss, some states permit recovery to the widow for mental anguish, emotional pain and suffering, loss of society, companionship, comfort, protection and marital care; and to the surviving children, recovery is allowed for loss of parental care, attention, advice, counsel, training, guidance or education (i.e. Maryland, Article 67–*Maryland Code Annotated,* Sec. 4).

Some states fix a maximum amount which may be recovered; consult your own state's code.

The present value of future earnings may be considered in arriving at the total pecuniary loss. (See *Federal Jury Practice and Instructions* by Mathes & Devitt, Sec. 76.12, pages 433-34) [original edition]. See also Sec. 13.9, infra.

There is authority which indicates that in arriving at pecuniary loss by the widow, any savings in income tax liability that the deceased would have incurred might be considered in favor of the defendant. *So. Pac. Co. v. Guthrie* (1951) (Calif. 9 C.A.), 186 F. 2d 926, cert. den. 341 U.S. 904, 71 S. Ct. 614. *Floyd v. Fruit Industries Inc.,* 144 Conn. 659 (1957); *Sipes v. Michigan Central Railway Co.,* 231 Mich. 404, 204 N.W. 84. On the other hand, it has been held that an award should not be decreased by reason of the fact that there are no income taxes to pay on it. *25 C.J.S.,* Sec. 87 page 967; *Jennings v. U.S.,* supra.

The majority rule seems to hold that future income taxes are too speculative and should not be deducted from an award. *Stokes v. U.S.* (1964) (2 C.A. N.Y.), 144 F. 2d 82; Speiser's *Recovery for Wrongful Death,* Sec. 8:13.

The Internal Revenue Code exempts monies received by way of damages for personal injuries, whether by suit or agreement. *28 U.S.C.A.,* Sec. 154; *IRC* 1954, Sec. 154.

The courts differ on whether counsel should be permitted even to mention income taxes in their closing arguments. Speiser's *Recovery for Wrongful Death,* Sec. 8:14.

For life expectancy and work career expectancy tables, see on this subject, Appendix A and Appendix B of this book.

probable increases, accumulations, and augmentations in earnings, savings, and investments had the deceased survived (see this chapter, footnote 23).

A sample request for such an instruction appears in this footnote.[23]

C. Household Services

Comment

Some courts hold that this is an item which may be considered to increase the amount of the award. See Sec. 12.10, "Comment", supra.

A sample request for such an instruction appears in this footnote.[24]

D. Inflationary Diminution of Values

Comment

There is authority that the diminution of the value of lost future earnings by inflationary forces occurring in the future may be considered and allowance made for it by adding to the aggregate loss sustained by the widow (see Sec. 13.9, footnote 13, infra).

A sample request for such an instruction appears in this footnote.[25]

---

23.   Sample Instruction

> If you shall find for the plaintiff, then in estimating the damages to which the widow is entitled, you may consider the value of probable future increases, accumulations and augmentations in earnings, savings and investments of the deceased husband had he not met his untimely death.

See Speiser's *Recovery for Wrongful Death*, Sec. 3:35, p. 190.

In recent years wrongful death actions involving persons of wealth are more frequent, as for example from airplane accidents. Hence, more attention must be given to accumulations and augmentations which the decedent would have acquired in his estate in increased earnings, savings, investments, etc., had he lived and which have been lost to the estate. There are numerous authorities on this point: *O'Toole v. U.S.* (1957, 3 C.A. Del.), 242 F. 2d 308 [it is error not to allow for accumulations in the estate of deceased husband who earned $250,000 per year]; *Martin v. Atlantic Coast Line R. Co.* (1959, 5 C.A. Fla.), 268 F. 2d 397, 91 A.L.R. 2d 472 [it was error not to allow for anticipated increases in earnings of deceased railroad employee]; *National Airlines Inc. v. Stiles* (1959, 5 C.A. La.) 268 F. 2d 400, cert. den. 361 U.S. 885, 4 L. Ed. 2d 121, reh. den. 361 U.S. 926, 80 S. Ct. 291 [widow entitled to lost accumulations to estate of deceased husband who was a lawyer]; *Circle Line Sightseeing Yachts Inc. v. Storebeck* (1963, 2 C.A. N.Y.), 325 F. 2d 338 [damages may be extended to the property or income which was devoted wholly or partly to the aid of the beneficiaries during deceased's lifetime]. See also: *91 A.L.R. 2d* 477 for state court decisions; *N.Y. Pattern Jury Instructions—Civil P.J.I.* 2:320 for other pattern instruction and legal explanation.

24.   Sample Instruction

> Should you find in favor of the plaintiff, then in estimating the damages to which she is entitled, you may consider as a factor in such award the value on an annual basis of the household services which were rendered by the husband in the nature, for example, of upkeep, maintenance and repair of their home, based on the evidence introduced about such services, and you may project this over the years in which he would have contributed those services, if he had lived, and make your award accordingly.

25.   Sample Instruction

> If you find for the plaintiff, then in estimating the damages to be awarded her, you may

E. Companionship Loss

Comment

Some states allow as an item of damage the loss of the deceased spouse's companionship, comfort, and protection; some states do so by virtue of statute and some on the basis of common law (see this chapter, footnotes 22 and 27).

A sample request for such an instruction appears in this footnote.[26]

F. Fringe Benefits

Comment

There is authority that future lost fringe benefits may be considered in the award of damages (see this chapter, footnote 22).

A sample request for such an instruction appears in this footnote.[26a]

G. Increases in Earnings and Promotions

Comment

There is authority that probable future increases in earnings and promotions may be considered in the award of damages (see this chapter, footnote 22).

A sample request for such an instruction appears in this footnote.[26b]

---

consider the inflationary forces in the future which will operate to diminish the value of the income which has been lost by the widow due to her husband's untimely death and to which income she is entitled as damages, and you may add a certain percentage to such lost income as you shall find fair and reasonable to offset the loss due to future inflation.

26.   Sample Instruction

If you shall find for the plaintiff, then in estimating the damages to which she is entitled, you may consider as a factor in such an award, the value of the mental anguish, emotional pain and suffering, the loss of society, companionship, comfort, protection and marital care which the widow has and will sustain as a consequence of the untimely death of her husband.

26a.   Sample Instruction

If you shall find for the plaintiff, then in estimating the damages to which the widow is entitled, you may consider the value of the fringe benefits (i.e. health and welfare, pension and vacation benefits) which have been lost to her on account of the untimely death of her husband.

26b.   Sample Instruction

If you shall find for the plaintiff, then in estimating the damages to which the widow is entitled, you may consider the value of probable future increases in earnings and probable future promotions which the deceased husband would have enjoyed except for his untimely death.

Sec. 12.11   Wrongful Death of Wife

Comment

[See discussion under Sec. 12.10, supra, "Wrongful Death of Husband."]

A. Sample Instruction of Widower's
Pecuniary Loss for Death of Wife

If you shall find a verdict in favor of the widower, in estimating the damages to be allowed to the widower for benefits lost as a consequence of the death of his wife in the accident, you may consider the pecuniary loss or the loss in money which he has sustained and will sustain by reason of the negligent killing of his wife, and in this connection, you may consider what would have been the reasonable possibilities of the continuance of the joint lives of the decedent and her widower but for her untimely death in this accident.[27]

[Note important discussion under footnotes 22 and 23 infra on legal ramifications pertaining to death of a spouse.]

> See: *West Key Number System on
> Death*, Section 104 (6); *Corpus
> Juris Secundum on Death*,
> Section 90.

B. Accumulations and Augmentations in
Earnings, Savings and Investments

[See Comment, Sec. 12.10 B, supra.]
A sample request for such an instruction appears in this footnote.[28]

C. Substitute Housekeeper and Mother

Comment

There is authority that a widower is entitled to damages to pay for a

---

27. Based on *Illinois Pattern Jury Instructions*, Sec. 31.01 [original edition]. Some states permit as an item of damages the value of the loss of the deceased spouse's society (see note 22 supra). However, there is authority that even without specific statutory directive, this item may be allowed if the society of the decedent was valuable as "services." *Sipes v. Michigan Central Ry. Co.*, 231 Mich. 404, 204 N.W. 84.

There is authority that where the death results in loss of a wife and mother who was the home member of the work team, a pecuniary loss exists which is recoverable, even though she was not employed. See *25A Corpus Juris Secundum*. Sec. 26 A, citing: *Cordts v. Vanderbilt*, 147 A. 464, 7 N.J. Misc. 856.

28. See footnote 23 supra.

person or persons to take over the work of housekeeper which his widow performed before her death, and for the expense of living persons to care for and to supervise their infant children since his wife's passing (see this chapter, footnote 27).

A sample request for such an instruction appears in this footnote.[29]

D. Companionship Loss

Comment

Some authorities, whether by statute or common law, allow as a damage item the value of the loss of the deceased spouse's society and companionship (See this chapter, footnotes 22 and 27).

A general sample request for such an instruction appears in this chapter at footnote 26.

E. Inflationary Diminution in Values

See Sec. 12.10 D, supra, for discussion and sample instruction.

F. Fringe Benefits

See Sec. 12.10 F, supra, for discussion and sample instruction.

G. Increases In Earnings and Promotions

See Sec. 12.10 G, supra, for discussion and sample instruction.

Sec. 12.12   Personal Representative's Claim for Death

Comment

The personal representative is entitled to sue for the out-of-pocket expenses and the pain and suffering of the deceased caused by his death (see Comment, Sec. 12.10, supra).

---

29.   Sample Instruction

If you shall find for the plaintiff, then in estimating the damages to which the widower is entitled, you may take into consideration the expenses to which he has been and will be put in order to pay others to assume the housekeeping duties which his deceased wife performed during the remainder of years of their joint lives had she survived, and for the care and supervision of the child (or children) of their home until they reached age 21 or were sooner emancipated.

Sample Instruction

If you shall find for the plaintiff, then in the claim by Jane Smith, as Administratrix of the Estate of John Smith, Deceased, in estimating the damages, you are to consider the medical, hospital, and drug expenses incurred as a consequence of the accident, which caused John Smith's death, and the funeral and burial expenses, and the expenses for a suitable tombstone or marker for the remains of the deceased, and you are to consider the pain and suffering which the deceased endured from the time of the accident up until the time of his death, all as a consequence of the said accident, and you are to allow such an amount as in your opinion will be fair and just compensation for such damages.[30]

> See: *West Key Number System on*
> *Death,* Sections 82 and 84;
> *Corpus Juris Secundum on*
> *Death,* Section 98 et seq.

Sec. 12.13   Child's Losses for Death of Parent

Comment

In the case of wrongful death of a parent, children are entitled to receive the pecuniary value of services from the parent which they would have received if the parent had not been killed.[31] In many states, pecuniary value is interpreted to cover also the value of the loss of the parental advice and training he otherwise would have had.[32]

Sample Instruction

If you shall find for the plaintiff, in estimating the damages which the minor, James Smith, has and will sustain as a result of the death of his father, John Smith, you may consider what pecuniary losses he has suffered and will suffer as a consequence of the negligent killing of his father, and the loss of the comforts, education, and position in society which he would have enjoyed if his father had lived and retained his income, and if he had

---

30. Based on *Jennings v. U.S.* (4 C.A.), 178 F.S. 516, 291 F. 2d 880, 207 F.S. 143, 318 F. 2d 718. Some states fix a maximum for the items of funeral and burial expenses and tombstone.

31. Speiser's *Recovery for Wrongful Death,* Sec. 3:36, citing: Cal.—*Sumrall v. Butler* (1955), 102 Cal. App 2d 515, 227 P. 2d 881; Minn.—*Bolinger v. St. Paul & D.R. Co.* (1887), 36 Minn. 418, 31 N.W. 856; *Thevenot v. Sieber* (1962 D.C. N.Y.), 204 F.S. 15; *Continental Bus System Inc. v. Biggers* (1959) (Tex. Civ. App.), 322 S.W. 2d (child may recover the value of father's training, advice and education).

32. See the *Biggers* case, supra, footnote 31 (Texas). In Maryland, this is provided by statute (Article 67, *Maryland Code Annotated,* Sec. 4).

continued to form part of his family, and the said prospects of damages are to be estimated up to the time when the minor, James Smith, reached his majority, namely the age of 21, or until he married.[33]

> See: *West Key Number System*
> *on Death,* Sections 85, 88
> and 89; *Corpus Juris*
> *Secundum on Death,* Sections
> 100, 101, 104 and 107.

Alternate Sample Instruction

If you shall find for the plaintiff, in estimating the damages which the minor, James Smith, has and will sustain as a result of the death of his father, John Smith, you may consider what pecuniary losses he has suffered and will suffer as a consequence of the negligent killing of his father, and you may consider the accumulations and augmentations of his parents' estate which he has lost by way of inheritance, and the loss of the comforts, education, and position in society which he would have enjoyed if his father had lived and retained his income, and if he had continued to form part of his family, and the said prospects of damages are to be estimated up to the time when the minor, James Smith, reached his majority, namely the age of 21, or until he married. [34]

A. Inflationary Diminution of Values

See Sec. 12.10 D., supra, for discussion and sample instruction.

B. Fringe Benefits

See Sec. 12.10 F, supra, for discussion and sample instruction.

C. Increases in Earnings and Promotions

See Sec. 12.10 G, supra, for discussion and sample instruction.

D. Accumulations and Augmentations in Earnings, Savings and Investments

See Sec. 12.10 B, supra, for discussion and sample instruction.

---

33. Based on the following cases:—*Chesapeake & Potomac Telephone Company of Baltimore City v. State, etc.,* 124 Md. 527, 93 A. 11; *Jennings v. U.S.* (4 C.A.), 178 F.S. 516, 291 F. 2d 880, 207 F.S. 143, 318 F. 2d 718.
 Some states allow the damage item of loss of parental care, guidance and attention (i.e. Maryland—Article 67, *Maryland Code Annotated,* Sec. 4).
 34. See footnote 23 supra.

Sec. 12.14   Parents' Losses for Death of Child

Comment

Many states hold that for the wrongful death of a child, the parents may recover the pecuniary value that the services of the child would have meant to the parents up to the time he reached 21 or was sooner emancipated.[35] Some of these same authorities allow for the deduction of the expenses that would have been incurred in the rearing of the child. Many states hold that the parents may recover benefits which, based on evidence, the parents might have reasonably expected after the child reached his majority.[36] Some states are allowing, in addition to pecuniary losses, the value of the mental pain and suffering of the parents.[37] Some states allow the parents to recover for the loss of an adult child, after his minority has terminated.[38] It is self-apparent that the law is in a state of ferment in respect to recovery for a child's wrongful death. There is a tendency to relax the harshness of the old rule that recovery is limited to the bare anticipated pecuniary losses only during minority. Alternate sample instructions will be presented to conform to these different state holdings, and the lawyer may choose the one which conforms with his state's law (or choose a more progressive one in order to advance the law in his state by the process of change by common law rather than by the cumbersome process of legislative change).

A. Sample Instruction

If you shall find for the plaintiffs, in estimating the damages to which the parents are entitled, you are to consider the services, earnings, and wages of the deceased minor that were lost and will be lost to the parents up until he would have reached the age of 21 years or up until the time he would have

---

35. Speiser's *Recovery for Wrongful Death*, Sec. 3:36; *14 A.L.R. 2d 485.* Many states hold that the expense of rearing the child is a deductible item. *Allen v. Moore* (1938), 109 Vt. 405, 199 A. 257. Some states do not make the deduction. See *State T/U Parr v. Board of County Commissioners* (1955) (Md.), 207 Md. 91, 113 A. 2d 397.

36. Speiser, supra, Sec. 4:21.

37. Speiser, supra, Sec. 4:16-4:20. Some states arrive at it by statute, i.e. Arkansas, Florida and Kansas, and other states by common law, i.e. Louisiana, Virginia, and West Virginia. See e.g. *Norfolk & W. Ry. Co. v. Cheatwood's Admr.* (1905), 103 Va. 356, 49 S.E. 489.

In the recent case of *Wycko v. Gnotke,* 105 N.W. 2d 118 (Sup. Ct. Mich. 1960), an award of $14,000 was allowed for the unlawful death of a fourteen year old boy, plus $979 funeral expenses. The court allowed for the "investment value" of the child (i.e. the amount spent for his birth, care, maintenance and education prior to death) and for loss of the child's companionship which was referred to as "value of the life."

See also Vols. 26-27 NACCA L.J. 206-14.

38. Speiser, supra, Sec. 4:34.

been otherwise emancipated from the control of his parents, all as a consequence of the death of the minor, and you shall allow such an amount as will be fair and just compensation for such damages suffered by the parents. [39]

> See: *West Key Number System on Death*, Sections 85, 88 and 89; *Corpus Juris Secundum on Death*, Sections 100, 101, 104 and 107.

B. Alternate Sample Instruction

If you shall find for the plaintiffs, in estimating the damages to which the parents are entitled, you are to consider the services, earnings, and wages of the deceased minor that were lost and will be lost to the parents up until he would have reached the age of 21 years or up until the time he would have been otherwise emancipated from the control of his parents, and you may consider what amounts the parents might have reasonably expected to receive by inheritance from the child, all as a consequence of the death of the minor, and you shall allow such an amount as will be fair and just compensation for such damages suffered by the parents. [40]

C. Alternate Sample Instruction

If you shall find for the plaintiffs, in estimating the damages to which the parents are entitled, you are to consider the services, earnings, and wages of the deceased minor that were lost and will be lost to the parents up until he would have reached the age of 21 years or up until the time he would have been otherwise emancipated from the control of his parents, and you may consider the services, earnings, and wages of the deceased minor that will be lost to the parents after the minor would have reached the age of 21, provided you find from the evidence that there was a reasonable basis for the parents to have expected support from the minor after he attained age 21. [41]

D. Alternate Sample Instruction

If you find for the plaintiffs, in estimating the damages you are to

---

39. Based on *State T/U Parr v. Board of County Commissioners* (Md.), 113 A. 2d 397.

40. Based on holdings in *Connaughton v. Sun Printing & Pub. Assn.* (1902), 73 App. Div. 316, 76 N.Y.S. 755. See also: *New York Pattern Jury Instructions–Civil* (1965), p. 519.

41. Based on the holding in *U.S. v. Sabine Towing Co. v. Brennan* (1936 C.A.I. Texas), 85 F. 2d 478, cert. den. 299 U.S. 599, 57 S. Ct. 191, reh. den. 299 U.S. 624, 57 S. Ct. 234 (FELA). See discussion in Speiser, supra, Sec. 4:21.

consider, in addition to the strictly pecuniary losses which the parents will have sustained, the grief and anguish which the untimely death of their child caused them.[42]

E. Alternate Sample Instruction

If you find for the plaintiffs, in estimating the damages you are to consider, in addition to the strictly pecuniary losses which the parents will have sustained, their loss of the comfort, society, companionship, and protection of the minor.[43]

Sec. 12.15   Mortality Tables and Discounting– Death of Husband

Comment

Use of mortality tables is advisable in wrongful death cases.[44]

For mortality tables, see Appendix A, infra.

Also, the lost future earnings are to be discounted to arrive at the present value of these future earnings. In other words, it is as though a sum of money were set aside now by the jury verdict to create an annuity which will produce these future earnings with regularity and periodically.[45] See also discussion in Sec. 13.9, infra.

For discount tables, see Appendix C, infra.

Sample Instruction[46]

If you find for the plaintiff, then in assessing damages, you may consider how long the widow (and next-of-kin)[47] would be likely to have received pecuniary benefits from the decedent, considering how long he was likely to have lived and how long she (or they) was likely to live.

According to a table of mortality in evidence, the life expectancy of a person (the decedent) aged . . . years is . . . years. That of a person (the widow) aged . . . years is . . . years. These figures are not conclusive. They

---

42. Based on the holding in *Norfolk & W. Ry. Co. v. Cheatwood's Admr.* (1905), 103 Va. 356, 49 S.E. 489; *Black v. Peerless Elite Laundry Co.* (1933), 113 W.Va. 828, 169 S.E. 447. See discussion in Speiser, supra, Sec. 4:21.

43. Based on the holding in *Fuentes v. Tucker* (1947), 31 Cal. 2d 1, 187 Pac. 2d 752. See discussion in Speiser, supra, Sec. 4:18.

44. *Calvert v. Springfield Electric Light & Power Co.*, 236 Ill. 290, 83 N.E. 184, 14 L.R.A. N.S. 782, 12 Ann. Cas. 423 (1907); *Allendorf v. Elgin J. & E.R. Co.*, 8 Ill. 2d 164, 133 N.E. 2d 288 (1956), cert. den. 352 U.S. 833, 77 S. Ct. 99, 1 L. Ed. 2d 53, reh. den. 352 U.S. 937, 77 S. Ct. 219, 1 L. Ed. 2d 170 (1956).

45. *Allendorf v. Elgin J. & E.R. Co.*, see footnote 44 supra.

46. Based on *Illinois Pattern Jury Instructions, Civil,* Sec. 34.05 (original edition).

47. Omit it if not applicable to your case.

are the average life expectancies of persons who have reached those ages. They may be considered by you in connection with other evidence relating to the probable life expectancies of the decedent and his widow (and his next-of-kin), including evidence of the decedent's occupation, health, habits, and activities, bearing in mind that some persons live longer and some persons less than the average.

In calculating the amount of these pecuniary benefits, you should determine the then present cash value, which means the sum of money needed now, which together with what that sum will earn in the future, will equal the amounts of the pecuniary benefits at the times in the future when they would have been received.

> See: *West Key Number System*
> *on Death,* Section 65;
> *Corpus Juris Secundum on*
> *Death,* Sections 82, 83 and
> 85.

Sec. 12.16   Comparative Negligence Instruction
(i.e. F.E.L.A.; Jones Act Cases)

Comment

The comparative negligence doctrine permits plaintiff a recovery in tort even though both plaintiff and defendant were negligent. However, the amount of the verdict should reflect the apportionment of negligence. For example, if plaintiff's negligence was 50 percent responsible for the accident and the defendant was 50 percent accountable for it, then plaintiff would be entitled to only 50 percent of the total damages to which he would have been otherwise entitled.

This doctrine is applicable to cases filed under the Federal Employers Liability Act (F.E.L.A.), *45 U.S.C.A.,* Sec. 53, on account of injuries to railroad workers during employment, and to suits under the Jones Act (*46 U.S.C.A.,* Sec. 688) on account of injuries occurring to merchant seamen in their employment.

In the ordinary personal injury case, the majority of the state courts still follow the more restrictive contributory negligence doctrine which bars recovery if plaintiff was negligent, regardless of the fact that defendant was negligent.

Sample Instruction

This case is controlled by the comparative negligence rule. In other words, if you shall find that the accident and the resulting injuries to plaintiff were caused by the negligence of both parties, the plaintiff would still be entitled to a verdict. The method which you would use in arriving at how much plaintiff is entitled to would be as follows:

> First, determine the full amount of all damages sustained by the plaintiff as a proximate result of the accident;
>
> Second, compare the negligence or fault of the parties, by determining in what proportion, figured in percentage, plaintiff's own fault contributed to the accident and the resulting injuries, and in what proportion the defendant contributed;
>
> Third, then reduce the full amount of plaintiff's damages by subtracting a sum equal to the percentage of plaintiff's negligence;
>
> Fourth, return a verdict in favor of the plaintiff for the amount remaining.

However, if you shall find from the evidence that the accident and the resulting injuries to plaintiff were caused solely by defendant's negligence, your verdict should reflect this and the plaintiff would be entitled to a verdict in an amount of all the damages sustained by him without reduction.

On the other hand, if you shall find that the accident and the resulting injuries to plaintiff were caused solely by plaintiff's negligence, your verdict should be for the defendant.[48]

> See: *West Key Number System,*
> *Master & Servant,* Sections
> 227 (1) and 228 (1); *Corpus*
> *Juris Secundum, Master &*
> *Servant,* Section 421 et seq.

Sec. 12.17   Federal Tort Claims Act Instructions

Comment

The U.S. Government is liable on account of its torts "in the same manner and to the same extent as a private individual under like circumstances," *28 U.S.C.A.* Sec. 2674. The trials are without jury. Hence, instructions would

---

48. Based on *Federal Jury Practice and Instructions,* by Mathes & Devitt, Sec. 84.20 (original edition).

See *Dennis v. Denver & R.G. W.R. Co.* (Utah, 1963), 375 U.S. 208, 11 L. Ed. 256, 84 S.Ct. 291; *Bly v. So. R. Co.,* 183 Va. 162, 168, 31 S.E. 2d 564, 567.

However, if the accident were caused by an improper safety appliance in a railroad case, then there is authority that defendant's liability is absolute and plaintiff is entitled to recover fully. See *Picard v. Pittsburgh & O.V. R.R. Co.* (D.C. Pa., 1957), 153 F.S. 583.

be addressed to the Court. The law of damages is similar to the usual common law tort case. However, the question arises, which guideposts to use in determining the measure of damages, since the Act does not fix a damage schedule. It has been held that the law of the state where the tort was committed shall apply, and the same prevails as to aggravation of a pre-existing condition. While the collateral benefits doctrine, which favors the injured plaintiff (see Sec. 12.8, supra), does not apply in the main as to benefits received from the general treasury of the United States, it does apply to benefits received otherwise, and to benefits received from a special fund of the United States, i.e. for social security death benefits.[49]

Sample Instructions

A.

The law of damages applying to this case would be that of .... (the state where the tortious act was committed).

> Based on: *Hatahley v. U.S.,* 351 U.S.
> 173, 76 S. Ct. 745 (Utah)

B.

The aggravation of a pre-existing condition is compensable, according to the law of .... (if this is the law of the state where the tortious act was committed).

> Based on: *Bruce v. U.S.* (D.C. Cal., 1958),
> 167 F.S. 579

C.

There should be no reduction in the damages to which plaintiff is entitled even though he received benefits from collateral sources on account of his injuries, unless these benefits were received from the general treasury of the United States.

> Based on: *U.S. v. Harne Hayashi,* 282 F. 2d
> 599 (9 C.A., 1960)
>
> *Hughes v. Clinchfield R. Co.,* 289
> F.S. 374 (E.D. Tenn., 1968)
>
> *Sleeman v. Ches. & Ohio R. Co.,*
> 290 F.S. 817, 820 (W.D.
> Ohio, 1958)

---

49. For a general discussion, see "Personal Injury Damages" by Practising Law Institute, pages 194-196. See also this chapter, at footnote 13 supra.

Based on: *Feely v. U.S.* (C.A. Pa., 1964), 337
                    F. 2d 924

                    U.S. v. Brooks (4 C.A., 1949), 176
                    F. 2d 482, 485

Sec. 12.18   Economic Expert's Opinion

Comment

The majority trend is to admit into evidence the testimony of an economic expert on losses due to serious disability and death (see Sec. 9.4, supra, and Sec. 13.14, infra).

There is authority that such an opinion may encompass the following data: probable lost earnings, probable future increases in earnings, probable future promotions (Sec. 9.4 supra); also, such an opinion may cover the value of lost household services and inflationary diminution of future earning losses (Sec. 12.10 supra); also, it may embrace the loss of future fringe benefits (i.e. pension and social security retirement benefits—this chapter, footnote 22); accumulations and augmentations on savings and investments may also be considered (this chapter, footnote 23).

A sample request for such an instruction appears in this footnote.[50]

---

50.   Sample Instruction

If you shall find for the plaintiff, then in estimating the damages to which the widow is entitled, you may take into consideration the testimony of the economic expert who has testified on behalf of the plaintiff. While you are not necessarily bound by his testimony and conclusions, it is given to assist you in reaching a proper conclusion because where a matter of science or art is involved requiring special knowledge or skill not ordinarily possessed by the average person, an expert is permitted to state his opinion for the enlightenment of the court and jury.

Chapter 13

HOW DEFENDANT SHOULD WORD
REQUESTS FOR INSTRUCTIONS
ON DAMAGES

Sec. 13.1   Guideline to the Use of This Chapter

See previous discussion under Sec. 12.1, supra.

Sec. 13.2   Burden of Proof

Sample Instruction

The burden rests on the plaintiff to prove by a preponderance of the evidence the elements of his damages, if any. The mere fact that an accident happened, considered alone, would not support a verdict for any particular sum.[1]

> See: *West Key Number System on*
> *Damages,* Key #163; *Corpus*
> *Juris Secundum on Damages,*
> Section 144.

Sec. 13.3   The Meaning of "Preponderance of Evidence"

Comment

Preponderance of evidence has been succinctly defined as that weight of

---

1. Taken from *California Jury Instructions–Civil,* 3rd Revised Edition, Sec. 171-A. See also *California Jury Instructions,* 5th Edition, Sec. 2.60.

the evidence which, although it may not be enough entirely to free the mind from a reasonable doubt, is enough to persuade a reasonable mind to one side rather than to the other.[2]

Sample Instruction

The meaning of preponderance of evidence is to prove that something is more likely so than not so. In other words, it means such evidence as when considered and compared with that opposed to it, has more convincing force, and produces in your minds belief that what is sought to be proved is more likely true than not true. In determining whether any fact in issue has been proven by a preponderance of the evidence in the case, the jury may, unless otherwise instructed, consider the testimony of all witnesses, regardless of who may have called them, and all exhibits received in evidence, regardless of who may have produced them.[3]

> See: *West Key Number System on*
>   *Evidence,* Key #1017; *Corpus*
>   *Juris Secundum on Evidence,*
>   Section 1017, p. 632.

Sec. 13.3A   Contributory Negligence

Sample Instruction

If the jury believes from the evidence that the defendant was negligent and that such negligence was a proximate cause of the accident and injuries suffered by the plaintiff, and if you further believe from the evidence that the plaintiff was also negligent and that such negligence proximately contributed to cause the accident and injuries, then your verdict shall be in favor of the defendant.

The law does not undertake to apportion or balance the negligence of the parties where both are at fault, but the plaintiff is barred from recovery if he was guilty of any negligence which proximately contributed to cause the accident and injuries. [3a]

---

2. *Corpus Juris Secundum on Evidence,* Sec. 1017, p. 633.

3. Based on *Federal Jury Practice & Instructions–Civil and Criminal,* by Mathes & Devitt, Sec. 71.01, p. 384 [original edition].

3a. Based on *Virginia Practice,* Volume I, by Doubles, Emrich & Merhige, Sec. 12.03. Since this book deals primarily with damages, the species of contributory negligence (i.e. involved in automobile collisions) and the other forms of defenses (i.e. assumption of risk doctrine and fellow employee negligence doctrine), are not treated herein. For help on such instructions, see the sources referred to in Sec. 11.5, supra.

See: *West Key Number System on
Negligence,* Key No. 80, 82,
and 97; *Corpus Juris Secundum
on Negligence,* Sections 129,
130, 169 et. seq.

Sec. 13.4   No Speculative Damages

Sample Instruction

You are not permitted to award a party speculative damages, which means compensation for future loss or harm which, although possible, is conjectural or not reasonably certain.

However, if you determine that a party is entitled to recover, you should compensate him for loss or harm which is reasonably certain to be suffered by him in the future as a proximate result of the injury in question.[4]

See: *West Key Number System on
Damages,* Key #216 (7) and
on Trial at Key #216-239;
*Corpus Juris Secundum on
Damages,* Section 185 (3).

Sec. 13.5   Condition Not Caused by Defendant's Negligence

Sample Instruction

A person who has a condition or disability at the time of an injury is not entitled to recover damages therefor. However, he is entitled to recover damages for any aggravation of such pre-existing condition or disability proximately resulting from the injury.

That is true even if the person's condition or disability made him more susceptible to the possibility of ill effects than a normally healthy person would have been, and even if a normally healthy person probably would not have suffered any substantial injury.

Where a pre-existing condition or disability is so aggravated, the damages as to such condition or disability are limited to the additional injury caused by the aggravation.[5]

---

4. Taken from *California Jury Instructions–Civil,* 5th Edition, Sec. 14.60.
5. Taken from *California Jury Instructions–Civil,* 5th Edition, Sec. 14.65. See discussion on aggravation of injuries in Sec. 12.6, supra.

> See: *West Key Number System on*
>   *Damages,* Key #6; *Corpus*
>   *Juris Secundum on Damages,*
>   Section 28.

Sec. 13.6   Punitive Damages

Comment

See discussion in Sec. 12.9, supra.

Sample Instruction

You may not include in any award to the plaintiff any amount that you might add for the purpose of punishing the defendant or to make an example of him for the public good or to prevent other accidents. Such damages would be punitive and they are not authorized in this action.[6]

> See: *West Key Number System on*
>   *Damages,* Key #215; *Corpus*
>   *Juris Secundum on Damages,*
>   Section 188.

Sec. 13.7   Duty of Plaintiff to Mitigate Damages

Sample Instruction

It is the duty of one who claims to have been injured by the wrongful or negligent act of another to exercise reasonable care and diligence to avoid loss and to minimize or lessen the resulting damage, and to the extent that his damages are the result of his active and unreasonable enhancement thereof or are due to his failure to exercise such care and diligence, he cannot recover.

And if you believe from the evidence that the plaintiff, after he was injured, failed to exercise reasonable care and diligence in an attempt to lessen the resulting damages to him and that such failure enhanced his damages, then he cannot recover for such enhanced or increased damage.[7]

---

6. Taken from *California Jury Instructions—Civil,* 5th Edition, Sec. 14.61.
7. Taken from *Virginia Practice,* Volume I, by Doubles, Emrich & Merhige, Sec. 23.96, citing: *Haywood v. Massie,* 188 Va. 176, 182, 49 S.E. 2d 281, 284.

See: *West Key Number System on*
      Damages, Key #62 (1); *Corpus*
      Juris Secundum on Damages,
      Section 32 et seq.

Sec. 13.8 "Per Diem" Argument of Counsel

Comment

The majority of the states permit the per diem argument (daily allowance for past and future pain and suffering) [*60 A.L.R.* 2d 1333; *Culley v. Pennsylvania Railroad Company,* 244 F.S. 710, 715 (1965), (D.C. Del.); *Harper v. Higgs,* 225 Md. 24, 169 A. 2d 661; *Eastern Shore Public Service Co. v. Corbett,* 227 Md. 411, 177 A. 2d 701]. However, the defendant should have the opportunity to answer in its closing argument. Also the defendant is permitted a cautionary instruction that this constitutes argument and not evidence, and that the jury must decide the damages [*Eastern Shore* case, supra].

Some states have decided against permitting the per diem argument, i.e. New Jersey [*Botta v. Brunner,* 26 N.J. 82, 138 A. 2d 713, 60 A.L.R. 2d 1331], Delaware, Virginia, Missouri, and Wisconsin.

Sample Instruction

In respect to the argument [made or which may be made] by counsel for plaintiff as to the per diem or daily amount of money which you may allow for pain and suffering which the plaintiff has suffered and will suffer in the future as a consequence of the accident, you are instructed that this is a valid argument but that it is argument and not evidence and that only you, the jury, must determine the proper verdict.[8]

See: *West Key Number System on*
      Damages, Key #32-34, and *on*
      Trial Key #218; *Corpus Juris*
      Secundum on Damages, Sections
      62 and 135, p. 1204, and *on*
      Trial, Sections 294 and 321.

---

8. Based on *Eastern Shore Public Service Company v. Corbett,* 227 Md. 411, 177 A. 2d 701.

Sec. 13.9   Wrongful Death

A. Discounting Future Damages

Comment

The present value of future earnings may be considered in estimating the total money loss.[9] The discount tables appear in Appendix C, infra. The rule requires proof of probable contributions[10] and of probable accumulations to the estate had the decedent lived,[11] and of the value of probable services which the decedent would have contributed to the household had he survived.[12]

It is argued that if the defendant is to be allowed the advantage of the present worth of future earnings, the plaintiff should be allowed the benefit of adding the effects of inflation in computing the future value of the award.[13]

The damages are assessed in accordance with the cash value of the damage elements at the time of trial.[14] However, the present value should be computed from the date of death and interest should be computed from that date also, although there are authorities to the contrary.[15]

Where time has intervened between death and trial, present value should not be applied to that period because the plaintiff has not had the use of defendant's money.[16]

As to the tactical wisdom of using discount tables, it is probably helpful to the plaintiff in low verdict areas because it stresses the large amounts of

---

9. See Sec. 12.15, supra.

10. Speiser's *Recovery for Wrongful Death,* Sec. 8:1, citing: California—*Bond v. United Railroads of S.F.* (1911), 159 Cal. 270, 113 P. 366, 48 Crans. 687; Iowa—*Carnego v. Crescent Coal Co.* (1914), 164 Iowa 552, 146 N.W. 38; Texas—*Gulf C. & S.F.R. Co. v. Ballew* (1933) (Tex. Com. App.) 66 S.W. 2d 659 and other authorities.

11. Speiser, supra, footnote 10, Sec. 8:1, citing: *Picket v. Wilmington W.R. Co.* (1895), 17 N.E. 616, 23 S.E. 264, 30 L.R.A. 257.

12. Speiser, supra, footnote 10, Sec. 8:1, citing: *Coleman v. Moore* (1952 D.C. Dist. Col.), 108 F.S. 425; *Davis v. Guarineri* (1887), 450 Ohio St. 470, 15 N.E. 350.

13. Speiser, supra, footnote 10, Sec. 8:10, citing: *Furumizo v. U.S.,* 1965 (D.C. Hawaii), which mentioned the inflation factor as an item to increase the amount of an award in a Federal Tort Claims Act case. But see *Spell v. U.S.* (1947, D.C. Fla.), 72 F.S. 731, in which the court used the inflationary factor to reduce the amount of an award in a similar case.

The Consumer Price Index (C.P.I.) is the yardstick in the changes in purchasing power; it is obtainable at the U.S. Department of Labor, Bureau of Labor Statistics, Washington 25, D.C.

14. *Downs v. Sulphur Springs Val. Elec. Corp.* (1956 Ariz.), 80 Ariz. 286, 297 P. 2d 339; Speiser, supra, footnote 10, Sec. 8:1.

15. Speiser, supra, footnote 10, Sec. 8:3.

16. *Nollenberger v. United Airlines Inc.* (1963), (D.C. Cal.), 216 F.S. 734, aff'd in part and mod. in part on other grounds. *United Air Lines v. Wiener* (C.A. 9), 335 F. 2d 379, cert. den. 379 U.S. 951, 85 S. Ct. 452.

money involved even though the defendant is given the fullest advantages, and it is beneficial to the defendant in large verdict areas because it reduces the aggregate amounts to which plaintiff would be otherwise entitled.[17]

Sample Instruction

If the jury shall find that the plaintiff is entitled to a verdict, and further find that the evidence in the case establishes any one or more of the following items of actual damage: (1) a reasonable likelihood of future medical expenses, (2) a reasonable likelihood of loss of future earnings, (3) a reasonable likelihood of future pain or suffering or mental anguish; then it becomes the duty of the jury to ascertain the present worth in dollars of such future damage, since the award of future damages necessarily requires that payment be made now for a loss that will not actually be sustained until some future date.

Under these circumstances, the result is that the plaintiff will in effect be reimbursed in advance of the loss, and so will have the use of money which he would not have received until some future date, but for the verdict.

In order to make a reasonable adjustment for the present use, interest free, of money representing a lump sum payment of anticipated future loss, the law requires that the jury discount, or reduce to its present worth, the amount of the anticipated future loss, by taking (1) the interest rate or return which the plaintiff could reasonably be expected to receive on an investment of the lump sum payment, together with (2) the period of time over which the future loss is reasonably certain to be sustained, and then reduce, or in effect deduct from, the total amount of anticipated future loss, whatever that amount would be reasonably certain to earn or return, if invested at such rate of interest over such future period of time, and include in the verdict an award for only the present worth—the reduced amount—of the total anticipated future loss.

As already explained to you, this computation is readily made by using the so-called "present worth" tables, which the Court had judicially noticed and received in evidence in this case.[18]

> See: *West Key Number System on Damages,* Key #100; *Corpus Juris Secundum on Damages,* Section 87 (e).

---

17. *21 Ohio St. L.J. 204* (1960).

18. Taken from *Federal Jury Practice and Instructions—Civil and Criminal,* by Mathes & Devitt, Sec. 76.12 [original edition]. See Discount Tables at Appendix C, infra.

B. Consumption Expenditures

Comment

There are some jurisdictions which hold that allowance should be made for personal consumption expenditures in estimating future lost earnings in wrongful death cases.[19] This means that the estimated portion of the deceased's lost future earnings which he would have devoted to his own personal living expenses (i.e. food, clothing, etc.) should be deducted from the estimated aggregate loss.

A sample request for such an instruction appears in this footnote.[20]

C. Income Tax Deductions

Comment

There are some jurisdictions which hold that the estimated income taxes which the deceased would have paid had he lived should be deducted from the aggregate loss which the widow has sustained. This appears to be a minority view because of the speculative nature of such rates and amounts into the future.[21]

A sample request for such an instruction appears in this footnote.[22]

D. Diminution in Earnings

Comment

There is authority that the deciding tribunal may take into consideration the normal diminution in earnings which may have been expected had the

---

19. *Floyd v. Fruit Industries Inc.*, 144 Conn. 659 (1957); *Sipes v. Michigan Central Railway Co.*, 231 Mich. 404, 204 N.W. 84; *Jennings v. U.S.*, 178 F.S. 516 (D.C. Md.).

20.   Sample Instruction

Should you find in favor of the plaintiff, then in estimating the lost earnings which the widow has sustained, you may consider the consumption expenditures that her deceased husband would have had, if he had lived, namely, that portion or percentage of his annual income which he would have spent for his personal living expenses, such as for food, clothing and spending money; and you may deduct such an amount which is reasonable from the aggregate loss which the widow has sustained.

21. See discussion in Chapter 12, footnote 22, supra.

22.   Sample Instruction

Should you find in favor of the plaintiff, then in estimating the lost earnings which the widow has sustained, you may consider the annual liability of the husband for federal and state income taxes if he had lived, and this amount should be deducted from his probable gross earnings during his normal life span.

deceased not been killed, as for example from aging or ill-health (see chapter 12, footnote 22, supra).

A sample request for such an instruction appears in this footnote.[23]

E. Parents' Losses for Child's Death

Comment

There are many authorities which hold that the parents are confined to merely the anticipated pecuniary losses up to the time the child would have attained age 21 or would have been sooner emancipated from the parents, and also that from this amount must be deducted the expense of rearing the child [see discussion in Sec. 12.14, footnote 35, supra].

A sample request for such an instruction appears in this footnote.[24]

Sec. 13.10   Mortality Tables

Comment

Mortality tables are admissible in evidence in the determination of future loss of earnings. For a general discussion and sample instruction, see Sec. 12.15 supra.

The mortality tables are located in Appendix A, infra.

Sec.. 13.11   Work Career Expectancy Tables

Comment

The use of work career expectancy tables is advisable in serious disability and death cases. While the courts do not often differentiate between them

---

23.   Sample Instruction

Should you find for the plaintiff, then in estimating the damages with reference to the projected lost income in the future, you may take into consideration the normal diminution in earnings that might reasonably have been expected of the deceased had he not met his untimely end, such for example as from his advancing age and from the condition of his health.

24.   Sample Instruction

Should you find for the plaintiffs, then in awarding damages you are to consider the pecuniary losses, that is the monies which the deceased child would have contributed to his parents from his own earnings, had he not died, but only up to the time he would have attained age 21 or would have been sooner emancipated, as for example by marriage, whichever would have been sooner; and you are further instructed that you are to deduct from such an aggregate sum the anticipated expenses which the parents would have incurred in rearing him, as for example for food and clothes, over the same period of time.

and mortality tables, they are different nevertheless.[25] Their use would tend to favor defendants because the work expectancy period is usually somewhat shorter than the life expectancy period. However, it is well recognized that many persons continue to engage in gainful employment on a part-time if not on a full-time basis even after retirement.[26] Hence, the mortality tables should be considered in conjunction with the work expectancy tables. Neither is conclusive and other factors should be considered also, i.e. age, condition of health, type of employment, geographical location and employment opportunities, etc.

For the tables themselves, see Appendix B, infra.

Sample Instruction

If you shall find for the plaintiff, the widow, then, in estimating the damages to which she is entitled on account of pecuniary losses due to her husband's death, you may consider the work career expectancy table offered in evidence in determining the probable duration of future lost earnings. However, this table is not conclusive and may be considered along with other factors in estimating the extent and probable lost earnings, such as mortality tables, condition of the husband's health and strength, his type of employment, his geographical location and the job opportunities there.

> See: *West Key Number System on
> Death,* Key #67; *Corpus Juris
> Secundum on Death,* Section
> 123.

Sec. 13.12   Comparative Negligence

Comment

For application of this doctrine, see Sec. 12.16 supra.

Sample Instruction

If you shall find that the accident and the resulting injuries to plaintiff were caused solely by plaintiff's negligence, then your verdict must be for the defendant.[27]

---

25. Speiser, supra, footnote 10, Sec. 3:14.

26. "Immel's Actuarial Tables and Damage Awards", 19 Ohio St. L.J. 240 (1958), reprinted in *Trial & Tort Trends 1959,* Belli Seminar 347.

27. Based on *Federal Jury Practice and Instructions—Civil and Criminal,* by Mathes & Devitt, Sec. 84.20 [original edition].

See: *West Key Number System,*
           Master & Servant, Key #227 (1)
           and #228 (2); *Corpus Juris*
           Secundum, Master & Servant,
           Section 421 et seq.

Sec. 13.13   Nominal Damages

Comment

Compensatory damages are rendered to replace the loss caused by the wrong inflicted on the plaintiff by the defendant. Where there is proof of the wrong but none as to actual or substantial damage resulting therefrom, the jury may render a verdict in favor of the plaintiff but for a nominal amount, ranging from one cent to one dollar. Thus the rights as between the parties have been adjudicated and a basis for taxing the costs has been established. On the other hand, if the wrong complained of and if the damages are trivial, even nominal damages may be refused. *Corpus Juris Secundum on Damages,* Sec. 7-16.

Sample Instruction

If you shall find that there has been an invasion of plaintiff's rights by the act of the defendant, but that the plaintiff has not proven that he suffered any actual damages, you may award to the plaintiff nominal damages, for example $1.00, as the amount he should recover. Thus you will determine the rights of the parties.[28]

See: *West Key Number System on*
           Damages, Key #8; *Corpus Juris*
           Secundum on Damages, Sections
           8-16.

Sec. 13.14   Expert's Opinion

Comment

As special knowledge becomes professionalized, experts enter the field and their testimony becomes admissible in court. Generally speaking, the standard used by the courts to determine if an expert opinion should be allowed is if his testimony will be of assistance in aiding the judge or jury to

---

28. Based on *Connecticut Jury Instructions* by Wright, Sec. 255.

arrive at a verdict.[29] Such expert opinions are admissible, for example, to prove the cause of disability or of death where it is not answerable from common knowledge or where it is within the peculiar knowledge and training of a medical expert who may testify from first-hand knowledge[30] or in response to a hypothetical question.[31] While the court decides whether the witness is qualified to testify as an expert, it is for the jury to weigh the value of such testimony.[32] A new type of expert recently arisen in the legal firmament is the economist-statistician, and the majority rule is that his testimony is admissible.[33]

Sample Instruction

You will recall that the witness(es) [state name(s)] gave testimony concerning (his, her) qualifications as an expert(s) in the field(s) of [state profession(s)]. When a case involves a matter of science or art, requiring special knowledge or skill not ordinarily possessed by the average person, an expert is permitted to state his opinion for the information of the court and jury. The opinion(s) stated by (the, each) expert who testified before you (was, were) based on particular facts, as the expert himself observed them and testified to them before you, or as the attorney who questioned him asked him to assume. You may reject an expert's opinion if you find the facts to be different from those which formed the basis for the opinion. You may also reject his opinion if, after careful consideration of all the evidence in the case, expert and other, you disagree with the opinion. In other words, you are not required to accept an expert's opinion to the exclusion of the facts and circumstances disclosed by other testimony. Such an opinion is subject to the same rules concerning reliability as the testimony of any other witness. It is given to assist you in reaching a proper conclusion, is entitled to such weight as you find the expert's qualifications in his field warrant and must be considered by you, but is not controlling upon your judgment.[34]

> See: *West Key Number System on*
> *Evidence,* Key #508, 528-536;
> *Corpus Juris Secundum on*
> *Damages,* Section 162 (8), p. 105.

---

29. See Sec. 9.1, supra.
30. *Bethlehem-Sparrows Point Shipyard v. Scherpenisse* (1946), 187 Md. 375, 50 A. 2d 256; Speiser, supra, footnote 10, Sec. 12:12.
31. *Garmeda Coal Co. v. Davis* (1949) 310 Ky. 639, 221 S.W. 2d 622.
32. *Meiselman v. Crown Heights Hosp.,* 285 N.Y. 389, 398, 34 N.E. 2d 367.
33. See Sec. 9.4, supra.
34. Taken from *New York Pattern Jury Instructions,* Sec. 1:90.

Chapter 14

WHAT YOU SHOULD KNOW ABOUT

NO FAULT INSURANCE

Sec. 14.1   Complaints Against the Present System
in Automobile Accidents

Alfred Lord Tennyson wrote in his classic poem, Locksley Hall, "Let the world spin forever down the ringing grooves of change."

The negligence lawyer should take some time out from his exacting routine to observe the changing scene about him and to get a new prospective of his busy cosmos. Radical changes are being proposed and adopted, which will have a serious effect on the negligence practice in automobile accident cases.

The automobile is a necessity in modern life. It is estimated that in the U.S.A. there is one automobile for every 2.4 persons, and that the supply will be on the increase in the immediate future. It is understandable then that the number of accidents involving injuries and/or damages will be astronomical in such a large country. It is estimated that the average driver will have an accident every third year.[1]

A recent study revealed the following interesting data about automobile accident reparations in the state of Michigan, which is a fairly representative state of the union:[2]

1. Denenberg, *The Automobile Insurance Problems: Issues and Choices.* 1970 Ins. L.J. 455. See also Daniel's *Michigan's Auto Insurance Ills,* 53 Auto. Club of Mich. Motor News 10 (Jan. 1971.) See also "No-Fault Automobile Insurance" by Friedman, Notre Dame Lawyer, Spring 1971, Vol. 46:542.

2. *Automobile Accident Costs and Payments, Studies in the Economics of Injury Reparation,* by Conrad, Morgan, Pratt Jr., Voltz and Bombaugh, published by the University of Michigan Press, Ann Arbor (1964), at pages 1-6.

1. About one of every one hundred persons suffered some economic loss in a personal injury and about 60 percent had losses of less than $500; the proportion with losses under $3,000 was over 90 percent; 2 or 3 percent had losses over $10,000.

2. Less than 1 percent of the injury cases reach trial and substantially all were serious cases; a substantial majority of the serious cases were settled and the long delay in reaching trial was a major cause.

3. The smaller the loss the greater the chance of generous recovery. The more seriously injured are usually dissatisfied with the results.

4. The burden of reparation does not fall on the guilty driver but on his insurer, which in turn distributes the cost among its masses of insured. Hence, the tort liability system of punishing for fault as a deterrent against future accidents is somewhat dubious, but it does have some effect because of its influence on the driver's ego and because of the time and trouble consumed by an accident case, and because of the spectre of an increased premium rate or of no insurance at all.

5. Tort liability insurance coverage accounted for about 1/2 of the reparations and other types of insurance accounted for the remainder, i.e. life, health, and auto collision in which the victim's own insurer paid him. Social Security coverage was also a factor in permanent total disability cases.

6. The trend in the increase of insurance coverage in recent years is in the following sequence:
    a. Health
    b. Social (i.e. Social Security)
    c. Life
    d. Insured automobile liability
    e. Workmen's Compensation

The same trend is occurring in foreign countries, i.e. England, France, Germany and Sweden.

The same study found that the law was lacking in providing for: rehabilitation, damages for loss of use of the vehicle, and allowance for the subsistence and lost opportunities, i.e. promotion on the job.[3] The study concluded that there is room for both no fault and common law tort remedy.[4]

The U.S. Department of Transportation (DOT) has made a study of the problems affecting automobile accidents.[5] It made some pertinent findings,

3. Supra, at pages 81-86.

4. Supra, at page 128.

5. *Motor Vehicle Crash Losses and their Compensation in the United States—Department of Transportation;* U.S.A. Automobile Insurance and Compensation Study, March 1971. Available at Superintendent of Documents, Washington, D.C.

including the following: the public is demanding change against high cost of insurance, against fears of arbitrary insurance cancellation, and against delays in settlement.[6] Also there are complaints about injustices arising from the present tort system because of the necessity of proving fault and freedom from contributory negligence.

The DOT study made many recommendations, which in essence favor no fault insurance to be enacted by the states, with common law trial by jury to be reserved only in the more serious injury cases, thus to make payment for injuries and damages speedier and surer.[7]

Daniel P. Moynihan, while Director of the Harvard-M.I.T. Joint Center for Urban Studies and Chairman of the Health, Education and Welfare Secretary Advisory Committee on traffic safety, charged that the insurance companies were discriminating against Negroes and other disadvantaged groups, i.e. teenagers, bachelors and the poor, and were charging excessive premiums through unfair and spurious rate-making methods and that they were indulging in unwarranted cancellations. He further charged that some automobile negligence lawyers were exploiting the situation by inflating the value of an automobile damage case into a personal injury case and by unneeded medical attention.[8]

Federal legislation is now pending which will provide for a nationwide system of compulsory automobile liability insurance on a no fault basis, and it does away largely with the present tort liability system.[9]

No fault insurance systems have been enacted in Puerto Rico and Saskatchewan, Canada.

No fault insurance in different forms, varying from the stricter to the highly modified no fault systems, have been adopted more recently in Connecticut, Delaware, Florida, Illinois, Maryland, Massachusetts, New Jersey, Oregon and South Dakota.[10] More states undoubtedly will enact similar and diversified No Fault statutes.

Sec. 14.2   What is No Fault Insurance?

Simply stated, no fault insurance provides that the insured person can

---

6. Supra, at pages 80-88.

7. Supra, at pages 128-142.

8. *Baltimore Sunday Sun,* March 5, 1967, "The Automobile Insurance Mess" by James D. Dilts.

9. S. 945. It is known as the Hart-Magnuson-Moss Bill. It was recently reported on favorably by the Senate Commerce Committee. Its basic provisions are: the states may adopt their own no fault laws consistent with the guidelines established in this bill, else the federal no fault law would apply; minimum first party medical coverage of $25,000 for medical expenses and $25,000 for rehabilitation expenses; minimum coverage for economic losses of $75,000; tort liability is abolished except in cases of death, permanent significantly incapacitated loss of bodily function, permanent serious disfigurement, and injury resulting in more than six months' disability; severe limitations on the allowance of attorney's fees.

10. These state laws are discussed in more detail hereafter in Sec. 14.4.

recover from his own insurance company his net out-of-pocket losses, regardless of who was at fault for the automobile accident. The insurance premium rate is expected to be cheaper and the claim should be paid off very expeditiously. But in exchange for these advantages, some important advantages would be sacrificed, the most important of which would be the surrender of the right to damages suffered on account of pain and suffering and on account of permanent disabilities resulting from pain and suffering; under some plans and acts even further rights would be lost.

Sec. 14.3   The Basic No Fault Plans[11]

A. The Columbia Plan[12]

This was the first of the many plans and was introduced in 1932. It proposed a no fault system with compulsory insurance; it barred the right to recover at common law for tort, and it barred the right to recover for pain and suffering. It set up a schedule of benefits for specific injuries, as in workman's compensation insurance. It did not insure against property damage or against the uninsured or hit-and-run driver. It provided for the determination of lawyers' fees by the agency administering the plan. It came to nought.[13]

B. The Saskatchewan System[14]

This was adopted in 1946 by a province in Canada with a population of only about 888,000, covering 251,700 square miles, and apparently has worked there satisfactorily. It seems to have removed the pressure to settle because of need and it still preserves the common law remedy.

Bodily injury and property damage claims are paid without regard to fault. However, the victim can still avail himself of his common law remedy

---

11. This chapter does not cover all of the no fault plans and systems but attempts to mention some of the better known ones. For additional plans, see *No Fault Insurance* by Rokes, published by Insurors Press Inc., Santa Monica, California (1971) and see *The Automobile Insurance System: Current Status and Some Proposed Revisions* by *Institute For The Future WP-18*, published by Institute for the Future, Middletown, Connecticut.

12. *Columbia University Council for Research in the Social Sciences, Report of the Committee to Study Compensation for Automobile Accidents* 1932. See also Grad, *Recent Developments in Automobile Accident Compensation*, 50 Colum. L.R. 300 (1950).

13. For an excellent and detailed analysis of each of the basic no fault plans, see "An Outline of Leading Automobile Reparation Plans" by Professor William Schwartz, General Director of American Trial Lawyers Association (ATLA), 20 Garden Street, Cambridge, Massachusetts. See also *No Fault Insurance* by Rokes, published by Insurors Press Inc., Santa Monica, California.

14. The Automobile Accident Insurance Act, 1963, 12 Eliz. 2, C. 38 (Saskatchewan), as amended, 13 Eliz. 2, C. 51 (Saskatchewan, 1964); Revised Statutes of Saskatchewan, Chapter 409 (1965).

with the right of trial by jury, but the amount already received by him under the "first party" system will be deducted from the amount of the verdict. The insurance is written by the government, with the right reserved by the insured to have it written by a private insurer. The premium payments are made annually concurrently with license renewals to drive and registration of the vehicle. There is provided a schedule of limited benefits for specific injuries. Overlapping of benefits (i.e. from workman's compensation or unemployment insurance benefits or insurance under a private accident and illness policy) is not permitted, and same are deducted from the awards made. It covers where an uninsured driver is involved. Attorney's fees are administered and controlled by a committee of judges.[15]

C. Puerto Rico Act[16]

It has been operative since July 1, 1969. This is a social insurance scheme which has been tailored after the Saskatchewan Act, supra, and the Keeton-O'Connell Plan, infra. The premium is only $35.00 per year and is charged at the time of car registration; the cost is thus distributed among the general population. It has a schedule of limited benefits and is administered by a governmental agency. It contains unlimited comprehensive hospital, medical, surgical and rehabilitative coverage. It has no coverage for property damage. In substitution for liability in tort, the Act requires that benefits be paid up to the limits its schedule provides or up to the amount of benefits collected, whichever of the two is greater—subject, however, to a deductible.

The exemption from tort liability does not apply in cases where the recoverable loss exceeds: (a) the amount of $1,000 for pain and suffering, and of (b) the sum of $2,000 by reason of other damages or losses not included in pain and suffering. Most collateral benefits are deducted. If there is disagreement with the agency's findings, the claimant must first exhaust his administrative remedies and the board's findings of fact are final if supported by substantial evidence. Counsel fees for lawsuits filed are not chargeable against the benefits payable unless previously authorized by the agency. Suit may be brought directly against the insurer.

D. Keeton-O'Connell Plan[17]

It is known as the Basic Protection Plan and was proposed in 1965. It provides compulsory automobile insurance but limits recovery to net losses.

---

15. For a critical analysis of the Saskatchewan system, see 37 Australian L.J., p. 224 (Nov. 1963).
16. Automobile Accident Social Protection Act, Laws of Puerto Rico, Title 9, Chapter 17, Sec. 2058.
17. R. Keeton & J. O'Connell, *Basic Protection for the Traffic Victim, A Blueprint for Reforming Automobile Insurance,* 140-148 (1965); 51 Judicature 151-152 Dec. 1967.

Collateral source benefits are deducted so as not to permit overlapping of benefits. The common law tort remedy is excluded if the damages for pain and suffering would not exceed $5,000 and if losses for out-of-pocket expenses, i.e. medical, hospital expenses, and loss of income, do not exceed $10,000 per person. It contains no schedule of benefits as does the Saskatchewan law. In the more serious cases, the common law tort remedy is preserved but deductions are made for the amounts received under the Plan. Benefits are paid on a monthly basis, subject to a lump sum allowance in special cases. It covers against uninsured or hit-and-run drivers. Rehabilitation is provided for, including medical and occupational training. Attorneys are entitled to reasonable fees for advising and representing the claimant, and one-half of such fee is chargeable against benefits otherwise due; if overdue benefits are involved, the fee is charged against the insurer; if there is a dispute, it is submitted to a court. Property damage is covered by a separate new form of insurance (Property Dual Option Coverage). A modified or "optional" plan offers each bodily injury liability insurance policy holder the option of electing basic protection insurance also.

E. Cotter Plan[18]

It is a plan that was proposed by the insurance department of the State of Connecticut. It attempts to strike a middle course between no fault insurance and common law tort liability. Recently, Connecticut adopted a No Fault law which is somewhat different from the Cotter Plan.[19]

F. Miscellaneous Plans

Rockefeller-Stewart Plan[20]

It does away with common law tort liability and recovery for pain and suffering.

American Insurance Association (A.I.A.) Plan[21]

It provides for compulsory insurance and does away with all common law tort liability and recovery for pain and suffering. There would be no obligation on the insurer to pay attorney's fees, except where insurer unreasonably refused or delayed settlement.

---

18. Proposed by Insurance Department of Connecticut. For its details, see Schwartz article referred to in footnote 13 Supra.

19. See Sec. 14.4, infra.

20. *State of New York Insurance Department Rep. Automobile Insurance For Whose Benefit* (1970). See S.B. 8922 (1970 Session).

21. American Insurance Association, Personal and Property Protection Motor Vehicle Insurance Act (Draft #10, 1970).

The DOT Plan (Federal Department of Transportation)[22]

It presents guidelines for enactment of state legislation to create no fault insurance along the lines of the Keeton-O'Connell Plan.

The ATLA Plan (American Trial Lawyers Association)[23]

Its chief provisions are: federal regulation of automobile insurance; an ombudsman to oversee automobile insurance; prohibition against cancelling and refusing to renew policies and against arbitrary rejections; a federal corporation to pay automatically for medical expenses and wage losses, and it is to compete in the sale of automobile insurance with private companies; tax relief on insurance premiums paid; minimum insurance limits of $30,000 for injuries to one person and $60,000 for any one accident; $5,000 property damage; uninsured motorist coverage; retention of common law tort actions; comparative negligence doctrine; arbitration for small claims.

Dual Protection Plan (proposed by the National Association of Independent Insurers)[24]

Basically it provides for: compulsory no fault insurance for private passenger vehicles up to certain dollar limits to cover medical, income loss and substitute service expenses; tort recovery in many cases; mandatory arbitration for tort cases up to $3,000.

Responsible Reform (proposed by the Defense Research Institute)[25]

Its main provisions are: optional no fault insurance for non-fleet passenger vehicles; no fault benefits cover economic losses only within the limits and duration to be fixed at the local state level; tort remedy is possible in all cases; compulsory arbitration for all tort cases up to $3,000 in state jurisdictions where there is trial delay; judicial reforms (i.e. separate trials for liability and damage).

---

22. See footnotes 5 and 9 supra.

23. It is titled "Federal Automobile Insurance Reform Act" and appeared in " . . . in brief", No. 3, p. 1, October 1971 issue published by American Trial Lawyers Association. Also, it has two model statutes for consideration by state legislatures, entitled "Freedom of Choice No Fault Act" (which is an optional no fault plan) and "Triple Protection No Fault Act" (which provides for priorities in insurance policies). These are obtainable at ATLA, 20 Garden Street, Cambridge, Massachusetts 02138.

24. Proposed on December 14, 1970 by the Chicago-based National Association of Independent Insurers, which writes over ½ of the nation's automobile insurance through its affiliated companies.

25. *Vol. 1969, No. 8, Milwaukee, 1969.* "Responsible Reform, A Program to Improve The Liability Reparation System".

Uniform Motor Vehicle Accident Reparation Act (proposed by
the National Conference of Commissioners on Uniform
State Laws)[26]

"The main provisions proposed as a model law for states to adopt are: reimbursement up to an aggregate of $200 per week for lost wages and replacement services and in case of death payment up to $200 per week to survivors in accordance with the state's wrongful death laws (but with some limitations); tort liability is abolished except where damages for non-economic detriment is in excess of $5,000 if there is permanent significant loss of bodily function or death, or permanent serious desfigurement, or more than six months of total disability; insurance coverage for no fault and tort liability is required with a minimum of $25,000 per accident for bodily injury and $10,000 per accident for property damage; attorney's fees are payable by insurer for collection of overdue or disputed benefits."

Guaranteed Protection Plan (proposed by the American
Mutual Insurance Alliance)[27]

Basically, it provides: compulsory no fault insurance for all private passenger motor vehicles carrying coventional insurance; no fault benefits up to certain limits for economic losses necessitated by medical bills, income loss and substitute service expenses; tort remedy is possible in some cases; mandatory arbitration for tort cases up to $3,000.

American Bar Association Plan[27A]

Very recently it altered its position, which was against no fault automobile insurance, to a no fault plan, the main provisions of which are as follows: all states should adopt no fault automobile insurance; federal government should stay out of this area; recovery of up to $2,000 in medical payments and lost wages; common law remedy would be preserved for the most part.

Sec. 14.4   State Acts

The state acts are quite different from one another. They vary from the stricter no fault law, such as in Massachusetts, to the more modified and

---

26. Adopted August 1972. 1155 E. 60th Street, Chicago, Illinois.
27. Presented before the Senate Commerce Committee May 6, 1971. See also Insurance Information Institute, Existing and Proposed Auto Insurance Systems (Fall 1970).
27A. Adopted August 1972. 1155 E. 60th Street, Chicago, Illinois.

optional no fault laws, as in South Dakota. However, generally speaking, their contents are characterized by inclusion of the following categories:[28]

a. No fault availability (private passenger vehicles are covered; in some states commercial vehicles, trailers and motorcycles are covered also).

b. Eligibility for no fault benefits [usually, the person covered is the one injured if he is the driver, a passenger, a family member residing in the household, or a pedestrian; the injured person is ineligible if he engaged in gross misconduct (i.e. drunken driving)].

c. Limits of no fault (usually, it includes medical expenses, income loss and expense for substitute services, i.e. housekeeper; the amounts vary).

d. Deductibles (usually, workmen's compensation benefits received are deductible from no fault benefits).

e. Extent to which tort liability is preserved (usually, the exemption from no fault limits applies to death, serious permanent injuries, permanent significant disfigurement, fractures, loss of use of a body member, and to injuries where the expenses exceed the threshold no fault medical benefits, i.e. $500 in Massachusetts).

f. Provisions for payment (usually, the insurer is required to pay within thirty days from the date of notice of injury).

g. Regulation of insurers (protection is provided for the insured from abuses).

Connecticut Act[29]

Its basic features are: compulsory liability insurance, plus no fault coverage up to $5,000 per person per accident for economic losses; tort action remedy is preserved but with some limitations; limited comparative negligence doctrine is to apply in tort actions; a self-insurance system is permitted; insurer has subrogation rights in tort actions; there is to be a 10 percent reduction in insurance rates during the first year of the law.

Delaware Act[30]

Its basic features are: compulsory insurance; insurers must include certain no fault minimum coverage for economic losses and for certain

28. Based on chart entitled "Alternative No-Fault Automobile Insurance Legislation" prepared by Institute for the Future, Middletown, Connecticut.

29. Public Act. No. 273, Laws of Connecticut 1972. Effective January 1, 1973.

30. Delaware H.B. 270 House of Representatives, 126th Assembly, First Session 1971, as amended by House Amendment No. 2, Chapter 98 of Volume 58 of *Laws of Delaware* (also Title 21 of *Motor Vehicle Code*). Effective January 1, 1972.

types of property damage; bars overlapping of benefits (i.e. automobile liability insurance benefits and workmen's compensation); preserves tort action remedy; subrogation rights in insurer to damages obtained by the insured to extent of benefits paid. The rules implementing the law provide benefits for the victim of an uninsured motorist.

Florida Act[31]

Its basic features are: compulsory insurance; insurer must include certain minimum no fault coverage for economic losses embracing medical expenses, income losses, and funeral burial expenses; exemption from common law tort action except in cases where the medical expenses exceed $1,000 or if the injury or disease consists of permanent disfigurement, a fracture of a bone, loss of a body member, permanent injury within reasonable medical probability, permanent loss of a bodily function, or death; offset for workmen's compensation benefits collected; exemption from tort actions on account of property damage except in certain cases; reduction of insurance rates by not less than 15 percent.

Illinois Act[32]

Its basic features are: insurer must include a certain minimum no fault coverage for economic losses; some collateral benefits are not permitted to overlap the insurance benefits; the tort remedy is preserved with some limitations; arbitration procedure to settle claims which do not exceed $3,000.

This Act was ruled to be unconstitutional by the Illinois courts.[33] The rationale of the lower court was that the law discriminated against the poor and therefore violated the due process and equal protection clauses of the federal and state constitutions. The lower court reasoned that since the poorer people can afford less medical and hospital expenses and would lose less wages or income than the more affluent, they would be less likely to meet the threshold limit entitling the claimant to bring a tort action. The upper court relied on the denial of a jury trial in the cases of lesser amount as one of its reasons.

---

31. *Florida Insurance Code* 627.730-627.741, known as Florida Automobile Reparations Act.
32. Illinois Law S.B. 976; approved September 2, 1971.
33. *Grace v. Howlett* (71 C.H. 4737), Cir. Ct. Cook Co., Ill. Co. Dept., Chanc. Div., aff'd 283 N.E. 2d 474; rehearing denied May 25, 1972.

Maryland Act[34]

Its basic features are: insurer must include certain minimum coverage ($2,500) for its insured regardless of fault for economic losses (i.e. medical, hospital, wage losses, etc.); common law tort remedy is preserved; creation of a state-owned insurance fund to provide insurance for those whom the private insurers consider the less desirable risks; insurance coverage against damages from an uninsured motorist is optional.

Massachusetts Act[35]

It was adopted in 1970 and is patterned after the Keeton-O'Connell Plan. It provides principally as follows: an injured motorist can collect no fault benefits for bodily injury claims up to $2,000 on account of economic losses; unless he can show that he has incurred more than $500 for medical expenses, he is barred from claiming damages for pain and suffering in a common law action; a common law action will lie for pain and suffering before death, for bodily dismemberment, serious disfigurement, loss of sight or hearing, and fracture. It requires a 15 percent rate reduction for all coverages.[36] The constitutionality of the Act is being challenged.[37]

New Jersey Act[38]

Its basic features are: compulsory liability insurance with minimums of $15,000/$30,000/$5,000; no cancellations or refusals by insurers without consent of Commissioner of Insurance; no fault coverage for economic losses up to certain limits except for medical expenses, which have no limit; tort remedy is preserved with some limitations; compulsory uninsured motorist protection; evidence of no fault payments is inadmissible in tort remedy suits; insurance rates shall be reduced a minimum of 15 percent.

---

34. Maryland Law, Chapter 73 (HB 444), adopted 1972, amending and adding provisions in Articles 26, 48a, 66-½ and 75 in *Maryland Code Annotated.*

35. Massachusetts 1970 General Laws, G.L.C. 90, Sec. 34A [6 Advance Legislative Service 765 (August 13, 1970); Chapter 670, Acts of 1970].

36. Massachusetts General Laws Annotated, Ch. 175, Sec. 1136 [6A Advance Legislative Service 302-3 (August 13, 1970)].

37. See *Aetna Casualty & Surety Company v. Commissioners of Insurance* (Mass.), 263 N.E. 2d 698 (1970); *Pinnick v. Cleary* (Sup. Jd. Ct. Mass.), Equity 7550, Suffolk County, 271 N.E. 2d 592.

38. Assembly Bill No. 667, 2nd Official Copy Reprint, enacted 1972; known as the New Jersey Automobile Reparation Reform Act.

Oregon Act[39]

Its basic features are: insurer must include certain minimum no fault insurance coverage for economic losses sustained by its insured and others named, i.e. medical expenses ($3,000 per person for one year from the time of the accident), some lost wages and substitute service expenses; common law tort remedy is preserved but insurer is entitled to be reimbursed out of the damages recovered for its payments made; overlapping of benefits is barred; arbitration procedure is provided for; advance no fault payments are not admissible as evidence in tort suits.

Oregon has a modified comparative negligence law, which was passed in 1971.

Oregon has an uninsured motorist law, which was enacted in 1961.

South Dakota Act[40]

Its basic features are: optional supplemental insurance coverage for following minimums—$10,000 for death, lost income to the extent of $60.00 per week for 52 weeks with certain limitations, $2,000 for medical expenses within two years from the date of the accident.

Sec. 14.5   Observations

The fair-minded observer cannot deny that conditions call for a change in the automobile accident field. It seems that the pendulum is swinging to absolute liability, which is not foreign to our law.[41] However, frequently when the pendulum swings, it goes too far in the opposite direction in order to appease the vociferous critics. Most of the needed changes can be assimilated into the present common law tort liability system with the passage of legislation and by adjudications and administration by the courts, and by policy arrangements between the insurer and the insured.[42] A list of these changes and how they can be accomplished follows:

1. The comparative negligence doctrine should be substituted for the contributory negligence doctrine. This would tend to silence the cries of injustice under the present system, which is too harsh. The majority of the

---

39. Chapter 523, Oregon Laws, 1971, H.B. 1300, effective January 1, 1972.

40. South Dakota Compiled Laws 58-23-6, 7 & 8 "Supplemental Automobile Coverage"; known as Modified Voluntary No Fault Auto Insurance Coverage. Effective January 1, 1972.

41. "Negligence and Liability Without Fault in Tort Law" by Peck, 46 Wash. L.R., p. 225 (1971).

42. For a well-reasoned and scholarly article supporting this point, see the article by James Friedman cited in footnote 1 supra.

modern western European countries and England and Scotland have adopted it.[43] It works well in Wisconsin[44] where it was adopted, although in a modified form. More recently it was adopted in Connecticut and Oregon in a similar form.[45]

2. The high cost of and the arbitrary cancellation of insurance policies and the discrimination against the disadvantaged can and should be corrected. If need be, legislation would have to be resorted to. If necessary, the state should take over the insurance of vehicles, as was done in Saskatchewan Province and in Puerto Rico, assuming that the private insurance companies cannot charge affordable rates or will not cooperate.[46] In Maryland, a state-owned insurance fund has been created.[47] It can serve not only as the insurer for the undesirable risks, but also as a watchdog over the rates being charged by the private insurers so as to combat excessive premium rates.

3. Delays in paying out-of-pocket expenses until the litigation is disposed of could be resolved by arrangements in the insurance policy to pay them promptly, with the condition that it will be deducted from the settlement or verdict and that it cannot be considered as an admission of liability in the litigation. Certain courts have ruled this is not an admission of liability.[48] In New Jersey and Oregon, the No Fault Acts prohibit its admission in evidence.[49]

4. Court congestion accounting for delays in litigation could be greatly dissipated by following the Pennsylvania system of assignment to arbitration of small claims of $3,000 or less[50] and by the liberal use of pre-trial conferences as used in the federal court system to effectuate settlements. Some of the new state no fault laws provide for arbitration, i.e. Illinois and Oregon.[51]

5. Coverage for damages resulting from the uninsured motorist, the hit-and-run driver, and the insolvent insurer can be effectuated by special legislation providing for an uninsured fund to be contributed to by all motorists.

---

43. Belli–*Modern Trials*, Vol. IV, "History of the Law of Damages," pps. 64-147.

44. Wisconsin Stat. Ann., Sec. 331.045 (1958).

45. See Sec. 14.4 supra.

46. The scare-howl of socialism no longer registers with the American people where serious conditions warrant change. Examples where sweeping social changes were made in the face of expletives are: Social Security and unemployment insurance. Now there is a decided move in Congress to enact National Health Insurance, despite the spectre of social medicine raised by critics. See "Americans Now Favor a National Health Plan" by Richard D. Lyons, *New York Times* August 9, 1971.

47. See Sec. 14.4 supra.

48. *Edwards v. Passarelli Bros. Automative Service Inc.,* 8 Ohio St. 2d 6, 221 N.E. 2d 708 (1966); *Byrd v. Stewart,* 450 S.W. 2d 11 (1969) (Tenn.)

49. See Sec. 14.4 supra.

50. Ryan "Arbitration Cuts Philadelphia Backlog," 10 For The Defense 42, June (1969).

51. See Sec. 14.4 supra.

6. Collateral source benefits can be taken account of in the automobile insurance policy so as to avoid overlapping of benefits and thus to reduce the premium rate somewhat.

Nevertheless, a problem is presented where liability is a real issue. Only a collision clause and a medical payment clause in the automobile policy, plus an income loss policy in the event of accident, could cope with this problem. The high expense of such extensive insurance under present conditions is undeniable. No fault insurance supplies the easy solution, but it exacts a heavy toll on the insured's rights unless a fair and balanced no fault law is adopted. While the overall experience is too short to appraise the merits and demerits of the no fault laws adopted thus far, there are some interesting glimpses which can be made. In Massachusetts, there has been a drop in the insurance rates, but there has also been a harsh amputation of common law tort benefits. For example, a recent study of the Massachusetts law shows that deserving cases involving serious disabilities from pain and suffering, i.e. aggravation of an arthritic condition or synovitis (inflammation of knee), etc., which previous to the no fault law brought verdicts of $25,000 and more, would now be limited to $2,000.[52]

The criticism that the concept of pain and suffering in the determination of damages is an intangible and difficult one is not valid. It is intangible, but then many legal doctrines and theories are, and this does not deter courts and juries from rendering fair verdicts under instructions from the presiding judge. In our system of justice, each individual and his rights are precious, and the pain and suffering concept is an integral part of our democratic system of jurisprudence.

The tendency to relegate the assessment of damages to administrative tribunals in personal injury cases is prevalent, but not without danger. For example, this has been done in workmen's compensation, both state and federal, and in permanent total disability cases under the Social Security system. This is not an unmixed blessing. While results are arrived at with fair expedition, a heavy price is paid by the victim. The workmen's compensation statutes severely limit the benefits and, generally speaking, they do not keep up with the rising cost of living and the changes in the concepts of disability evaluations. Appeals to the courts are made more and more difficult and meaningless by the invocation of the "substantial evidence" doctrine and by the use of so-called "impartial doctors" chosen by the agency, as if there were such fictitious personages, and by intricate legal technicalities and interpretations.

---

52. *The Automobile Insurance System* by Institute For The Future, Middletown, Connecticut, pps. 40-42. See also *No Fault* by Gillespie, pps. 57-71, published by Praeger Publishers, 111 Fourth Avenue, New York.

There is the constant inclination in such legislation to emasculate proper legal representation for the injured victim by cutting down on counsel fees and by avoiding a lawyer's lien against the benefits accruing to the claimant. This has resulted in a lack of proper legal representation for the claimant, as for example under such administrative tribunals as the U.S. Employees Compensation Act, and the veterans disability and retirement laws; lawyers are discouraged from representing claimants because of the inadequate and insecure fees.

Serious constitutional questions confront no fault insurance plans. Do they wrongfully deprive claimants of right of trial by jury? Many states have provisions in their constitutions similar to the seventh amendment to the federal constitution, which guarantees jury trials in common lawsuits where the amount in controversy exceeds $20.00. Do no fault laws discriminate against the poor and minority segments of our population and thereby violate the due process and equal protection sections of the federal constitution? The courts of Illinois seem to think so.[53]

In spite of all of these valid arguments, the realistic lawyer can foresee more no fault insurance statutes being adopted by states which have not yet accepted them. If no fault legislation is to be adopted, it would seem prudent to compare the different plans and to argue for the most balanced plans. Certainly, the Oregon and Maryland Acts[54] are more acceptable than the others because they preserve the common law tort liability action with the right to trial by jury, and they preserve the right to sue for pain and suffering. To put it another way, Oregon, particularly, retains the best of the two systems. The Saskatchewan system does the same, except that it includes the complete paraphernalia of a workmen's compensation schedule of benefits for all types of injuries. The Puerto Rico Act also preserves the right of appeal to common law jury trials, but contains the schedule of benefits as in workmen's compensation cases and uses the "substantial evidence" doctrine, which will stifle appeals. Also, it puts severe limitations on the effective collection of counsel fees and would thus discourage adequate legal representation.

The Oregon No Fault Act, complemented by its separate comparative negligence statute plus its uninsured motorist's law, presents a fairly balanced automobile insurance reparation system. To complete the picture, there should be considered the Maryland feature of a state-owned insurance fund to make certain that the disadvantaged and the undesirable risks could get insurance and so that a watchdog is present to warn against excessive premium rates which might be charged by private insurers. There should also

---

53. See Sec. 14.4 supra
54. See Sec. 14.4 supra

be considered coverage against the insolvent insurer. A pure comparative negligence law, i.e. as in the F.E.L.A.[55] and Jones Acts,[56] would be preferable to the modified comparative negligence doctrines in Connecticut, Oregon and Wisconsin.

Eventually, the federal government may attempt to take over the control of automobile insurance, which it is now threatening to do if the states do not take prompt action. At this writing, it is still in state hands.

Finally, it should be borne in mind that the no fault plans are confined to automobile injury and damage cases and do not affect the multitude of tort cases arising from outside the automobile area of torts. At least, such is the state of things at this writing. No one can croak what the morrow may bring.

---

55. *45 U.S.C.A.*, Sec. 53.
56. *46 U.S.C.A.*, Sec. 688.

APPENDIX A

Mortality Tables

Comment

These tables are important in proving the extent of the losses to the survivors from the decedent's wages or income and from accumulations in the estate in wrongful death cases[1] and in proving the extent of wage loss plus the duration of pain and suffering in serious disability cases.

There are various mortality tables.[2] However, the most often used and the most acceptable table in court is that issued by the United States Department of Health, Education and Welfare, Public Health Service, National Center for Health and Statistics. The joint life table can be obtained by writing to Division of the Actuary, United States Department of Health, Education and Welfare, Social Security Administration, Washington, D.C. It is based on the most recent census statistics. In comparison, the other tables tend to be more conservative because predicated on older census figures.

To avoid problems presented by objections on account of authenticity, it is desirable to obtain a certified copy of the U.S. tables by writing to the United States Department of Health, Education and Welfare, Washington 25, D.C.

The other tables are usually admitted into evidence on a showing that they are in common use by life insurance companies.[3]

Frequently, the courts will take judicial notice of these tables.[4]

These tables are not conclusive as to life expectancy and other factors to be considered are such as age, health, and the habits of the individual.[5]

For a sample request for instruction on mortality tables, see Sec. 12.15, supra.

There follow the applicable tables from the following sources: the U.S. Mortality Table previously referred to for males and females; the U.S. joint

1. See Speiser "Recovery For Wrongful Death," Sec. 3:35, p. 190.

2. Samples of mortality tables are: The Carlisle Tables contained in *Encyclopaedia Britannica*: the American Experience tables contained in life insurance manuals; the Flatchcraft Insurance Manual.

Some states have codified their own mortality tables, so it is advisable to examine your own state's laws on this search.

See Immel, "Actuarial Tables and Damage Awards," 19 Ohio St. L.J. 240 (1958) and Duffey "Life Expectancy and Loss of Earning Capacity," 19 Ohio St. L.J. 314 (1958). Belli, *Trial & Tort Trends*, 1959 Seminar at Pp. 300 and 347. Speiser "Recovery for Wrongful Death," Sec. 3:8, p. 89.

3. *Gulf, C. & S. F.R. Co. v. Johnson* (1895), 10 Tex. Civ. App. 254, 31 S.W. 255.

4. *Gordon v. Tweedy* (1883), 74 Ala. 232; *Froeming v. Stockton Elec. R. Co.* (1915), 171 Cal. 401, 153 P. 712. Speiser "Recovery for Wrongful Death," Sec. 3:8, p. 90.

5. *Montellier v. U.S.* (1962 D.C. N.Y.), 202 F.S. 384, aff'd. CA 2, 315 F. 2nd 180.

life expectancy for white males and females; and a joint life table issued by Metropolitan Life Insurance Company for all persons.[6]

SECTION 5 - LIFE TABLES

57

Table 5-1. Abridged Life Tables for Total, Male, and Female Population: United States, 1968

Age interval	Proportion dying	Of 100,000 born alive		Stationary population		Average remaining lifetime
Period of life between two exact ages stated in years	Proportion of persons alive at beginning of age interval dying during interval	Number living at beginning of age interval	Number dying during age interval	In the age interval	In this and all subsequent age intervals	Average number of years of life remaining at beginning of age interval
(1)	(2)	(3)	(4)	(5)	(6)	(7)
x to x+n	$_nq_x$	l_x	$_nd_x$	$_nL_x$	T_x	$\overset{\circ}{e}_x$
TOTAL						
0-1	0.0218	100,000	2,177	98,062	7,017,538	70.2
1-5	.0034	97,823	337	390,485	6,919,276	70.7
5-10	.0022	97,486	211	486,860	6,528,791	67.0
10-15	.0021	97,275	203	485,917	6,041,931	62.1
15-20	.0054	97,072	527	484,151	5,556,014	57.2
20-25	.0071	96,545	687	481,059	5,071,863	52.5
25-30	.0071	95,858	680	477,614	4,590,824	47.9
30-35	.0087	95,178	827	473,918	4,113,210	43.2
35-40	.0126	94,351	1,187	468,984	3,639,292	38.6
40-45	.0190	93,164	1,772	461,706	3,170,308	34.0
45-50	.0292	91,392	2,671	450,769	2,708,602	29.6
50-55	.0450	88,721	3,989	434,222	2,257,833	25.4
55-60	.0678	84,732	5,745	410,090	1,823,611	21.5
60-65	.1005	78,987	7,937	376,047	1,413,521	17.9
65-70	.1461	71,050	10,382	330,279	1,037,474	14.6
70-75	.2134	60,668	12,944	271,915	707,195	11.7
75-80	.2913	47,724	13,905	204,453	435,280	9.1
80-85	.4076	33,821	13,784	133,946	230,827	6.8
85 and over	1.0000	20,057	20,057	96,881	96,881	4.8
MALE						
0-1	.0245	100,000	2,451	97,805	6,660,561	66.6
1-5	.0038	97,549	368	389,319	6,562,756	67.3
5-10	.0025	97,181	246	485,248	6,173,437	63.5
10-15	.0027	96,935	257	484,112	5,688,189	58.7
15-20	.0078	96,678	751	481,686	5,204,077	53.8
20-25	.0108	95,927	1,056	477,078	4,722,391	49.2
25-30	.0099	94,891	943	472,092	4,245,313	44.7
30-35	.0114	93,948	1,069	467,176	3,775,221	40.2
35-40	.0159	92,879	1,475	460,955	3,306,045	35.6
40-45	.0241	91,404	2,201	451,925	2,845,090	31.1
45-50	.0377	89,203	3,363	438,249	2,393,165	26.8
50-55	.0596	85,840	5,112	417,188	1,954,916	22.9
55-60	.0916	80,728	7,396	386,109	1,537,728	19.0
60-65	.1366	73,332	10,021	342,649	1,151,619	15.7
65-70	.1950	63,311	12,216	296,774	808,970	12.8
70-75	.2784	51,095	14,222	220,314	522,196	10.2
75-80	.3557	36,873	13,115	151,497	301,882	8.2
80-85	.4597	23,758	10,922	90,429	150,385	6.3
85 and over	1.0000	12,836	12,836	59,956	59,956	4.7
FEMALE						
0-1	.0189	100,000	1,890	98,332	7,395,849	74.0
1-5	.0051	98,110	305	391,702	7,296,917	74.4
5-10	.0018	97,805	175	488,545	6,905,215	70.6
10-15	.0015	97,630	148	487,799	6,416,670	65.7
15-20	.0030	97,482	296	486,717	5,928,871	60.8
20-25	.0037	97,186	357	485,067	5,442,154	56.0
25-30	.0043	96,829	419	483,144	4,957,087	51.2
30-35	.0061	96,410	588	480,662	4,473,943	46.4
35-40	.0094	95,822	902	477,001	3,993,281	41.7
40-45	.0142	94,920	1,349	471,450	3,516,280	37.0
45-50	.0212	93,571	1,988	463,209	3,044,830	32.5
50-55	.0311	91,583	2,852	451,179	2,581,621	28.2
55-60	.0454	88,731	4,028	434,195	2,130,442	24.0
60-65	.0672	84,703	5,696	410,099	1,696,247	20.0
65-70	.1051	79,007	8,303	375,423	1,286,148	16.3
70-75	.1611	70,704	11,391	326,474	910,725	12.9
75-80	.2424	59,313	14,379	261,976	584,251	9.9
80-85	.3702	44,934	16,657	182,916	322,275	7.2
85 and over	1.0000	28,297	28,297	139,359	139,359	4.9

6. The complete tables are titled as follows: "Vital Statistics of the United States, 1968–Volume II–Sec. 5 Life Tables"; Statistical Bulletin of July 1966 "Years of Joint Expectation of Life for Men and Women, United States 1959-61" issued by Metropolitan Life Insurance Company. Actuarial Note Number 14, March 1965, U.S. Department of Health, Education and Welfare, Social Security Administration, "Joint-Life Immediate Annuities Based On The United States Life Tables For White Persons, 1959-61" by Francisco Bayo, Division of the Actuary.

SECTION 5 - LIFE TABLES

Table 5-2. Abridged Life Tables by Color and Sex: United States, 1968

Age interval — Period of life between two exact ages stated in years (1) $_nq_x$	Proportion dying (2) $_nq_x$	Of 100,000 born alive — Number living at beginning of age interval (3) l_x	Of 100,000 born alive — Number dying during age interval (4) $_nd_x$	Stationary population — In the age interval (5) $_nL_x$	Stationary population — In this and all subsequent age intervals (6) T_x	Average remaining lifetime (7) $\overset{o}{e}_x$
WHITE						
0-1	0.0192	100,000	1,919	98,266	7,110,424	71.1
1-5	.0030	98,081	299	391,617	7,012,158	71.5
5-10	.0020	97,782	199	488,375	6,620,541	67.7
10-15	.0019	97,583	190	487,487	6,132,166	62.8
15-20	.0051	97,393	499	485,815	5,644,679	58.0
20-25	.0064	96,894	619	482,937	5,158,864	53.2
25-30	.0059	96,275	569	479,961	4,675,927	48.6
30-35	.0069	95,706	663	476,950	4,195,966	43.8
35-40	.0103	95,043	982	472,934	3,719,016	39.1
40-45	.0163	94,061	1,534	466,769	3,246,082	34.5
45-50	.0262	92,527	2,421	457,047	2,779,313	30.0
50-55	.0416	90,106	3,744	441,741	2,322,266	25.8
55-60	.0635	86,362	5,484	418,902	1,880,525	21.8
60-65	.0953	80,878	7,705	386,155	1,461,623	18.1
65-70	.1384	73,173	10,124	341,609	1,075,490	14.7
70-75	.2074	63,049	13,076	283,621	733,881	11.6
75-80	.2919	49,973	14,586	214,083	450,260	9.0
80-85	.4133	35,387	14,625	139,628	236,177	6.7
85 and over	1.0000	20,762	20,762	96,549	96,549	4.7
WHITE, MALE						
0-1	0.0219	100,000	2,186	98,216	6,754,209	67.5
1-5	.0033	97,814	326	390,494	6,655,993	68.0
5-10	.0024	97,488	232	486,822	6,265,699	64.3
10-15	.0025	97,256	239	485,758	5,778,877	59.4
15-20	.0073	97,017	710	483,469	5,293,119	54.6
20-25	.0098	96,307	943	479,189	4,809,650	49.9
25-30	.0083	95,364	794	474,815	4,330,461	45.4
30-35	.0091	94,570	860	470,790	3,855,646	40.8
35-40	.0131	93,710	1,232	465,691	3,384,856	36.1
40-45	.0208	92,478	1,927	457,959	2,919,165	31.6
45-50	.0341	90,551	3,088	445,656	2,461,206	27.2
50-55	.0557	87,463	4,876	425,885	2,015,550	23.0
55-60	.0872	82,587	7,198	395,926	1,589,665	19.2
60-65	.1320	75,389	9,949	353,163	1,193,739	15.8
65-70	.1864	65,440	12,197	297,539	840,576	12.1
70-75	.2722	53,243	14,494	230,495	543,037	10.2
75-80	.3571	38,749	13,835	159,109	312,542	8.1
80-85	.4675	24,914	11,646	94,307	153,433	6.2
85 and over	1.0000	13,268	13,268	59,126	59,126	4.5
WHITE, FEMALE						
0-1	0.0164	100,000	1,637	98,551	7,488,111	74.9
1-5	.0027	98,363	270	392,806	7,389,580	75.1
5-10	.0017	98,093	165	490,015	6,996,774	71.3
10-15	.0014	97,928	139	489,310	6,506,759	66.4
15-20	.0029	97,789	281	488,281	6,017,449	61.5
20-25	.0032	97,508	314	486,773	5,529,168	56.7
25-30	.0035	97,194	344	485,143	5,042,395	51.9
30-35	.0048	96,850	465	483,154	4,557,252	47.1
35-40	.0076	96,385	731	480,224	4,074,098	42.3
40-45	.0119	95,654	1,141	475,624	3,593,874	37.6
45-50	.0186	94,513	1,762	468,460	3,118,250	33.0
50-55	.0280	92,751	2,599	457,623	2,649,790	28.6
55-60	.0412	90,152	3,715	442,080	2,192,167	24.3
60-65	.0616	86,437	5,323	419,749	1,750,087	20.2
65-70	.0965	81,114	7,828	387,198	1,330,338	16.4
70-75	.1554	73,286	11,392	339,521	943,140	12.9
75-80	.2426	61,894	15,013	273,446	603,619	9.8
80-85	.3749	46,881	17,578	190,304	330,173	7.0
85 and over	1.0000	29,303	29,303	139,869	139,869	4.8

Age interval — Period of life between two exact ages stated in years (1) $_nq_x$	Proportion dying (2) $_nq_x$	Of 100,000 born alive — Number living at beginning of age interval (3) l_x	Of 100,000 born alive — Number dying during age interval (4) $_nd_x$	Stationary population — In the age interval (5) $_nL_x$	Stationary population — In this and all subsequent age intervals (6) T_x	Average remaining lifetime (7) $\overset{o}{e}_x$
ALL OTHER						
0-1	0.0345	100,000	3,451	97,055	6,573,079	63.7
1-5	.0055	96,549	527	384,582	6,276,024	65.0
5-10	.0029	96,022	276	479,334	5,891,142	61.4
10-15	.0030	95,746	283	478,087	5,411,788	56.5
15-20	.0074	95,463	705	475,738	4,933,701	51.7
20-25	.0123	94,760	1,163	471,047	4,457,963	47.0
25-30	.0159	93,597	1,492	464,411	3,986,916	42.6
30-35	.0217	92,105	1,996	455,780	3,522,505	38.2
35-40	.0294	90,109	2,650	444,300	3,066,725	34.0
40-45	.0411	87,459	3,592	428,744	2,622,425	30.0
45-50	.0559	83,867	4,685	408,283	2,193,681	26.2
50-55	.0762	79,182	6,034	381,586	1,785,398	22.5
55-60	.1085	73,148	7,935	346,609	1,403,812	19.2
60-65	.1528	65,213	9,966	301,676	1,057,203	16.2
65-70	.2294	55,247	12,621	244,985	755,527	13.7
70-75	.2667	42,626	12,219	182,322	510,542	12.0
75-80	.2835	30,407	8,619	130,263	328,220	10.8
80-85	.3330	21,788	7,255	90,377	197,957	9.1
85 and over	1.0000	14,533	14,533	107,580	107,580	7.4
ALL OTHER, MALE						
0-1	0.0578	100,000	3,778	96,750	6,005,398	60.1
1-5	.0060	96,222	576	383,447	5,908,648	61.4
5-10	.0054	95,646	522	477,364	5,526,201	57.8
10-15	.0038	95,324	364	475,808	5,048,837	53.0
15-20	.0107	94,960	1,015	472,538	4,573,029	48.2
20-25	.0182	93,945	1,706	465,670	4,100,491	43.6
25-30	.0225	92,239	2,077	456,152	3,634,821	39.4
30-35	.0293	90,162	2,642	444,470	3,178,669	35.3
35-40	.0380	87,520	3,322	429,747	2,734,199	31.2
40-45	.0521	84,198	4,387	410,541	2,304,452	27.4
45-50	.0701	79,811	5,591	385,837	1,893,911	23.7
50-55	.0956	74,220	7,092	354,205	1,508,074	20.3
55-60	.1344	67,128	9,023	315,793	1,153,871	17.2
60-65	.1830	58,105	10,633	264,584	840,078	14.5
65-70	.2605	47,472	12,368	206,585	575,494	12.1
70-75	.3524	35,104	12,370	143,923	368,901	10.5
75-80	.3393	22,734	7,713	93,993	224,978	9.9
80-85	.3669	15,021	5,512	60,881	130,985	8.7
85 and over	1.0000	9,509	9,509	70,104	70,104	7.4
ALL OTHER, FEMALE						
0-1	0.0311	100,000	3,114	97,369	6,753,955	67.5
1-5	.0049	96,886	476	386,361	6,656,586	68.7
5-10	.0024	96,410	229	481,410	6,270,225	65.0
10-15	.0021	96,181	202	480,432	5,788,815	60.2
15-20	.0041	95,979	390	479,017	5,308,383	55.3
20-25	.0069	95,589	660	476,399	4,829,366	50.5
25-30	.0100	94,929	948	472,422	4,352,967	45.9
30-35	.0151	93,981	1,417	466,573	3,880,545	41.3
35-40	.0222	92,564	2,055	457,991	3,413,972	36.9
40-45	.0317	90,509	2,866	445,721	2,955,981	32.7
45-50	.0432	87,643	3,790	429,285	2,510,260	28.6
50-55	.0589	83,853	4,935	407,593	2,080,975	24.8
55-60	.0846	78,918	6,675	378,573	1,673,382	21.2
60-65	.1245	72,243	8,996	339,115	1,294,809	17.9
65-70	.1987	63,247	12,569	285,260	955,694	15.1
70-75	.2327	50,678	11,794	224,049	670,434	13.2
75-80	.2406	38,884	9,354	171,059	446,385	11.5
80-85	.3054	29,530	9,020	124,764	275,346	9.3
85 and over	1.0000	20,510	20,510	150,582	150,582	7.3

SECTION 5 - LIFE TABLES

Table 5-4. Expectation of Life at Single Years of Age, by Color and Sex: United States, 1968

Age	Total			White			All other		
	Both sexes	Male	Female	Both sexes	Male	Female	Both sexes	Male	Female
0	70.2	66.6	74.0	71.1	67.5	74.9	63.7	60.1	67.5
1	70.7	67.3	74.4	71.5	68.0	75.1	65.0	61.4	68.7
2	69.8	66.4	73.5	70.6	67.1	74.2	64.2	60.6	67.9
3	68.9	65.4	72.5	69.6	66.2	73.3	63.2	59.7	66.9
4	67.9	64.5	71.6	68.7	65.2	72.3	62.3	58.7	66.0
5	67.0	63.5	70.6	67.7	64.3	71.3	61.4	57.8	65.0
6	66.0	62.6	69.6	66.7	63.3	70.4	60.4	56.8	64.1
7	65.0	61.6	68.7	65.8	62.4	69.4	59.4	55.9	63.1
8	64.1	60.6	67.7	64.8	61.4	68.4	58.5	54.9	62.1
9	63.1	59.7	66.7	63.8	60.4	67.4	57.5	53.9	61.2
10	62.1	58.7	65.7	62.8	59.4	66.4	56.5	53.0	60.2
11	61.1	57.7	64.7	61.9	58.4	65.5	55.5	52.0	59.2
12	60.1	56.7	63.8	60.9	57.5	64.5	54.6	51.0	58.2
13	59.2	55.7	62.8	59.9	56.5	63.5	53.6	50.1	57.3
14	58.2	54.8	61.8	58.9	55.5	62.5	52.6	49.1	56.3
15	57.2	53.8	60.8	58.0	54.6	61.5	51.7	48.2	55.3
16	56.3	52.9	59.8	57.0	53.6	60.6	50.7	47.2	54.3
17	55.3	52.0	58.9	56.1	52.7	59.6	49.8	46.3	53.4
18	54.4	51.0	57.9	55.1	51.8	58.6	48.9	45.4	52.4
19	53.5	50.1	57.0	54.2	50.9	57.7	48.0	44.5	51.5
20	52.5	49.2	56.0	53.2	49.9	56.7	47.0	43.6	50.5
21	51.6	48.3	55.0	52.3	49.0	55.7	46.1	42.8	49.6
22	50.7	47.4	54.1	51.4	48.1	54.8	45.2	41.9	48.6
23	49.8	46.5	53.1	50.4	47.2	53.8	44.4	41.1	47.7
24	48.8	45.6	52.2	49.5	46.3	52.8	43.5	40.2	46.8
25	47.9	44.7	51.2	48.6	45.4	51.9	42.6	39.4	45.9
26	47.0	43.8	50.2	47.6	44.5	50.9	41.7	38.6	44.9
27	46.0	42.9	49.3	46.7	43.6	49.9	40.8	37.7	44.0
28	45.1	42.0	48.3	45.7	42.6	49.0	40.0	36.9	43.1
29	44.2	41.1	47.4	44.8	41.7	48.0	39.1	36.1	42.2
30	43.2	40.2	46.4	43.8	40.8	47.1	38.2	35.3	41.3
31	42.3	39.2	45.5	42.9	39.8	46.1	37.4	34.4	40.4
32	41.4	38.3	44.5	42.0	38.9	45.1	36.5	33.6	39.5
33	40.4	37.4	43.6	41.0	38.0	44.2	35.7	32.8	38.6
34	39.5	36.5	42.6	40.1	37.0	43.2	34.9	32.0	37.7
35	38.6	35.6	41.7	39.1	36.1	42.3	34.0	31.2	36.9
36	37.7	34.7	40.7	38.2	35.2	41.3	33.2	30.5	36.0
37	36.7	33.8	39.8	37.3	34.3	40.4	32.4	29.7	35.2
38	35.8	32.9	38.9	36.3	33.4	39.4	31.6	28.9	34.3
39	34.9	32.0	38.0	35.4	32.5	38.5	30.8	28.1	33.5
40	34.0	31.1	37.0	34.5	31.6	37.6	30.0	27.4	32.7
41	33.1	30.3	36.1	33.6	30.7	36.6	29.2	26.6	31.8
42	32.3	29.4	35.2	32.7	29.8	35.7	28.4	25.9	31.0
43	31.4	28.5	34.3	31.8	28.9	34.8	27.7	25.2	30.2
44	30.5	27.7	33.4	30.9	28.0	33.9	26.9	24.4	29.4
45	29.6	26.8	32.5	30.0	27.2	33.0	26.2	23.7	28.6
46	28.8	26.0	31.7	29.2	26.3	32.1	25.4	23.0	27.9
47	27.9	25.2	30.8	28.3	25.5	31.2	24.7	22.3	27.1
48	27.1	24.4	29.9	27.4	24.7	30.3	24.0	21.7	26.3
49	26.3	23.6	29.0	26.6	23.8	29.4	23.3	21.0	25.6
50	25.4	22.8	28.2	25.8	23.0	28.6	22.5	20.3	24.8
51	24.6	22.0	27.3	25.0	22.3	27.7	21.9	19.7	24.1
52	23.8	21.2	26.5	24.1	21.5	26.8	21.2	19.0	23.3
53	23.1	20.5	25.7	23.3	20.7	26.0	20.5	18.4	22.6
54	22.3	19.8	24.8	22.6	20.0	25.2	19.8	17.8	21.9
55	21.5	19.0	24.0	21.8	19.2	24.3	19.2	17.2	21.2
56	20.8	18.3	23.2	21.0	18.5	23.5	18.6	16.6	20.5
57	20.0	17.7	22.4	20.3	17.8	22.7	18.0	16.0	19.8
58	19.3	17.0	21.6	19.5	17.1	21.9	17.4	15.5	19.2
59	18.6	16.3	20.8	18.8	16.5	21.0	16.8	15.0	18.5
60	17.9	15.7	20.0	18.1	15.8	20.2	16.2	14.5	17.9
61	17.2	15.1	19.3	17.4	15.2	19.5	15.7	14.0	17.3
62	16.5	14.5	18.5	16.7	14.6	18.7	15.1	13.5	16.7
63	15.9	13.9	17.7	16.0	14.0	17.9	14.6	13.0	16.1
64	15.2	13.3	17.0	15.3	13.4	17.1	14.1	12.5	15.6
65	14.6	12.8	16.3	14.7	12.8	16.4	13.7	12.1	15.1
66	14.0	12.2	15.6	14.1	12.3	15.7	13.3	11.7	14.7
67	13.4	11.7	14.9	13.4	11.7	14.9	12.9	11.4	14.3
68	12.8	11.2	14.2	12.8	11.2	14.2	12.6	11.0	13.9
69	12.2	10.7	13.5	12.2	10.7	13.5	12.3	10.8	13.5
70	11.7	10.2	12.9	11.6	10.2	12.9	12.0	10.5	13.2
71	11.1	9.8	12.2	11.1	9.7	12.2	11.7	10.3	12.9
72	10.6	9.4	11.6	10.5	9.3	11.6	11.5	10.2	12.6
73	10.1	9.0	11.1	10.0	8.9	10.9	11.3	10.1	12.2
74	9.6	8.6	10.4	9.5	8.5	10.3	11.0	10.0	11.9
75	9.1	8.2	9.9	9.0	8.1	9.8	10.8	9.9	11.5
76	8.6	7.8	9.3	8.5	7.7	9.2	10.5	9.8	11.1
77	8.2	7.4	8.7	8.0	7.3	8.6	10.2	9.6	10.7
78	7.7	7.1	8.2	7.6	6.9	8.1	9.9	9.5	10.2
79	7.3	6.7	7.7	7.1	6.5	7.6	9.5	9.0	9.8
80	6.8	6.3	7.2	6.7	6.2	7.0	9.1	8.7	9.3
81	6.4	6.0	6.7	6.2	5.8	6.6	8.7	8.4	8.9
82	6.0	5.7	6.2	5.8	5.5	6.1	8.3	8.1	8.4
83	5.6	5.3	5.8	5.4	5.1	5.6	8.0	7.9	8.0
84	5.2	5.0	5.3	5.0	4.8	5.2	7.7	7.6	7.6
85	4.8	4.7	4.9	4.7	4.5	4.8	7.4	7.4	7.3

Table 5-5. Life Table Values by Color and Sex: Death-Registration States, 1900-1902 to 1919-21, and United States, 1929-31 to 1968

[Alaska and Hawaii included for 1959 and 1960. For decennial periods prior to 1929-31, data are for groups of registration States as follows: 1900-1902 and 1909-11, 10 States and the District of Columbia; 1919-21, 34 States and the District of Columbia. For 1900-1902 to 1929-31, figures for "all other, male" and "all other, female" cover only Negroes. However, in no case did the Negro population comprise less than 95 percent of the corresponding "all other" population]

Age, color, and sex	Number of survivors out of 100,000 born alive (l_x)									Average number of years of life remaining ($\mathring{e}_x$)								
	1968	1967	1959-61	1949-51	1939-41	1929-31	1919-21	1909-11	1900-1902	1968	1967	1959-61	1949-51	1939-41	1929-31	1919-21	1909-11	1900-1902
WHITE, MALE																		
0	100,000	100,000	100,000	100,000	100,000	100,000	100,000	100,000	100,000	67.5	67.8	67.55	66.31	62.81	59.12	56.34	50.23	48.23
1	97,814	97,768	97,408	96,931	95,188	93,768	91,975	87,674	86,655	68.0	68.3	68.34	67.41	64.98	62.04	60.24	56.26	54.61
5	97,488	97,436	97,015	96,403	94,150	91,738	88,842	82,972	80,864	64.3	64.6	64.61	63.77	61.68	59.38	58.31	55.37	54.43
10	97,256	97,213	96,758	96,069	93,601	90,810	87,530	81,519	79,109	59.4	59.7	59.78	58.98	57.03	54.96	54.15	51.32	50.59
15	97,017	96,976	96,503	95,728	93,089	90,074	86,546	80,549	78,037	54.6	54.9	54.93	54.18	52.33	50.39	49.74	46.91	46.25
20	96,307	96,298	95,908	95,104	92,293	88,904	84,997	79,116	76,376	49.9	50.2	50.25	49.52	47.76	46.02	45.60	42.71	42.19
25	95,364	95,421	95,106	94,294	91,241	87,371	83,061	77,047	73,907	45.4	45.7	45.65	44.93	43.28	41.78	41.60	38.79	38.52
30	94,570	94,656	94,401	93,489	90,092	85,707	80,888	74,810	71,219	40.8	41.0	40.97	40.29	38.80	37.54	37.65	34.87	34.88
35	93,710	93,812	93,589	92,543	88,713	83,812	78,441	72,108	68,245	36.1	36.4	36.31	35.68	34.36	33.33	33.74	31.08	31.29
40	92,478	92,583	92,427	91,173	86,880	81,457	75,733	68,848	64,954	31.6	31.8	31.73	31.17	30.03	29.22	29.86	27.43	27.74
45	90,551	90,692	90,533	89,002	84,285	78,345	72,696	65,115	61,369	27.2	27.4	27.34	26.87	25.87	25.28	26.00	23.86	24.21
50	87,463	87,632	87,424	85,601	80,521	74,288	69,107	60,741	57,274	23.0	23.3	23.22	22.83	21.96	21.51	22.22	20.39	20.76
55	82,587	82,831	82,463	80,496	75,156	68,981	64,574	55,622	52,491	19.2	19.5	19.45	19.11	18.34	17.97	18.59	17.03	17.42
60	75,389	75,692	75,485	73,172	67,787	61,933	58,498	48,987	46,452	15.8	16.1	16.01	15.76	15.05	14.72	15.25	13.98	14.35
65	65,440	65,990	65,834	63,541	58,305	52,964	50,663	40,862	39,245	12.8	13.0	12.97	12.75	12.07	11.77	12.21	11.25	11.51
70	53,243	53,962	53,825	51,735	46,739	41,880	40,873	31,527	30,640	10.2	10.4	10.29	10.07	9.42	9.20	9.51	8.83	9.03
75	38,749	39,716	40,207	38,104	33,404	29,471	29,205	21,585	21,387	8.1	8.2	7.92	7.77	7.17	7.02	7.30	6.75	6.84
80	24,914	25,904	25,993	24,005	19,860	17,221	17,655	12,160	12,266	6.2	6.2	5.89	5.88	5.38	5.26	5.47	5.09	5.10
85	13,268	13,896	13,065	12,015	9,013	7,572	8,154	5,145	5,252	4.5	4.5	4.34	4.35	4.02	3.99	4.06	3.88	3.81
ALL OTHER, MALE																		
0	100,000	100,000	100,000	100,000	100,000	100,000	100,000	100,000	100,000	60.1	61.1	61.48	58.91	52.33	47.55	47.14	34.05	32.54
1	96,222	96,080	95,301	94,911	91,696	91,268	89,499	78,065	74,674	61.4	62.6	63.50	61.06	56.05	51.08	51.63	42.53	42.46
5	95,646	95,498	94,570	93,921	89,920	88,412	85,195	68,589	64,385	57.8	59.0	59.98	57.69	53.13	48.69	50.18	44.25	45.06
10	95,324	95,184	94,734	93,453	89,211	87,311	83,768	66,377	61,730	53.0	54.2	55.19	52.96	48.54	44.27	45.99	40.65	41.90
15	94,960	94,870	93,874	92,965	88,417	86,152	82,332	64,478	59,667	48.2	49.4	50.39	48.23	43.95	39.83	41.75	36.77	38.26
20	93,945	93,982	93,108	91,941	86,770	83,621	79,057	61,426	56,733	43.6	44.8	45.78	43.73	39.74	35.95	38.36	33.46	35.11
25	92,239	92,432	91,825	90,285	84,055	79,516	74,540	57,736	53,285	39.4	40.5	41.38	39.49	35.94	32.67	35.54	30.44	32.21
30	90,162	90,499	90,270	88,327	80,865	75,083	70,344	54,073	49,867	35.3	36.3	37.05	35.31	32.25	29.45	32.51	27.33	29.25
35	87,520	88,080	88,331	85,940	77,185	70,049	65,873	49,865	46,541	31.2	32.2	32.81	31.21	28.67	26.39	29.54	24.42	26.16
40	84,198	85,013	85,744	82,832	72,830	64,710	61,353	45,414	42,989	27.4	28.3	28.72	27.29	25.23	23.36	26.53	21.57	23.12
45	79,811	80,882	82,075	78,686	67,514	58,432	56,589	40,563	39,230	23.7	24.6	24.89	23.59	22.02	20.59	23.55	18.85	20.09
50	74,220	75,675	77,239	72,891	60,766	51,748	51,880	35,427	34,766	20.3	21.1	21.28	20.25	19.18	17.92	20.47	16.21	17.34
55	67,128	68,720	70,351	65,122	52,867	44,436	46,581	29,754	29,987	17.2	18.0	18.11	17.36	16.67	15.46	17.50	13.82	14.69
60	58,105	59,951	61,669	55,535	44,370	36,790	40,506	23,750	24,194	14.5	15.3	15.29	14.91	14.38	13.15	14.74	11.67	12.62
65	47,472	50,180	51,392	45,198	35,912	29,314	34,042	17,806	19,015	12.1	12.7	12.84	12.75	12.18	10.87	12.07	9.74	10.38
70	35,104	37,539	39,914	35,018	27,688	21,741	26,923	12,295	13,829	10.5	11.2	10.81	10.74	10.06	8.78	9.58	8.00	8.33
75	22,734	25,605	29,064	25,472	19,765	14,419	18,854	7,494	8,892	9.9	10.3	8.93	8.83	8.09	6.99	7.61	6.54	6.60
80	15,021	17,348	19,994	16,904	12,352	8,239	11,615	3,894	4,831	8.7	9.0	6.87	7.07	6.46	5.42	5.83	5.23	5.12
85	9,509	11,344	11,620	9,898	6,492	3,660	5,605	1,747	2,030	7.4	7.5	5.08	5.38	5.08	4.30	4.53	4.48	4.04
WHITE, FEMALE																		
0	100,000	100,000	100,000	100,000	100,000	100,000	100,000	100,000	100,000	74.9	75.1	74.19	72.03	67.29	62.67	58.53	53.62	51.08
1	98,363	98,318	98,036	97,645	96,211	95,037	93,608	89,774	88,939	75.1	75.3	74.68	72.77	68.93	64.93	61.51	58.69	56.39
5	98,093	98,053	97,709	97,199	95,309	93,216	90,721	85,349	83,426	71.3	71.5	70.92	69.09	65.57	62.17	59.43	57.67	56.03
10	97,928	97,891	97,525	96,960	94,890	92,466	89,564	83,979	81,723	66.4	66.7	66.05	64.26	60.85	57.65	55.17	53.57	52.15
15	97,789	97,754	97,375	96,756	94,534	91,894	88,712	83,093	80,680	61.5	61.7	61.15	59.39	56.07	53.00	50.67	49.12	47.79
20	97,508	97,486	97,135	96,454	93,984	90,939	87,281	81,750	78,978	56.7	56.9	56.29	54.56	51.38	48.52	46.46	44.88	43.77
25	97,194	97,179	96,844	96,072	93,228	89,524	85,163	79,865	76,588	51.9	52.1	51.45	49.77	46.78	44.25	42.55	40.88	40.05
30	96,850	96,841	96,499	95,605	92,320	87,972	82,740	77,676	73,887	47.1	47.2	46.63	45.00	42.21	39.99	38.72	36.96	36.42
35	96,385	96,382	96,026	94,977	91,211	86,248	80,206	75,200	70,971	42.3	42.5	41.84	40.28	37.70	35.73	34.86	33.09	32.82
40	95,654	95,662	95,326	94,080	89,805	84,256	77,624	72,425	67,935	37.6	37.8	37.13	35.64	33.25	31.52	30.94	29.26	29.17
45	94,513	94,550	94,228	92,725	87,920	81,780	74,871	69,341	64,677	33.0	33.2	32.53	31.12	28.90	27.39	26.98	25.45	25.51
50	92,751	92,822	92,522	90,685	85,267	78,572	71,547	65,629	61,005	28.6	28.7	28.08	26.76	24.72	23.41	23.12	21.74	21.89
55	90,152	90,293	89,967	87,699	81,520	74,321	67,323	61,053	56,509	24.3	24.5	23.81	22.58	20.73	19.60	19.40	18.18	18.43
60	86,437	86,647	86,339	83,279	76,200	68,462	61,704	54,900	50,752	20.2	20.4	19.69	18.64	17.00	16.05	15.93	14.92	15.23
65	81,114	81,486	80,739	76,773	68,701	60,499	54,299	47,086	43,806	16.4	16.5	15.88	15.00	13.56	12.81	12.75	11.97	12.23
70	73,286	73,682	72,507	67,545	58,363	49,932	44,638	37,482	35,206	12.9	13.0	12.38	11.68	10.50	9.98	9.94	9.38	9.59
75	61,894	62,403	60,461	54,397	44,685	37,024	32,777	26,569	25,362	9.8	9.9	9.28	8.87	7.92	7.56	7.62	7.20	7.33
80	46,881	47,554	44,676	38,026	28,882	23,053	20,492	15,929	15,349	7.0	7.1	6.67	6.59	5.88	5.63	5.70	5.35	5.50
85	29,303	29,886	26,046	21,348	14,487	10,937	9,909	7,152	7,149	4.8	4.8	4.66	4.83	4.34	4.24	4.24	4.06	4.10
ALL OTHER, FEMALE																		
0	100,000	100,000	100,000	100,000	100,000	100,000	100,000	100,000	100,000	67.5	68.2	66.47	62.70	55.51	49.[illegible]1	46.92	37.67	35.04
1	96,886	96,761	96,172	95,913	93,318	92,796	91,251	81,493	78,525	68.7	69.5	68.10	64.37	58.47	52.33	50.39	45.15	43.54
5	96,410	96,291	95,543	95,055	91,710	90,185	87,149	72,768	68,056	65.0	65.8	64.54	60.93	55.47	49.81	48.70	46.42	46.04
10	96,181	96,062	95,265	94,679	91,092	89,201	85,607	70,508	65,111	60.2	61.0	59.72	56.17	50.83	45.33	44.54	42.84	43.02
15	95,979	95,867	95,057	94,343	90,363	88,088	83,954	68,218	62,384	55.3	56.1	54.85	51.36	46.22	40.87	40.36	39.18	39.79
20	95,589	95,485	94,660	93,544	88,505	85,078	80,154	64,764	59,053	50.5	51.3	50.07	46.77	42.14	37.22	37.15	36.14	36.89
25	94,929	94,848	94,005	92,336	85,961	81,067	75,359	61,430	55,795	45.9	46.6	45.40	42.35	38.31	33.93	34.35	32.97	33.90
30	93,981	93,950	93,070	90,799	83,147	76,816	70,633	58,281	52,773	41.3	42.1	40.83	38.02	34.52	30.67	31.48	29.61	30.70
35	92,564	92,525	91,670	88,805	79,879	72,192	65,857	54,595	49,567	36.9	37.7	36.41	33.82	30.83	27.47	28.58	26.44	27.52
40	90,509	90,529	89,676	86,052	75,908	67,271	61,130	50,568	46,146	32.7	33.4	32.16	29.82	27.31	24.30	25.60	23.34	24.37
45	87,643	87,879	86,793	82,257	71,061	61,365	56,230	45,947	42,279	28.6	29.4	28.14	26.07	24.00	21.39	22.61	20.43	21.36
50	83,853	84,239	82,979	77,007	64,886	54,920	50,780	40,886	37,681	24.8	25.5	24.31	22.67	21.04	18.60	19.76	17.65	18.67
55	78,918	79,359	77,362	70,196	57,419	47,074	44,742	35,415	33,124	21.2	21.9	20.89	19.62	18.44	16.27	17.09	14.98	15.88
60	72,243	72,756	69,941	61,758	49,102	38,761	37,954	28,908	27,524	17.9	18.7	17.83	16.95	16.14	14.22	14.69	12.78	13.60
65	63,247	64,255	60,825	52,358	40,718	30,852	31,044	22,302	21,995	15.1	15.8	15.12	14.54	13.95	12.24	12.41	10.82	11.38
70	50,678	52,087	51,274	42,612	32,579	23,341	24,107	15,871	16,140	13.2	13.9	12.46	12.29	11.81	10.38	10.25	9.22	9.62
75	38,884	41,069	40,540	32,981	24,668	16,576	17,216	10,657	11,066	11.5	12.0	10.10	10.15	9.80	8.62	8.37	7.55	7.90
80	29,530	31,595	30,315	23,712	17,157	10,822	11,151	6,324	6,708	9.3	9.8	7.66	8.15	8.00	6.90	6.58	6.05	6.48
85	20,510	22,565	19,744	15,550	10,658	6,033	5,972	3,029	3,567	7.3	7.7	5.44	6.15	6.38	5.48	5.22	5.09	5.10

TABLE 1
JOINT-LIFE IMMEDIATE ANNUITIES
UNITED STATES WHITE PERSONS: 1959-61 – AT 0% INTEREST RATE

Age of Male	Female older than male by												
	-16	-14	-12	-10	-8	-6	-4	-2	0	2	4	6	8
25	43.6783	43.4438	43.1658	42.8439	42.4752	42.0515	41.5618	40.9996	40.3589	39.6353	38.8267	37.9337	36.9576
26	42.7598	42.5237	42.2470	41.9286	41.5632	41.1403	40.6510	40.0890	39.4484	38.7252	37.9182	37.0274	36.0541
27	41.8356	41.5994	41.3253	41.0106	40.6474	40.2249	39.7360	39.1742	38.5339	37.8118	37.0068	36.1188	35.1487
28	40.9078	40.6729	40.4022	40.0909	39.7287	39.3066	38.8181	38.2566	37.6170	36.8965	36.0940	35.2090	34.2426
29	39.9791	39.7467	39.4798	39.1706	38.8088	38.3873	37.8992	37.3381	36.6996	35.9814	35.1817	34.3000	33.3378
30	39.0517	38.8227	38.5590	38.2508	37.8895	37.4685	36.9807	36.4204	35.7837	35.0679	34.2713	33.3933	32.4360
31	38.1267	37.9013	37.6398	37.3320	36.9714	36.5507	36.0634	35.5043	34.8698	34.1569	33.3635	32.4897	31.5381
32	37.2046	36.9824	36.7218	36.4146	36.0545	35.6342	35.1477	34.5903	33.9583	33.2484	32.4587	31.5898	30.6443
33	36.2858	36.0656	35.8055	35.4989	35.1392	34.7194	34.2341	33.6789	33.0496	32.3430	31.5575	30.6940	29.7554
34	35.3701	35.1509	34.8913	34.5853	34.2259	33.8070	33.3234	32.7706	32.1443	31.4412	30.6605	29.8031	28.8718
35	34.4574	34.2386	33.9797	33.6741	33.3152	32.8975	32.4160	31.8659	31.2428	30.5438	29.7684	28.9177	27.9961
36	33.5479	33.3297	33.0713	32.7661	32.4080	31.9919	31.5128	30.9656	30.3459	29.6515	28.8820	28.0384	27.1231
37	32.6424	32.4249	32.1668	31.8621	31.5052	31.0911	30.6146	30.0704	29.4547	28.7654	28.0023	27.1662	26.2595
38	31.7419	31.5248	31.2671	30.9632	30.6078	30.1960	29.7222	29.1813	28.5700	27.8854	27.1301	26.3019	25.4042
39	30.8471	30.6303	30.3731	30.0702	29.7168	29.3074	28.8364	28.2993	27.6928	27.0153	26.2662	25.4463	24.5577
40	29.9587	29.7423	29.4857	29.1843	28.8329	28.4261	27.9582	27.4252	26.8241	26.1531	25.4115	24.6001	23.7209
41	29.0774	28.8614	28.6059	28.3061	27.9571	27.5529	27.0885	26.5600	25.9647	25.3035	24.5667	23.7640	22.8944
42	28.2040	27.9886	27.7343	27.4366	27.0898	26.6885	26.2280	25.7045	25.1153	24.4581	23.7324	22.9386	22.0788
43	27.3390	27.1245	26.8718	26.5761	26.2318	25.8337	25.3774	24.8594	24.2764	23.6266	22.9091	22.1243	21.2749
44	26.4831	26.2698	26.0189	25.7254	25.3837	24.9891	24.5375	24.0251	23.4488	22.8065	22.0973	21.3218	20.4829
45	25.6371	25.4252	25.1762	24.8849	24.5462	24.1555	23.7089	23.2023	22.6329	21.9982	21.2975	20.5316	19.7025
46	24.8013	24.5910	24.3439	24.0550	23.7195	23.3332	22.8917	22.3913	21.8289	21.2020	20.5099	19.7539	18.9327
47	23.9763	23.7677	23.5227	23.2364	22.9046	22.5228	22.0868	21.5928	21.0374	20.4184	19.7353	18.9984	18.1734
48	23.1638	22.9569	22.7141	22.4307	22.1028	21.7258	21.2955	20.8079	20.2596	19.6486	18.9747	18.2350	17.4254
49	22.3653	22.1602	21.9197	21.6397	21.3159	20.9438	20.5193	20.0382	19.4971	18.8943	18.2287	17.4946	16.6908

TABLE 1 (continued)
JOINT-LIFE IMMEDIATE ANNUITIES
UNITED STATES WHITE PERSONS: 1959-61 - AT 0% INTEREST RATE

Age of Male	Female older than male by												
	-16	-14	-12	-10	-8	-6	-4	-2	0	2	4	6	8
50	21.5820	21.3788	21.1409	20.8644	20.5449	20.1779	19.7592	19.2846	18.7508	18.1564	17.4972	16.7676	15.9714
51	20.8146	20.6135	20.3785	20.1056	19.7906	19.4289	19.0160	18.5479	18.0215	17.4345	16.7800	16.0554	15.2694
52	20.0629	19.8641	19.6322	19.3632	19.0527	18.6962	18.2892	17.8276	17.3088	16.7274	16.0768	15.3587	14.5856
53	19.3257	19.1295	18.9009	18.6359	18.3302	17.9790	17.5778	17.1229	16.6108	16.0335	15.3870	14.6781	13.9194
54	18.6016	18.4082	18.1831	17.9223	17.6213	17.2754	16.8802	16.4322	15.9252	15.3512	14.7105	14.0134	13.2692
55	17.8895	17.6991	17.4777	17.2212	16.9251	16.5847	16.1957	15.7539	15.2505	14.6801	14.0478	13.3641	12.6339
56	17.1889	17.0017	16.7842	16.5321	16.2410	15.9060	15.5235	15.0864	14.5859	14.0208	13.3994	12.7292	12.0122
57	16.5005	16.3167	16.1032	15.8556	15.5695	15.2404	14.8636	14.4298	13.9325	13.3751	12.7661	12.1090	11.4042
58	15.8262	15.6459	15.4364	15.1934	14.9124	14.5892	14.2167	13.7854	13.2928	12.7454	12.1489	11.5039	10.8107
59	15.1683	14.9917	14.7863	14.5479	14.2721	13.9541	13.5844	13.1558	12.6701	12.1340	11.5494	10.9154	10.2335
60	14.5287	14.3557	14.1543	13.9204	13.6500	13.3357	12.9680	12.5434	12.0666	11.5417	10.9680	10.3441	9.6743
61	13.9074	13.7380	13.5407	13.3115	13.0457	12.7338	12.3682	11.9495	11.4828	10.9685	10.4043	9.7905	9.1341
62	13.3038	13.1380	12.9448	12.7203	12.4577	12.1474	11.7851	11.3743	10.9176	10.4128	9.8576	9.2543	8.6127
63	12.7170	12.5549	12.3658	12.1455	11.8849	11.5762	11.2191	10.8173	10.3700	9.8738	9.3272	8.7359	8.1092
64	12.1461	11.9876	11.8029	11.5854	11.3261	11.0201	10.6701	10.2773	9.8386	9.3502	8.8130	8.2350	7.6222
65	11.5901	11.4354	11.2545	11.0388	10.7808	10.4795	10.1375	9.7533	9.3222	8.8415	8.3150	7.7504	7.1517
66	11.0488	10.8981	10.7197	10.5051	10.2495	9.9546	9.6209	9.2444	8.8203	8.3480	7.8335	7.2814	6.6986
67	10.5221	10.3748	10.1980	9.9845	9.7331	9.4455	9.1196	8.7501	8.3328	7.8701	7.3677	6.8284	6.2633
68	10.0094	9.8645	9.6886	9.4773	9.2316	8.9516	8.6328	8.2695	7.8598	7.4079	6.9169	6.3920	5.8440
69	9.5098	9.3662	9.1914	8.9838	8.7449	8.4720	8.1594	7.8023	7.4013	6.9604	6.4810	5.9722	5.4396
70	9.0220	8.8793	8.7064	8.5041	8.2721	8.0056	7.6988	7.3485	6.9574	6.5268	6.0605	5.5675	5.0507
71	8.5453	8.4036	8.2340	8.0378	7.8124	7.5517	7.2505	6.9081	6.5271	6.1071	5.6555	5.1766	4.6790
72	8.0792	7.9392	7.7745	7.5846	7.3651	7.1097	6.8147	6.4814	6.1097	5.7017	5.2647	4.8002	4.3257
73	7.6244	7.4874	7.3283	7.1444	6.9302	6.6799	6.3921	6.0680	5.7059	5.3114	4.8872	4.4403	3.9935
74	7.1820	7.0494	6.8960	6.7175	6.5080	6.2633	5.9837	5.6680	5.3168	4.9355	4.5243	4.0986	3.6835
75	6.7535	6.6258	6.4777	6.3040	6.0990	5.8608	5.5894	5.2823	4.9433	4.5733	4.1781	3.7780	3.3921

YEARS OF JOINT EXPECTATION OF LIFE FOR MEN AND WOMEN
United States, 1959-61

Age of Male	When Male is YOUNGER than Female by (Years)		Male Same Age as Female	When Male is OLDER than Female by (Years)				
	5	2		2	4	5	10	15
18	44.4	45.6	46.4	47.0	47.6	—	—	—
20	42.6	43.8	44.6	45.2	45.8	46.0	—	—
22	40.8	42.0	42.8	43.4	44.0	44.3	—	—
25	38.1	39.4	40.1	40.7	41.3	41.6	42.6	—
30	33.6	34.9	35.6	36.2	36.8	37.0	38.1	38.8
35	29.2	30.4	31.1	31.7	32.3	32.5	33.6	34.3
40	25.0	26.1	26.8	27.4	27.9	28.2	29.2	29.9
45	21.0	22.1	22.7	23.2	23.7	24.0	24.9	25.6
50	17.3	18.3	18.9	19.4	19.9	20.1	21.0	21.6
55	14.0	14.9	15.5	16.0	16.4	16.6	17.4	18.0
60	11.0	11.9	12.4	12.9	13.3	13.5	14.2	14.8
65	8.5	9.3	9.7	10.2	10.5	10.7	11.4	11.9

APPENDIX B

Work Career Tables

Comment

These are issued by the United States Department of Labor. These tables may be used in conjunction with the Life Expectancy Tables, Appendix A, supra. They may become important in proving wage loss in a serious disability or death case by projecting realistically how long the average person is expected to engage in gainful occupation. It can be argued, of course, that the tables are not necessarily conclusive and that the subject, if in good health at the time of his accident and injuries, could have worked beyond the period fixed in the tables, either on a full-time or part-time basis.

It is advisable to obtain a certified copy of the U.S. Tables by writing to the U.S. Department of Labor, Bureau of Labor Statistics, Washington, D.C. 20212. This should overcome an objection to its admissibility predicated on lack of authenticity.

Frequently, the courts will take judicial notice of such tables.[1]

There now follow the applicable tables from the U.S. Government-issued Work Career Tables.[2]

Expectations of years of life, worklife, and retirement for men in the labor force at selected ages and years

Age	Expectation of life				Expectation of worklife				Expectation of retirement			
	1940	1950	1960	1968	1940	1950	1960	1968	1940	1950	1960	1968
16	50.4	52.6	53.3	52.9	44.8	46.8	46.3	45.3	5.6	5.8	7.0	7.6
25	42.4	44.4	45.0	44.7	36.7	38.5	37.9	37.0	5.7	5.9	7.1	7.7
35	33.7	35.2	35.7	35.6	27.8	29.3	28.6	27.7	5.9	5.9	7.1	7.9
45	25.5	26.6	26.9	26.8	19.7	20.6	19.7	18.9	5.8	6.0	7.2	7.9
55	18.3	19.0	19.2	19.0	12.4	13.0	11.9	11.0	5.9	6.0	7.3	8.0
65	12.2	12.7	12.8	12.8	6.8	7.4	6.3	5.5	5.4	5.3	6.5	7.3
75	7.3	7.8	8.0	8.2	4.5	4.7	5.1	4.9	2.8	3.1	2.9	3.3

---

1. See footnote 4, Appendix A, Supra. The same holding should apply to government-issued Work Career Tables.

2. The applicable tables for men have been taken from a government-issued pamphlet entitled "A Table of Expected Working Life For Men, 1968" by Howard N. Fullerton. The applicable tables for women have been taken from a government issued pamphlet entitled "Manpower Report", Number 12, May 1967."

Table 2. Working life for males, 1968

Year of age	Number living of 100,000 born alive — In population L_x	In labor force — Percent of population w_x	In labor force — Number Lw_x	Accessions to the labor force (per 1,000 in population) $1{,}000\,A_x$	Separations from the labor force (per 1,000 in labor force) — Due to all causes $1{,}000\,S_x$	Due to death $1{,}000\,S_x$	Due to retirement $1{,}000\,S_x$	Average number of remaining years — Life $\overset{\circ}{e}_x$	Labor force participation $\overset{\circ}{e}w_x$
				In year of age				At beginning of year of age	
16 to 19 years	385,064.9	58.10	223,723.4	489.7	1.7	1.7	0	52.9	45.3
16 years	96,499.9	40.69	39,267.5	125.9	1.4	1.4	0	52.9	45.3
17 years	96,356.1	53.30	51,359.6	112.5	1.6	1.6	0	52.0	44.3
18 years	96,193.3	64.57	62,113.2	93.4	1.8	1.8	0	51.0	43.4
19 years	96,015.6	73.93	70,983.0	52.6	1.9	1.9	0	50.1	42.5
20 to 24 years	477,078.0	86.34	411,933.0	78.6	2.0	2.0	0	49.2	41.5
20 years	95,831.8	79.20	75,898.6	33.8	2.2	2.2	0	49.2	41.5
21 years	95,629.6	82.59	78,979.8	41.6	2.2	2.2	0	48.3	40.6
22 years	95,418.0	86.77	82,789.6	40.8	2.2	2.2	0	47.4	39.7
23 years	95,403.0	90.86	86,500.4	15.3	2.2	2.2	0	46.5	38.8
24 years	94,994.6	92.39	87,764.5	16.0	2.2	2.2	0	45.6	37.9
25 to 29 years	472,092.0	95.01	448,558.1	7.0	2.0	2.0	0	44.7	37.0
25 years	94,795.0	93.98	89,090.8	5.7	2.1	2.1	0	43.8	37.0
26 years	94,602.6	94.55	89,450.0	5.2	2.1	2.1	0	43.8	36.1
27 years	94,416.5	95.07	89,766.1	4.6	1.9	1.9	0	42.9	35.1
28 years	94,232.3	95.54	90,027.7	4.0	2.0	2.0	0	42.0	34.2
29 years	94,045.6	95.94	90,223.5	3.2	2.0	2.0	0	41.1	33.2
30 to 34 years	467,176.0	96.53	450,982.4	0	2.5	2.3	.2	40.2	32.3
30 years	93,850.8	96.26	90,340.5	2.3	2.1	2.2	0	40.2	32.3
31 years	93,651.8	96.49	90,367.4	.3	2.2	2.2	0	39.2	31.4
32 years	93,445.6	96.63	90,296.9		2.3	2.2	0	38.3	30.4
33 years	93,228.2	96.67	90,123.1	.3	2.7	2.4	.3	37.4	29.5
34 years	92,999.0	96.62	89,854.6	0	3.4	2.5	.9	36.5	28.6
35 to 39 years	460,955.0	96.25	443,652.7	0	4.4	3.2	1.2	35.6	27.7
35 years	92,757.6	96.50	89,510.2	0	4.1	2.7	1.4	35.6	27.7
36 years	92,495.3	96.35	89,121.3	0	4.4	2.9	1.5	34.7	26.8
37 years	92,213.0	96.22	88,723.6	0	4.4	3.2	1.2	33.8	25.9
38 years	91,908.7	96.12	88,341.6	0	4.3	3.4	.9	32.9	25.0
39 years	91,580.4	96.04	87,956.1	0	4.7	3.7	1.0	32.0	24.1
40 to 44 years	451,925.0	95.63	432,184.9	0	6.5	4.9	1.6	31.1	23.2
40 years	91,240.6	95.93	87,518.0	0	5.4	4.1	1.3	31.1	23.2
41 years	90,766.6	95.79	87,012.5	0	6.4	4.4	1.6	30.3	22.4
42 years	90,421.6	95.63	86,472.9	0	6.4	4.8	1.6	29.4	21.5
43 years	89,965.8	95.48	85,899.9	0	6.9	5.3	1.6	28.5	20.6
44 years	89,470.1	95.32	85,282.6	0	7.6	5.8	1.8	27.7	19.8
45 to 49 years	438,249.0	94.58	414,507.8	0	10.9	7.7	3.1	26.8	18.9
45 years	88,933.5	95.13	84,599.6	0	8.6	6.3	2.2	26.8	18.9
46 years	88,346.9	94.89	83,835.7	0	9.6	7.6	2.7	26.0	18.1
47 years	87,707.8	94.62	82,990.0	0	10.7	7.6	3.1	25.2	17.2
48 years	87,010.7	94.31	82,056.0	0	12.0	8.4	3.6	24.4	16.4
49 years	86,250.0	93.94	81,026.6	0	13.6	9.2	4.4	23.6	15.6

Table 2. Working life for males, 1968—Continued

Year of age	In population L_x	In labor force — Percent of population w_x	In labor force — Number Lw_x	Accessions to the labor force (per 1,000 in population) $1{,}000\,A_x$	Separations — Due to all causes $1{,}000\,S_x$	Due to death $1{,}000\,S_x$	Due to retirement $1{,}000\,S_x$	Life $\overset{o}{e}_x$	Labor force participation $\overset{o}{ew}_x$
				In year of age				At beginning of year of age	
50 to 54 years	417,188.0	92.49	385,862.1	0	18.4	12.4	6.0	22.8	14.8
50 years	85,399.0	93.50	79,846.2	0	15.5	10.1	5.4	22.8	14.8
51 years	84,498.5	92.96	78,547.3	0	16.8	11.1	5.6	22.0	14.1
52 years	83,521.4	92.45	77,211.8	0	17.4	12.2	5.2	21.2	13.3
53 years	82,457.3	92.00	75,861.1	0	18.6	13.5	5.1	20.5	12.5
54 years	81,311.8	91.49	74,395.8	0	24.1	14.6	9.5	19.8	11.7
55 to 59 years	386,109.0	88.32	341,008.8	0	33.7	19.7	14.0	19.0	11.0
55 years	80,074.2	90.26	72,272.5	0	25.4	16.1	9.3	19.0	11.0
56 years	78,747.1	89.82	70,730.9	0	26.4	17.5	8.9	18.3	10.3
57 years	77,324.0	88.64	68,540.5	0	32.4	19.2	13.2	17.7	9.5
58 years	75,798.3	87.46	66,296.1	0	40.5	21.0	19.6	17.0	8.8
59 years	74,165.5	85.17	63,168.8	0	46.0	23.1	23.0	16.3	8.2
60 to 64 years	342,649.0	75.79	259,677.5	0	94.1	32.5	61.6	15.7	7.5
60 years	72,445.0	83.49	60,483.3	0	49.6	25.1	24.5	15.7	7.5
61 years	70,590.1	80.98	57,166.3	0	81.3	27.5	53.8	15.1	6.9
62 years	68,628.3	74.59	51,189.3	0	89.2	30.6	58.6	14.5	6.4
63 years	66,568.0	72.16	48,032.8	0	87.3	32.2	55.1	13.9	6.0
64 years	64,417.7	66.45	42,805.9	0	187.5	35.5	152.0	13.3	5.5
65 to 69 years	286,774.0	41.93	120,258.4	0	176.3	60.0	116.3	12.8	5.5
65 years	62,135.7	51.47	31,980.7	0	244.1	41.9	202.2	12.8	5.5
66 years	59,831.9	45.45	27,193.2	0	155.4	41.8	113.6	12.2	5.9
67 years	57,448.9	40.96	23,531.4	0	156.5	44.6	111.9	11.7	5.8
68 years	54,971.3	36.07	19,826.4	0	146.4	49.2	97.2	11.2	5.7
69 years	52,386.2	33.84	17,726.7	0	145.5	52.1	93.4	10.7	5.5
70 to 74 years	220,314.0	23.62	52,047.7	0	179.8	86.6	93.2	10.2	5.3
70 years	49,764.8	29.47	14,666.4	0	205.4	59.9	145.5	10.2	5.3
71 years	46,960.3	24.92	11,703.0	0	212.8	66.3	146.5	9.8	5.4
72 years	44,084.3	21.97	9,686.4	0	156.7	70.2	86.4	9.4	5.4
73 years	41,187.0	21.05	8,665.9	0	136.3	71.8	64.5	9.0	5.4
74 years	38,318.0	19.11	7,324.1	0	158.2	78.1	80.1	8.6	5.1
75 to 79 years	151,497.0	15.42	23,363.0	0	169.3	104.1	65.3	8.2	4.9
75 years	35,635.9	17.82	6,351.0	0	150.3	80.8	69.5	8.2	4.9
76 years	32,894.6	16.46	5,415.1	0	163.0	85.7	77.3	7.8	4.7
77 years	30,229.0	15.17	4,585.6	0	172.3	90.9	81.4	7.4	4.4
78 years	27,633.8	13.88	3,834.9	0	183.7	97.3	86.5	7.1	4.2
79 years	25,103.7	12.65	3,176.3	0	196.6	104.6	92.0	6.7	3.9
80 to 84 years	90,429.0	9.42	8,516.1	0	240.4	155.5	84.9	6.3	3.6
80 years	22,623.3	11.43	2,585.8	0	212.3	113.3	99.0	6.3	3.6
81 years	20,240.2	10.27	2,078.5	0	228.4	122.5	105.9	6.0	3.4
82 years	17,955.6	9.11	1,636.1	0	251.0	132.4	118.5	5.7	3.1
83 years	15,799.4	7.96	1,257.3	0	269.6	142.0	127.6	5.3	2.9
84 years	13,810.5	6.94	958.2	0	285.8	148.0	137.8	5.0	2.6
85 years and over	59,956.0	3.26	1,956.9	0				4.7	2.3

Average Number of Years of Labor Force Activity Remaining for Selected Groups of Women in the Labor Force, 1960

Age	Single women	Married, husband present, no children	Married, husband present, in labor force after birth of last child	Widowed	Divorced
20	45.3	34.9	(1)	41.8	43.3
25	40.5	30.1	(1)	37.0	38.5
30	35.7	26.6	(1)	32.1	33.6
35	31.2	24.4	23.8	27.3	28.8
40	26.3	20.8	19.1	22.5	24.1
45	21.6	16.7	14.5	17.8	19.7
50	17.1	13.7	11.9	13.4	15.5
55	13.1	10.9	9.4	9.8	11.6
60	10.0	8.7	6.9	7.1	8.4
65	7.8	6.5	5.9	6.0	6.7

[1] Amounts not significant.

SOURCE: Based on data from U. S. Department of Commerce; Bureau of the Census; and U. S. Department of Health, Education, and Welfare; Public Health Service.

APPENDIX C

Discount Tables

Comment

The discount tables are important in the determination of damages in wrongful death cases.[1] Courts may allow a reduction from the aggregate future lost earnings, accumulations, and services to the extent of the interest that would accrue on a lump sum paid out now to provide for the future annual lost installments which the decedent would have contributed if he had lived. In other words, there is authority that the suing survivor is entitled only to the present value of the future earnings.[2] For a general discussion on future income, see Sec. 13.9 supra.

There are some authorities which hold that the computation need not be predicated on legal rate of interest or on any basis of annuities or mathematical measurements.[3]

There follows a mathematical discount table.[4]

---

1. See Sec. 12, footnote 22, and Sec. 13.9. There is authority that discount tables are not to be considered in arriving at wage losses in wrongful personal injury as distinguished from wrongful death cases. *Hutzell v. Boyer,* 252 Md. 227, 249 A. 2d 449.

2. See footnote 1, supra.

3. Speiser's *Recovery For Wrongful Death,* Sec. 8:4. *Louisville & N.R. Co. v. Halloway,* (1918) 246 U.S. 525, 62 L. Ed. 867, 38 S. Ct. 379, 17 NACCA 578.

4. From Sun Life Insurance Discount Table. In the table, the column "Yrs." represents the number of years over which the computation is made (i.e. the life expectancy of the decedent); the succeeding columns with the "%" mentioned at the top is the interest rate used; the resulting figure on the table is the value of one dollar now based on that interest rate and life expectancy. For example, if the future contributions to survivors would have been $5,000 per year, and the life expectancy of the decedent were 15 years, then the present value on the table of $5,000 @ 3-½% interest per year is $59,605.

TABLE 5
PRESENT VALUE OF ONE DOLLAR PER YEAR
Payable at the Beginning of Each Year for a Term of
Years and Discounted at the Rate of Interst Shown

Yrs.	3%	3½%	4%	4½%	5%	5½%	6%	6½%	7%	7½%	8%	Yrs.
1	1.000	1.000	1.000	1.000	1.000	1.000	1.000	1.000	1.000	1.000	1.000	1
2	1.971	1.966	1.962	1.957	1.952	1.948	1.943	1.939	1.935	1.930	1.926	2
3	2.913	2.900	2.886	2.873	2.859	2.846	2.833	2.821	2.808	2.796	2.783	3
4	3.829	3.802	3.775	3.749	3.723	3.698	3.673	3.648	3.624	3.601	3.577	4
5	4.717	4.673	4.630	4.588	4.546	4.505	4.465	4.426	4.387	4.349	4.312	5
6	5.580	5.515	5.452	5.390	5.329	5.270	5.212	5.156	5.100	5.046	4.993	6
7	6.417	6.329	6.242	6.158	6.076	5.996	5.917	5.841	5.767	5.694	5.623	7
8	7.230	7.115	7.002	6.893	6.786	6.683	6.582	6.485	6.389	6.297	6.206	8
9	8.020	7.874	7.733	7.596	7.463	7.335	7.210	7.089	6.971	6.857	6.747	9
10	8.786	8.608	8.435	8.269	8.108	7.952	7.802	7.656	7.515	7.379	7.247	10
11	9.530	9.317	9.111	8.913	8.722	8.538	8.360	8.189	8.024	7.864	7.710	11
12	10.253	10.002	9.760	9.529	9.306	9.093	8.887	8.689	8.499	8.315	8.139	12
13	10.954	10.663	10.385	10.119	9.863	9.619	9.384	9.159	8.943	8.735	8.536	13
14	11.635	11.303	10.986	10.683	10.394	10.117	9.853	9.600	9.358	9.126	8.904	14
15	12.296	11.921	11.563	11.223	10.899	10.590	10.295	10.014	9.745	9.489	9.244	15
16	12.938	12.517	12.118	11.740	11.380	11.038	10.712	10.403	10.108	9.827	9.559	16
17	13.561	13.094	12.652	12.234	11.838	11.462	11.106	10.768	10.447	10.142	9.851	17
18	14.166	13.651	13.166	12.707	12.274	11.865	11.477	11.111	10.763	10.434	10.122	18
19	14.754	14.190	13.659	13.160	12.690	12.246	11.828	11.432	11.059	10.706	10.372	19
20	15.324	14.710	14.134	13.593	13.085	12.608	12.158	11.735	11.336	10.959	10.604	20
21	15.877	15.212	14.590	14.008	13.462	12.950	12.470	12.019	11.594	11.194	10.818	21
22	16.415	15.698	15.029	14.405	13.821	13.275	12.764	12.285	11.836	11.413	11.017	22
23	16.937	16.167	15.451	14.784	14.163	13.583	13.042	12.535	12.061	11.617	11.201	23
24	17.444	16.620	15.857	15.148	14.489	13.875	13.303	12.770	12.272	11.807	11.371	24
25	17.936	17.058	16.247	15.495	14.799	14.152	13.550	12.991	12.469	11.983	11.529	25
26	18.413	17.482	16.622	15.828	15.094	14.414	13.783	13.198	12.654	12.147	11.675	26
27	18.877	17.890	16.983	16.147	15.375	14.662	14.003	13.392	12.826	12.299	11.810	27
28	19.327	18.285	17.330	16.451	15.643	14.898	14.211	13.575	12.987	12.441	11.935	28
29	19.764	18.667	17.663	16.743	15.898	15.121	14.406	13.746	13.137	12.573	12.051	29
30	20.188	19.036	17.984	17.022	16.141	15.333	14.591	13.907	13.278	12.696	12.158	30
31	20.600	19.392	18.292	17.289	16.372	15.534	14.765	14.059	13.409	12.810	12.258	31
32	21.000	19.736	18.588	17.544	16.593	15.724	14.929	14.201	13.532	12.917	12.350	32
33	21.389	20.069	18.874	17.789	16.803	15.904	15.084	14.334	13.647	13.015	12.435	33
34	21.766	20.390	19.148	18.023	17.003	16.075	15.230	14.459	13.754	13.107	12.514	34
35	22.132	20.701	19.411	18.247	17.193	16.237	15.368	14.577	13.854	13.193	12.587	35
36	22.487	21.001	19.665	18.461	17.374	16.391	15.498	14.687	13.948	13.273	12.655	36
37	22.832	21.290	19.908	18.666	17.547	16.536	15.621	14.791	14.035	13.347	12.717	37
38	23.167	21.571	20.143	18.862	17.711	16.674	15.737	14.888	14.117	13.415	12.775	38
39	23.492	21.841	20.368	19.050	17.868	16.805	15.846	14.979	14.193	13.479	12.829	39
40	23.808	22.103	20.584	19.230	18.017	16.929	15.949	15.065	14.265	13.539	12.879	40
41	24.115	22.355	20.793	19.402	18.159	17.046	16.046	15.146	14.332	13.594	12.925	41
42	24.412	22.599	20.993	19.566	18.294	17.157	16.138	15.221	14.394	13.646	12.967	42
43	24.701	22.835	21.186	19.724	18.423	17.263	16.225	15.292	14.452	13.694	13.007	43
44	24.982	23.063	21.371	19.874	18.546	17.363	16.306	15.359	14.507	13.739	13.043	44
45	25.254	23.283	21.549	20.018	18.663	17.458	16.383	15.421	14.558	13.780	13.077	45
46	25.519	23.495	21.720	20.156	18.774	17.548	16.456	15.480	14.606	13.819	13.108	46
47	25.775	23.701	21.885	20.288	18.880	17.633	16.524	15.535	14.650	13.855	13.137	47
48	26.025	23.899	22.043	20.415	18.981	17.714	16.589	15.587	14.692	13.888	13.164	48
49	26.267	24.091	22.195	20.536	19.077	17.790	16.650	15.636	14.730	13.919	13.189	49
50	26.502	24.277	22.341	20.651	19.169	17.863	16.708	15.682	14.767	13.948	13.212	50
51	26.730	24.456	22.482	20.762	19.256	17.932	16.762	15.725	14.801	13.975	13.233	51
52	26.951	24.629	22.617	20.868	19.339	17.997	16.813	15.765	14.832	14.000	13.253	52
53	27.166	24.796	22.748	20.969	19.418	18.058	16.861	15.803	14.862	14.023	13.272	53
54	27.375	24.957	22.873	21.066	19.493	18.117	16.907	15.838	14.890	14.045	13.288	54
55	27.578	25.113	22.993	21.159	19.565	18.173	16.950	15.872	14.916	14.065	13.304	55
56	27.774	25.264	23.109	21.248	19.633	18.225	16.991	15.903	14.940	14.084	13.319	56
57	27.965	25.410	23.220	21.333	19.699	18.275	17.029	15.932	14.963	14.101	13.332	57
58	28.151	25.550	23.327	21.414	19.761	18.322	17.065	15.960	14.984	14.117	13.344	58
59	28.331	25.686	23.430	21.492	19.820	18.367	17.099	15.986	15.003	14.132	13.356	59
60	28.506	25.818	23.528	21.567	19.876	18.410	17.131	16.010	15.022	14.146	13.367	60

INDEX

259

SUPPLEMENTAL INDEX

(Authors, Sources, and Cases)*

[References are to chapter and section]

AUTHORS AND SOURCES

A

Alexander: *Jury Instructions on Medical Issues* (1966), published by Allen Smith Co., Indianapolis, Indiana   11.5

Alternative No-Fault Automobile Insurance Legislation (chart), prepared by Institute For The Future, Middletown, Connecticut   14.4

American Medical Association (A.M.A.)   4.2

American Statistical Association, 1757 K Street, N.W., Washington, D.C.   9.8

American Trial Lawyer's Journal (NACCA Law Journal), published by W.H. Anderson Co., Cincinnati   1.2

Appleman: "Cross-Examination of Physicians," *Successful Jury Trials, A Symposium* (Appleman ed. 1952)   4.3

Aristotle: "Government of Athens," translated by Kenyon, Atkeniesium Respublica 63-69 (Oxford 1920), Belli—*Modern Trials*, Vol. 4, pps. 64-107   10.1

Associated Appraisers of Impaired Earning Capacity, P.O. Box 7131, Berkeley, California   9.8

Averbach, Albert: *Handling Accident Cases* (1958), published by Lawyers Cooperative Publishing Company, Rochester, New York   1.3, 1.5, 1.6, 4.5

B

Bayo, Francisco: Actuarial Note Number 14, March 1965, U.S. Department of Health, Education and Welfare, Social Security Administration, "Joint Life Immediate Annuities Based On The United States Life Tables For White Persons, 1959-61"   Appendix A

Becker, Sprechter & Savin: *Legal Checklists*, published by Callaghan & Company, Chicago, Illinois   2.5

Belli, Melvin: *Modern Trials*, published by Bobbs-Merrill, Indianapolis, Indiana   1.3, 4.3
   Volume 1   2.5, 2.7
   Volume 4   2.1, 10.1

---

*Omitted are citations of law encyclopedias (i.e. West's *Key Number Digest, Corpus Juris Secundum, Am. Jur.*, etc.) and statutes. These may be found in the respective chapters and in the footnotes there, under the proper title.

H

Harper & James: *The Law of Torts,* Volume 2, published by Little, Brown & Company, Boston, Massachusetts (1956), Section 25.22   12.8

Horsley, Jack E.: "Persuasion in the Voir Dire: The Defendant's Approach," appearing in *Persuasion: The Key To Damages,* published by The Institute for Continuing Legal Education, Ann Arbor, Michigan (1969)   6.3, 6.6

Houts, Marshall: *Lawyers Guide to Medical Proof,* published by Matthew Bender, Albany, New York (1966)   1.3, 4.3

I

Ideal Pictures Corp., 58 E. South Walter Street, Chicago, Illinois, or 233-239 W. 42nd Street, New York, New York (kinescope of television program showing open heart surgery on 8-year-old boy; and other similar movies)   1.6

Iglehart, Francis N.: "Loss of Earning Capacity in Personal Injury and Wrongful Death Cases," *Daily Record* July 6, 1970, Baltimore, Maryland   9.4, 12.10A

Illinois Pattern Jury Instructions-Civil-I.P.I., published by Burdette Smith Company, Chicago, Illinois (1961); 2nd edition recently published by West Publishing Company, St. Paul, Minnesota   11.5
Section 30.07   12.5
Section 31.01   12.10A, 12.11A
Section 32.04   12.3
Section 34.05   12.15

Immel's *Acuarial Tables and Damage Awards,* 19 Ohio St. L.J. 240 (1958), reprinted in *Trial & Tort Trends* 1959, Belli Seminar 347   13.11, Appendix A

J

Jones, Burr W.: *The Law of Evidence: Civil and Criminal,* published by Bancroft-Whitney Company, San Francisco (1958), 5th ed., Section 412   9.1

Jury Verdict Research, Inc., Cleveland, Ohio   2.7

K

Keeton, R. & O'Connell, Jr.: *Basic Protection for the Traffic Victim, A Blueprint for Reforming Automobile Insurance* (1965)   14.3D

Kelly, Joseph B.: "Direct Examination of Medical Experts in Personal Injury Actions," appearing in the *Daily Record,* Baltimore, Maryland, September 29, 1970   4.3, 4.4

Key & Conwell: *Management of Fractures, Dislocations and Sprains,* 7th edition (pps. 300, 301), published by the C.V. Mosby Company, St. Louis, Missouri   4.9

L

Langerman, Samuel: "Persuasion in the Closing Argument: The Plaintiff's Approach," appearing in *Persuasion: The Key to Damages,* published by The Institute of Continuing Legal Education, Ann Arbor, Michigan   10.3

Lawyer's Medical Cyclopedia, published by The Allen Smith Company, Indianapolis, Indiana (1962)   1.3

Lederle Laboratories, Division of the American Cyanamid Company, Pearl River, New York ("Atlas of the Human Anatomy")   1.6

Louisell & Williams: *Medical Malpractice,* published by Matthew Bender, New York, New York (1970)   4.1

CASES

A

Aetna Casualty & Surety Company v. Commissioners of Insurance (Mass.), 263 N.E. 2d 698 (1970)   14.4

Allen v. Moore (1938),109 Vt. 405, 199 A. 257   12.14

Allendorf v. Elgin J. & E. R. Co., 8 Ill. 2d 164, 133 N.E. 2d 288 (1956), cert. den. 352 U.S. 833, 77 S. Ct. 99, 1 L. Ed. 2d 53, reh. den. 352 U.S. 937, 77 S. Ct. 219, 1 L. Ed. 2d 170 (1956)   12.15

Armour & Co. v. Tomlin, 60 S.W. 2d 204   12.6

B

Baker v. Salvation Army (1940), 91 N.H. 1, 12A. 2d 514   12.10

Ballard v. Moore-McCormack Lines, Inc. (D.C. N.Y. 1968), 285 F.S. 290   5.1

Baltimore City Passenger Railway Company v. Kemp, 61 Md. 74, 81 (1883)   12.6

Barnes v. Graham Va. Quarries Inc., 204 Va. 414, 420, 132 S.E. 2d 395, 398   12.7

Barnes v. Smith (1962 CA 10, N.M.), 305 F. 2d 226   9.4

Battala v. State, 10 N.Y. 2d 237, 176 N.E. 2d 729, 219 N.Y.S. 2d 34 (1961)   12.6A

Bethlehem-Sparrows Point Shipyard v. Scherpenisse (1946), 187 Md. 375, 50A 2d 256   13.14

Black v. Peerless Elite Laundry Co. (1933), 113 W. Va. 828, 169 S.E. 447   12.14D

Blair v. Bloomington & Normal Ry. Elec., etc., 131 Ill. App. 400 (3 Dist.) (1906)   12.3

Bly v. So. R. Co., 183 Va. 162, 168, 31 S.E. 2d 564, 567   12.16

Bolinger v. St. Paul & D.R. Co. (1887), 36 Minn. 418, 31 N.W. 856   12.13

Bond v. United Railroads of S.F. (1911), 159 Cal. 270, 113 P. 366, 48 Crans. 687   13.9A

Botta v. Brunner, 26 N.J. 82, 138 A. 2d 713, 60 A.L.R. 2d 1331   13.8

Bradburn v. G. & W.R. Co., L.R. 10 Ex. 1 (1874)   12.8

Brooks v. U.S. (1967) (D.C. S.C.), 273 F.S. 619   9.2

Brown v. DuFrey, 1 N.Y. 2d 190, 195-196; 151 N.Y. 2d 649, 654; 134 N.E. 2d 469   11.2

Bruce v. U.S. (D.C. Cal., 1958), 167 F.S. 579   12.17B

Bryant v. Woodlief (1960), 252 N.C. 488, 114 S.E. 2d 241, 81 A.L.R. 2d 939, noted in 27 NACCA L.J. 205 (1961); 39 N.C. L. Rev. 107 (1960)   9.2

Byrd v. Stewart, 450 S.W. 2d 11 (1969) (Tenn.)   14.5

C

Calvert v. Springfield Electric Light & Power Co., 236 Ill. 290, 83 N.E. 184, 14 L.R.A. N.S. 782, 12 Ann. Cas. 423 (1907)   12.15

Campbell v. Sutliff, 193 Wis. 370, 214 N.W. 374   12.8

Carnego v. Crescent Coal Co. (1914), 164 Iowa 552, 146 N.W. 38   13.9A

Central Foundry Co. v. Bennett (1906), 144 Ala. 184, 39 So. 574   9.5

Chapman v. McCormick, 86 N.Y. 479   11.2

Chesapeake & Potomac Telephone Company of Baltimore City v. State T/U Carry, 124 Md. 527, 93A 11   12.10A, 12.13

Chic. I. & L.R. Co. v. Ellis (1925), 83 Ind. App. 701, 149 N.E. 909   9.5

Christastie v. Elmira Water Co. (3rd Dept. 1922), 202 AD 270-272, 195 N.Y.S. 156, 157, 136 ALR 965, 66 ALR 2d 1082   4.8